W9-BRQ-037

WEiRD N.J.

WEiRD N.J.

Your Travel Guide to New Jersey's Local Legends and Best Kept Secrets

MARK SCEURMAN

MARK MORAN

For information on *Weird NJ* magazine please write to:
Weird NJ, P. O. Box 1346, Bloomfield, NJ 07003,
or visit us on the Web at WeirdNJ.com.

WEIRD N.J.

Copyright © 2004 by Barnes & Noble.
Photographs © 2004 by Mark Sceurman and Mark Moran.
Additional photography and illustration credits are found on page 272
and constitute an extension of this copyright page.

All rights reserved under International and Pan American Copyright Conventions.
Published in the United States by Barnes & Noble, New York, NY.
No part of this book may be reproduced or transmitted in any form or
by electronic or mechanical means, including information storage and
retrieval systems, without permission in writing from the publisher,
with the exception of brief passages used in a critical review or article.

For information contact:
Barnes & Noble, 122 Fifth Avenue, New York, NY 10011
212 633-4000

Barnes & Noble and colophon are registered trademarks.

Publisher:	Barbara J. Morgan
Editor:	Matt Lake
Design:	Richard J. Berenson
	Berenson Design & Books, Ltd., New York, NY
Production:	Della R. Mancuso
	Mancuso Associates, Inc., North Salem, NY

Library of Congress Cataloging-in-Publication Data is available on request.

ISBN 0-7607-3979-X

Printed in the U.S.A.

Sixth Printing

DEDICATION

We would like to dedicate this book to everyone who has ever written to us over the years, contributed a story, shared an experience, or just sent us off to parts unknown. Whether your tale is included in this book or not, we're glad that you all came along for the ride.

We would also like to thank longtime *Weird NJ* cohort and collaborator Chris Gethard, without whose invaluable assistance the research, writing, and editing of this material would have been a lot more work, and not nearly as much fun as it was.

And last but not least, to our families and friends, who have put up with this all-consuming hobby of ours all these years, even when it meant vacationing in Shellpile, New Jersey, instead of Disney World.

–Mark and Mark

CONTENTS

Introduction

*"New Jersey—the most American of all states.
It has everything from wilderness to the Mafia.
All the great things and all the worst, for example, Route 22."*

—Jean Shepherd

Greetings, fellow travelers, and welcome to *Weird NJ*. We began our *Weird NJ* adventure back in 1990, when we sent our first stapled newsletter to friends to let them know where our travels had taken us. It became a yearly mailing, and related the many sites and eccentricities overlooked by our various state tour guides. The pass-around rate of these newsletters was surprisingly high, and soon strangers were sharing their own adventures with us.

It didn't take long to discover that the residents of our little Garden State had some very strange life experiences and tall tales to tell.

The newsletter grew into a self-published journal that we distributed through the mail. It's now evolved into a full-fledged magazine, sold in weird places and normal places, and bought by tens of thousands of people as fascinated as we are by our state's modern folklore.

There is a certain pride that our readers share in telling us about something strange that lurks in their neighborhood. Some stories are personal, many are unbelievable, and others are just downright outrageous! And while many readers send us stories that we publish, more often they tell us something like, "Hey, have you guys ever seen this place? It's really weird, and you should go check it out!" So, armed with little more than our Hagstrom maps and the question, "What's weird around here?" we set out one day a week in search of New Jersey's local legends and best-kept secrets.

The sites you'll find in this book are a culmination of over ten years of research, interviews, and road trips. Many of the legends are localized, and their tales have never before been heard outside the town in which they originated. Though we've sought to find truth behind the legends, we've often found that truth is not always an essential ingredient for a good story.

Although *Weird NJ* is a journal of strange travels, we also like to churn up the historical muck. By reinvestigating the history that we thought we knew, we've found some very weird facts that have somehow been swept under the rug. Where the line between history and legend begins to blur is the tightrope that we like to tread.

Readers ask why there are often no directions given to the sites we write about. Although *Weird NJ* is a travel guide, we wouldn't want to lead others to trespass on private property or into a situation that might be dangerous. Some sites are better left to the imagination. But most sites are accessible to travelers, and we encourage everyone to get out there and see them before they disappear. Sadly, many have already vanished. But we are confident that as long as there are folks who still possess that irrepressible and indefinable New Jersey spirit, there will always be new oddities popping up for the weird traveler to investigate.

Weird NJ is not about the weirdest things or people. That stuff is fodder for the tabloids. We're interested in those little things that are slightly offbeat or left of center. It might be an odd roadside site that you drive past every day and really never gave a second thought to. Then, one day, you see it as if for the first time, and ask yourself, "Just what the hell is that thing, anyway?"

We do our best to reflect the rhythms, tastes, and smells of the state. Whether it's an abandoned village for epileptics or just a greasy hot dog stand alongside Route 1, it's all part of the unique culture of this state that we are proud to call home. With that in mind, we now present for your consideration this collection of shared tales that make up the *Weird NJ* experience.

One can only imagine the countless tales yet to be told. Even after years of traveling, we know that we've only scratched the surface. *Weird NJ* is a lot like life; it's the journey itself, not the destination, that is really important. So come take a ride with us as we hit the roads less traveled throughout New Jersey to see just what our strange state has to offer.

—Mark and Mark

Local Legends
Tales of Suburban Youth

"Myth helps you to put your mind in touch with this experience of being alive." —Joseph Campbell, *The Power of Myth*

There is an old stone clock tower high atop the New Jersey Palisades where you can go and meet the devil himself. There is a tunnel in Clifton well known to the local teenage population as a portal to hell. There is an ancient stone altar on a wooded hillside in Mount Holly that echoes with the mournful cries of witches who were executed there for their evil ways. You don't believe it? Go there alone sometime around midnight and see for yourself—if you dare!

There are sites throughout New Jersey that have attained legendary status, even though in some cases the location consists of nothing more than a gnarly old tree, or a large sewer tunnel. The stories that have grown out of these humble landmarks are the stuff of nightmares. How is it that a lonely oak tree standing in an otherwise empty field earns the moniker the "Devil's Tree"? Of all the trees in New Jersey, what is it about this particular tree that inspires tales of murder and mayhem? Are the stories associated with such sites merely the product of over-active youthful imaginations, or is there more to it than that?

People need mythology in their lives. Whether they admit it or not, most folks still want to believe that even in our technologically advanced society, there are still places of mystery and wonder. Sites such as the Devil's Tower and Demon's Alley represent physical manifestations of our mythological nature. They are like springboards for our collective unconscious and serve to fuel the dark side of our imagination. Most people just love a good scary story. Hearing that the frightening fable took place at a location you can actually visit just adds to the thrill.

Almost everyone has heard of urban legends—erroneous tales which are unknowingly told as if true. They are told by someone who professes that the story actually happened to a "friend of a friend," or swears that they heard it from a legitimate news source. Unbeknownst to the storyteller is that there are hundreds of tried and untrue urban legends that continually circulate around the country, with only slight variations. The stories differ primarily by changed locations and changed names of principal characters. Our local legends are site-specific and never change locale. There is only one Devil's Tower, for example, and it can be found nowhere else but in the town of Alpine in Bergen County.

After a decade of publishing *Weird NJ*, we have become all too familiar with your run-of-the-mill urban legends, and we have little or no use for them. Although this sort of mythology can be entertaining, and at times touch on archetypal fears, the stories are nothing more than modern-day morality tales, with little or no basis in fact.

Local legends, like folktales, are passed down as part of an oral tradition. They become the modern folklore of our state. But how do these dark and disturbing legends start, and why do they continue to be told from one generation to the next? The answer might lie in the need for people to prove themselves to their peer group and to themselves.

Every culture has its own rites of passage for its young adults; some primitive tribes practice scarification, circumcisions, or even knock the teeth out of their young. Joseph Campbell, a preeminent scholar of mythology, said, "The rituals of primitive initiation ceremonies are all mythologically grounded and have to do with killing the infantile ego and bringing forth an adult, whether it's the girl or the boy." After undergoing the ordeal the young man or woman is changed forever and emerges as a full-fledged member of the tribe, ready to take their place in the society.

In modern Western culture we have, for the most part, done away with such painful and traumatic practices, adopting the more genteel (though sometimes still harrowing) traditions of bar mitzvahs and confirmation ceremonies to mark one's passage into adulthood. But are these rituals enough to usher in manhood and womanhood, or are they merely compulsory formalities? Sometimes it takes a little more than facing a banquet hall full of your relatives to test one's mettle. Sometimes a late night ride to come face to face with the devil himself is what is really needed to separate the men from the boys.

The Devil's Tower

On a public road called The Esplanade, accessible from Route 9W, about a mile north of the Tenafly–Alpine border in Bergen County, stands the Devil's Tower. This stone clock tower looked unassuming enough to us on a recent drive-by—but the devil does work in mysterious ways.

According to the Alpine Historical Society, the Devil's Tower began in the first half of the 1900s as the centerpiece of an estate called Rio Vista. A Spanish businessman named Manuel Rionda, who made a fortune from sugarcane plantations in Cuba, built a mansion on the site of the present-day Alpine Lookout. His estate included a clock tower and a nearby chapel with a mausoleum that once contained the bodies of the owner's wife and sister. (They were removed after Rionda's death in 1943.) The Rio Vista estate was subdivided after Rionda's death and remained mostly just woodlands through the 1970s.

But dozens of stories that our readers have told us about this evil edifice tell a different tale. If you drive around the tower at night three times in reverse (some say six times), then turn off your headlights, the ghost of Rionda's wife will appear—or worse, take control of your car and drive it into a tree. Others say that if you walk six times around the tower backward at midnight, the devil himself will appear to you.

One thing's for sure: Kids used to break into the clock tower, party, and leave graffiti, sometimes of a diabolical nature, so eventually the tower was sealed up. But that doesn't stop people from visiting it to this day.

Devil's Tower Figures

My friends and I went to Devil's Tower in Alpine. We decided to drive around, what we thought was the correct number—six times in reverse. We got to the last time around and stopped. To our amazement me and my friend May saw what we thought were white eyes in the top middle window.

As I started to drive away, May turned around and looked at the tower. This is when the screaming started. I looked in my rearview mirror and noticed a bright white object in the round window on the second floor that started to fade toward the back. I immediately floored it as the screaming continued. The girls both agreed that they saw a white figure in the top window immediately move to the second floor, get really bright white, and then as we pulled away, it moved to the back of the tower and faded.—*Anonymous*

Ghostly Figures Haunt the Tower

We recently visited the Devil's Tower and heard a loud strange noise coming from within. The noise sounded almost like creaky steps, but we have no idea what it actually was. We got to the right side of it and parked the car because we saw something in the window on the right—not the very top one, the one that's a good number of feet under it, all the way to the right. It looked like there was a broken window, but the window kept going up and down, up and down. It disappeared for a couple seconds, and then a blurry figure of a person in all white leaned out and looked down at us, but there were no facial features! It almost looked like it was wearing a veil or cape. It was grayish white and very distorted.—*Michele*

Death at the Tower

The Devil's Tower was owned by a rich married man. He built the tower so his wife could see New York without really going to New York. One night, his wife was looking out of the top of the tower and she saw her husband with another woman, so she jumped right down the center of the tower. The husband was so upset that he stopped all the work on the tower. —*Nick G.*

Apparently his wife hung herself in the tower, and if you drive around it three times backward, you will see her apparition hanging in the tower. —*Susan*

The tower was started as a birthday gift for Rionda's wife, but she passed away before its completion. The tower was completed and fitted with a clock that never was used but was set to the time of her death. When strolling through the woods at night, the tower clock could actually be heard to ring at the appropriate hour on Halloween night! —*Letter via e-mail*

Red Eyes and Growls in the Dark Tower

Even into the early 1980s, the estate grounds were largely undeveloped, and the property was criss-crossed with old gravel roads intersecting with the roughed-out new roads being laid for the current development.

During a late summer evening in 1980, my friends and I were driving around looking for something to do. We hadn't gone up to the tower in a while, and off we went. I and another friend were looking in the window of the dark wing on the south side of the tower, and our other friends joined us. It was then that we had what I'll call a mass hallucination. As we stood there, we all heard growls come from the darkened chamber, and as we looked into the darkness, we saw in the right corner a pair of red eyes looking back at us. —*Alan M.*

The Devil Don't Pose for Pictures

We parked on a side street and made our way down the road with a flashlight and a couple of cameras. We snapped a bunch of pictures and took about fifteen minutes of video footage. As we began to speak louder, a banging sound began to emanate from the right side of the tower. We paused, and the sound stopped immediately. We checked around the tower for any sign of life, but no one else was around.

My friend said he saw a white object hanging out of one of the openings in the tower. As we all looked up, we saw the white object move back from the window. We stood there taping as the banging became louder, then became silent once more. At this point, the video camera died, and we ran for the car. —*Andrew F.*

The Devil's Tower Fog

I grew up in the area where Devil's Tower is located. Before all the houses were built around it, there was just a road that cut through the woods. There used to be a very small church there. Outside, someone had painted upside-down crosses everywhere. Where the altar was were remnants of a bonfire, so all the ash and heat blackened paintings.

I went there one night years ago to play an "I stalled the car" bit on a girlfriend, and she freaked out, screaming, "Get me out of here now!" When I turned the lights back on to start the car, what I saw made the hair on the back of my neck stand on end. There was a fog that I didn't see while driving in creeping toward the car, about waist high. I backed the car out of there as fast as I could. We laughed afterward, but for that moment, wow! —*Ed S.*

The Smell of Dirt and Flowers

There was one time when a bunch of us were at Devil's Tower goofing around. We had gone there with four cars, and someone tried the "driving around the tower backward three times" bit. While the one person was driving around, the rest of us stood looking at the tower waiting for something to happen. After the driver stopped and got out of his car, we noticed the wind was picking up, but only from the right side of the tower. Soon after, there was a dark, cloudlike shape forming overhead, with the strongest aroma of dirt and flowers. Suddenly there was a humongous gust of wind that sent the feeling of death right through us all! That was when we hightailed it out of there. Each car still smelled like dirt and flowers until we reached New Milford. —*José*

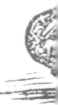

When the Devil's Tower Calls, Don't Answer the Phone

I grew up and still live in the Alpine area and have been to the tower several times. One of my friends drove around the circle six times backward. After that the wind kicked up, leaves started to swirl, we heard strange, faint wailing noises, and the lights in the gated area of the tower switched on and off. When we pulled away, we saw an image in the narrow window above the clock and felt a bigger chill. The wind picked up even more.

We sped off toward Route 9W. Just as we reached the intersection with the blinking light, my sister's cell phone started to beep. She had a message. The call was from her home phone. The message was garbled and could not be made out. My sister said the message sounded like a young girl giving a warning of some sort. The eight of us were standing around when one of the other cell phones started to ring. The call had come from another one of my sorority sisters who was standing right there and had not made any phone calls!–*Beth*

Mr. Rionda Still Hangs Around the Tower

When they knocked down the mansion, they attempted to knock down the tower also, but crew members started to quickly die off in odd and painful ways. Supposedly the ghost of the man still haunts the tower, keeping everyone away from his body up inside the tower.–*Mike P.*

The Devil's Tree

Alpine is by no means the only place in the state to meet the devil. He is also said to frequent a certain tree in the Martinsville section of Bernards Township, Somerset County. This is one sinister-looking tree. It stands all alone in the middle of a large field off Mountain Road. Its trunk has been severely scarred by axes and chain saws. Some of the wounds appear to be quite old.

Everyone in the vicinity seems to have a story about this evil arbor. They say that a farmer once killed his entire family, then went to the tree to hang himself. According to some, numerous suicides and murders occurred there. Supposedly anyone who tries to cut down the tree comes to an untimely end, as it is now cursed. And the souls of those killed at the spot, they say, give the tree an unnatural warmth. Even in the dead of winter, no snow will fall around it.

According to one *Weird NJ* reader, the tree is a portal to hell that's guarded by a sentinel who drives an old black pickup truck—who will chase you down the road before suddenly vanishing. You will see headlights one second, and the next, nothing. Other stories turn out to be less menacing. One reader described seeing bodies hanging from the tree, but on closer inspection found they were dummies in high school football uniforms, hung in effigy by the local team.

When Weird NJ visited the Devil's Tree, we didn't encounter any sentinels or linebacker effigies, but we did notice evidence that many attempts had been made over the years to fell the unholy oak. We also met locals who shared their tales of the tree. One told us that the inherent unholiness of the Devil's Tree is the result of the evil that men do, and should not be blamed on the devil.

Devil's Tree Is a K.K.K. Hangout

There is a very evil truth to the mythology of the Devil's Tree. At one time, Bernards Township was one of the central headquarters of the K.K.K. in New Jersey—they held many demonstrations in our town and held many meetings throughout the hills. As per K.K.K. policy, often they would lynch local African Americans to set an example of their principles and resolve.

The Devil's Tree was more secluded in those times, before the developments spread across the rural countryside. It stood in a very isolated area of woods and fields, far from the prying eyes of the police. The evil energy around the tree comes from the souls of dead men and women who were killed by this vile organization. If you look at the tree, you can see the leftmost branch extends almost parallel to the ground. This was the hanging branch. When the moon is a full red harvest moon and the wind is blowing just right, it looks like there might be bodies hanging from the branch, slowly swaying in the breeze.—*Rob S.*

The Devil's Tree Will Break You

At the time of our arrival [at] the Devil's Tree, there was a six-foot noose hanging from the big branch, which extends out of one side. We noticed what looked like claw marks from a person or very large animal. To get a better view, myself and a friend climbed the tree to see if any unique marks were further up.

After we climbed up, we were sitting on the branch trying to remove the noose. As we sat on the branch, we began to hear noises coming from inside the tree. When these noises grew even louder, a big bang sounded and a burst of energy came from the tree, sending myself and my friend flying into the air. When I crashed to the ground, I landed on my ankle, breaking it in two places.—*Steve K.*

The Devil's Tree and Heat Rock

Right next to the Devil's Tree there is a rock. It is very warm. Some people call it Heat Rock. People say it is the gate to hell.—*Elmo M.*

No Snow at the Devil's Tree

We went to the Devil's Tree in December when the ground was snow-covered. However, an eight- by twelve-foot circle of ground around the tree was totally bone-dry. Later, when we were driving home, one of our friends thought he was cool because he took a piece of bark off of the tree and had it on him in the car. We pulled the car over, yelled at him, and made him throw it out the window!—*Damian*

The Mark of the Devil

My friends and I went up to the Devil's Tree one night and got out of the car and touched it. Afterward, we went to Applebee's to get something to eat, and everyone that was sitting at the table suddenly had all of our hands turn black! We don't know why, but it took us two and a half hours to get the blackness off of our hands!—*Melissa C.*

The Children of the Tree

We have all heard the story of not messing with Devil's Tree, so we were smart and didn't mock the tree. We went right next to the tree and put our ears next to the bark. We heard sounds of screaming and children playing. —*Matt W.*

A Shocking Experience

I went up to the Devil's Tree this past Mischief Night with two of my friends. I told them all the stories and tall tales that went along with it. I got within arm's distance and reached out and touched it, as I had many times before. It's kind of like a ritual I have.

When I placed my hand on the tree, a single strike of lightning illuminated the sky. I don't know what caused it to happen, but when I touched the tree, the lightning struck, and when I took my hand off, the lightning disappeared. It could've been coincidence, or it could have been paranormal proof of the legend's truth. Either way, I thought it was cool, and it scares the hell out of me now. —*Brian D.*

Don't Pee on the Devil's Tree!

I am reminded of an incident which occurred about eight years back, when I was in high school. This guy and a carload of other rowdy types decided to go up to see the tree that weekend. On Friday night, they began their journey up the mountain to see what it was all about. A friend of mine was in that car, and his story is as follows.

After cruising back and forth several times, the kids were getting bad vibes and wanted to leave. The kid who was driving became angry at the "wimps" for having bad feelings. He stated to his friends that he was going to prove once and for all that the story was nothing and that he wasn't fazed by it. He pulled his car over on the side of the road, right before the bend, and got out. Marching up to the tree, he began yelling challenges to the so-called spirits. Nothing happened, so to further prove his fearlessness, he pulled down his pants and urinated all over the base of the tree. Still, nothing happened. He muttered an "I told you so" and got back into the car.

After starting the car, he began to drive toward the bend in the road slowly. Suddenly, without warning, the gas pedal of the car became floored and the car sped up all by itself. Surprised at what was happening, the guy was unable to control the car, and it skidded out and collided into a tree. The kids in the car sustained minor injuries, but the car was totaled. —*Anonymous*

The JL Tree

In the town of Lakewood, Ocean County, just off East County Line Road, is another tree famous in local lore. The JL Tree's legend is not nearly as sinister as that of the Devil's Tree, but it does tell the tragic tale of the violent murder of a young local lad and the tree that has immortalized his initials.

Jimmy's Tale

Jimmy Lynch was a high school student in Lakewood in the 1970s. He was in the park one October night when he was confronted by four youths. They had made fun of Jimmy in school, and when they found him in the park, they stabbed him to death.

The next morning, his neighbors found him there dead. His girlfriend carved his initials in the tree. Over the next few years, the branches at the top of the tree grew in the shape of JL. It is plainly visible and can't be mistaken as anything else but the letters JL.

If you ask old-timers around here if they remember Jimmy Lynch from the '70s, they will tell you the story. I went to Lakewood High School, and mostly all the teachers have been there since the '60s. If you ask if they knew Jimmy Lynch, most will become very uneasy and tell you it is only folklore.–*J220king*

Jimmy Lynch Still Wanders Lakewood

There used to be a park on the corner, but recently it was leveled. If you drive down the road, you have to look at the trees right before the left into the municipal garage. For some reason, the initials JL seem to grow up and over the rest of the other trees. I've also known people to actually drive up to the base of the tree, and their car stalled. The initials are still carved into the tree, and people have claimed to see a shadowy figure in a hooded sweatshirt walking around the area of the former park.–*Brianne D.*

Demon's Alley

Sometimes a place can become a local legend by simply lying dormant. Such is the case with a neighborhood of less than a dozen abandoned houses known as Demon's Alley.

Located just off the major thoroughfare of Route 23 on the border of Morris and Passaic counties, near the border of West Milford and Kinnelon, Demon's Alley lies in the woods on a poorly paved strip of asphalt called New City Road. The New City Colony was originally built in the early twentieth century to house workers constructing the numerous reservoirs and viaducts of the Newark Watershed, which owns the property. It was abandoned in the mid-1980s, and before long, this isolated former community gave rise to some of the most potent modern folktales in northern New Jersey lore.

The first question that people would ask themselves while traversing the short span of New City Road while taking the shortcut from Germantown to Route 23 is, Why? Why was this perfectly inhabitable neighborhood left out here in the woods to deteriorate? The houses spread out over ten acres — large and well-constructed wood frame and masonry cottages with spacious porches and slate roofs. Those who ventured into the abandoned houses of Demon's Alley often emerged with strange tales of their interiors. Most agreed that an inordinate number of personal belongings remained — clothes in the closets, furniture, kitchenware, and even TVs. One adventurer told us that he even discovered a kitchen table set for a meal, as if the family who once occupied the house might walk in at any moment and take their places to eat dinner.

To make the whole scene even more surreal, at

some point somebody painted crude renderings of windows and doors on the plywood boards that were nailed up over the *actual* windows and doors. The stark white frames of these painted windows had white window shades and pull strings, dangling half drawn over a black interior. By day, it was a puzzling and disturbing scene to behold. In the dead of night, though, the scene seemed nothing short of pure evil.

Demon's Alley is gone now, claimed by a number of suspicious fires within the last few years. The remainder of the buildings, which had suffered decades of severe neglect, were demolished in 2002, burying the unanswered questions and secrets forever beneath the unholy ground on which they once stood.

The Cult Killings at Demon's Alley

I had always heard this spot was being preserved for some historical reasons. I recently brought a friend of mine who is a well-known photographer, and he was very impressed. He went back on his own to shoot some pictures, and the camera's shutter would not open (and there was nothing wrong with it). His camera's inability to work when photographing the houses made him stop at some of the small-town stores on Route 23 to try to get some more information on the group of houses. An old man told him quite a tale of the village.

He claimed a man moved into the town in the early '80s who seemed to be a typical person and a normal resident. Shortly after his arrival, weird things started happening—small pranks, I assume. The residents suspected that it was kids coming off Route 23 to play jokes on the odd street.

The new resident decided to hold a town meeting at his house to decide what to do about the pranksters. Little did the small community know about this man's history or the plans for all the people of the town. The old-timer claimed this man had been a cult leader in the Midwest and had a large following. He had perpetrated the pranks in a plot to get all the town members together under the roof of his home. Once all were gathered in the downstairs, cult members stampeded from the upper level and engaged in a massacre of every member of the town.

Supposedly the cult fled and were never caught.

The old man said no one in the town talks about the incident, and most deny it ever happened.—*Ralph Sinisi*

The Killer Down in the Basement

I was told the real name of the Demon's Alley murderer. He lived in the big brick house with the white pillars. He should be about eighty-five years old by now. I was told it all happened on January 9, 1940. I heard that if you go there at midnight, lights go on in the man's basement and there is a lot of banging around. It goes on until five a.m. There are bloodstains in one house in the upstairs bedroom.

My friend told me he saw a ghost there, supposedly the guy involved in the killings. He had a white T-shirt on and dark pants. He also said he saw or heard some big creature or something come out of the house with bloodstains, and it ran up into the woods. It was too big to be a dog.—*Desiree*

The Kid from Demon's Alley

I first went to Demon's Alley about four years ago, when I was a freshman in high school. This was before the windows were painted, and most of the houses didn't even have wood covering the doors and windows. I had heard earlier accounts of the area but still had no idea what to expect. We first had to park away from it to keep the car at a safe distance.

We ran up through the woods and into the second house on the left. Inside, it was still furnished, yet obviously trashed. We went upstairs to where there were broken TV sets, clothes, and paper everywhere. We reluctantly ventured down to the basement, where it was extremely hot and smelled much worse. My friend found a large knife on the dirt-covered basement floor. I'm doubtful it was one of the knives used in any slayings at these houses, but who knows?—*Chverb*

Demon's Alley Not for the Chicken

Two months ago, I took my friends to Demon's Alley. As we pulled onto the street, we noticed tiny reflectors on the road. Upon closer inspection, we saw they were tiny candles in the shape of upside-down crosses.

After that, I told my friend to get the hell back in the car. I had had enough. Then things got real weird! Across our path, as we were driving out, walked six people dressed in black cloaks carrying a cage containing a live chicken. They walked into the building marked 48. They did not even pay attention to us! I did like ninety miles per hour out of the damn compound.—*district2fd51*

Demon's Alley Breath

The first house really intrigued me. I stared at the dwelling for a good five minutes before I rolled down the window. I was contemplating going up to it. The passenger in front also rolled his window down. We gazed in awe, when something really weird happened. A blast of hot air slammed my face. It had no odor, but it sent chills from my neck down to my lower back and up again. It was as though something had entered me and exited me through my face.

Needless to say, we flipped out, but that wasn't enough for my friends. They had to feel it.

We drove up and came around again. I shifted to the other side of the back seat, and we both opened our windows. I figured I would test it this time, so we waited. I had my head sticking out the window like a dog, and the car was completely silent. It struck again. This time I took a huge breath as it entered me—no smell. My friend spazzed out. He suddenly became Rainman.

"Yeah, of course, we definitely can't stay here. Yeah, definitely gotta go," he said.

So we got out of there in a hurry. The two of them talked about it for a while. They were loving it. I wasn't. I got sick to my stomach so damn fast it wasn't funny. It was like someone stuck their fist into my gut and was twisting it around. It hurt a lot. I was immobile, and they kept saying that I was possessed. As soon as I got home, I was fine.—*Jim D.*

The Dempsey House

Like Demon's Alley, the Dempsey House in the Leonardo section of Middletown in Monmouth County sat quietly in the woods for many years. Nothing more than a large pump house, the dark and rustic-looking stone building is one of the last remnants of the vast Dempsey estate that once occupied the surrounding grounds. Locals recount how the Dempsey children used to use the building as a playhouse.

Today, with suburban neighborhoods encroaching all around the wooded lot on which the Dempsey House stands, locals wonder what this unkempt relic from another age is still doing in the middle of their well-manicured community. Those who have grown up in those suburban neighborhoods know a different history of the house, and why no one dares disturb it.

Death at the Dempseys'

There was an old couple living in this house years ago. They were the Dempseys. The old man was quite ill. He was bedridden in their second-floor master bedroom. The old woman tended to her husband, bringing him food and water, bathing him, and nurturing him. She would run up and down the stairs twenty-plus times a day. Then one day she went downstairs to begin the same daily tasks but never returned upstairs. The old man waited helplessly for his caregiver to return, but she never did. He slowly died of starvation and dehydration.

Apparently, after a while a call was received by the local police. I am not sure who tipped them off, but nevertheless a response was made. An officer went to investigate. He entered the house. As I recall, the story goes that whatever he had observed or experienced inside drove him to come outside and immediately hang himself on a tree [on] an embankment not far from the house.

The noose was cut down at the time that they took the officer's body away, but the remains of that rope still sway in the breeze to this day.—*S. Gold*

Dr. Dempsey's Acid Overdose

Legend has it that an old doctor lived there with his wife and young daughter. One night the doctor took his daughter and killed her in the basement. Then when his wife came home, he murdered her, too, then drank acid to kill himself.—*Greg A.*

Mr. Dempsey's Ghost Still Roams Leonardo

The house has been condemned for years, and the reason it's standing is still a mystery. Supposedly a Mr. Dempsey and his family lived there. One Halloween, Mr. Dempsey lost it and killed his whole family. After realizing what he did, he hung himself from a tree in the middle of the street at the end of his property. All the kids on Halloween thought his body was just a decoration. Little did they know until daylight that it was his corpse. Some say at night you can still see the noose hanging from the tree.

I personally believe Mr. Dempsey still roams his property. An evil feeling comes over everyone who sets foot on the property. The front of the house is guarded by a spooky-looking rusted gate with a stone wall bordering the outskirts of the property. In the back of the building, there is a part that is open and leads to the basement. There is also a stench that smells like a rotting corpse.

Another legend about the house was that after he killed his wife and three kids, Mr. Dempsey buried the bodies in the basement. Maybe that explains the stench! I have yet to go inside the house, nor would I really want to.–*George G.*

The Gates of Hell

There is no better way to prove one's courage than by walking straight into the gaping maw of hell—the gates of which can be found in the town of Clifton, in Passaic County. This legendary passageway leads to a network of underground tunnels and storm sewers, and some say to the lair of the Evil One himself.

You might think that Gates of Hell would be a common nickname for any dark and foreboding entrance to the underground, but in all of our years of research we have found no other subterranean passage in the state with the same moniker as this Clifton site. It is a very old tunnel with an arched stone ceiling about eight feet high. The light quickly vanishes behind you as you enter, and you are soon enveloped in

total darkness. Even without the presence of Satan, it can be an extremely dangerous place. The tunnel system was built as a drainage runoff for a stream called Weasel Brook, and during heavy rain, the usual trickle of water through the tunnel can almost instantly turn into a raging torrent.

Generations of local teenagers have told stories of what lay deep inside these darkened corridors. Are their tales an accurate depiction of what lies beyond the murky threshold of the Gates of Hell, or are they a window into the dark fears inside us all? Only those who are brave enough, or foolhardy enough, to enter those gates can say for sure.

Enter the Gates of Hell

My first recollections of this place were from the kids at the local BMX bike jumps. They would tell stories of people entering these tunnels and never returning. Satanic sacrifices, decaying carcasses, upside-down crosses, satanic graffiti—anything dealing with the darkness in human nature was down there. Most chilling to me was a secret room many layers under the ground. This room was only to be entered if you possessed powers that enabled you to lift axes that weighed thousands of pounds and blocked the door. Inside this room was a dungeon that housed a human skull, or so it was said. There were seven layers of tunnels under the ground, and the lower you got, the closer you came to meeting the devil.

When I was sixteen, I was introduced to the Gates for the first time. After a few dead ends, we finally found a route to the tunnels. It was dark from all of the tree cover, and my stomach began to drop as we climbed down to the level that the tunnel entrances were located on. I could feel the fear running from my feet straight to my shoulders. All that I had heard and envisioned for the last half of my life was hitting me at once.

Looking at the entrance was more terrifying than anything else. Unlike the other tunnels, which were round and had streams of water flowing from them, this entrance was square and had no water flow. At this point, I was ready to leave and go home. I had seen the entrance, and I now believed everything I heard just by looking at it. It was pure evil. But I realized that the only way to conquer the Gates was to enter the tunnels.

Deep inside the dark tunnel, we started to hear a strange knocking sound. This was a shock to the system, since it had been totally quiet except for the flow of the water. That's when we ran and got the hell out of there. I wasn't sure what we had heard. My friend swears it was someone whispering some chant deeper in the tunnels. Years later, I made several trips back to the Gates of Hell. However, after telling my story, I could never convince anyone to venture into the tunnels as far as my friend and I did that one summer day.—*Ralph Sinisi*

The Portal to Hell Is Down in the Groove

There's supposed to be an area within the Gates that has some very disturbing decor. There are dead trees planted exactly three feet apart from one another with dead cats and birds tied around their trunks.

Another story I've heard is that at the very end of the Gates is the actual portal to hell. There is a groove about twenty feet deep and about forty feet across. At the very center of the groove is a smoothed-out granite manhole, which is supposed to be one of the portals leading to hell.—*Richard M.*

Red-eyed Mike Guards the Gates of Hell

I have explored every inch of Clifton, and nowhere is as eerie as the Gates of Hell! It's said that a spirit, known as Red-eyed Mike, guards the tunnel. If you knock on the railroad ties above the entrance in groups of three, you will hear a loud horn sound from within the tunnel. I have heard this horn on occasion, and have seen rocks hurling themselves out of the tunnel with no person visible inside. I also once witnessed a small human-shaped figure run out of the tunnel toward Weasel Brook Park with superhuman speed. I have been told that this is Red-eyed Mike.—*Jeff H.*

Ancient Mysteries

When you think of ancient structures and cryptic inscriptions from lost civilizations, you usually think of remote areas of the world. But all this and more can be found right in your own New Jersey backyard.

Over millions of years, New Jersey has weathered into a place of great topographical complexity. Formed seventy million years ago from the sands, clay, and marls of the shoreline (which at that time was located around Camden), its earliest landscapes emerged from the highlands. The mountainous, rugged terrain of northwestern New Jersey is sliced through by the ancient Appalachian Mountains on their way from Canada to the Gulf coast of Alabama.

But there is more to New Jersey's ancient past than what appears on the surface. Of course, there are Native American petroglyphs found in caves, crevices, and rock shelters throughout the state. But there is also evidence that Europeans visited or even settled here long before the travels of Christopher Columbus. Inscriptions found on rocks and shelters have turned up ancient languages like Libyan, Celtic, and Phoenician.

These ancient New Jerseyans have left us with their sacred sites, power points, and messages. All that's left for us is to decipher them.

The Stone Living Room *really is a room with a view. Every piece of the Flintstone furniture offers a breathtaking vista of the surrounding mountains of West Milford, Bloomingdale, and New York State.*

Tripod Rocks and Standing Stones

Perched rocks, or dolmens, are found all over the world. These awesome sites feature huge rock structures whose origins have been debated countless times. Were they formed by nature or by man? If glacial movement formed them during an Ice Age forty thousand years ago, it's wondrous that they have remained intact for aeons. If prehistoric cultures constructed them, they remain a testament to the ingenuity of primitive man. And many of them do show evidence that some ancient civilization had a hand in placing them. Some feature drill holes, and others line up with the rising and setting of the sun. This is the case with Tripod Rock on top of Pyramid Mountain, near the Kinnelon/Montville border in Morris County.

Kinnelon's Morris Stonehenge

Kinnelon's Tripod Rock is a massive boulder balanced precariously upon three smaller stones. The formation seems to defy gravity, and looks as if it might just topple over and tumble down the mountain at any moment. When looking north from the dolmen, you can see two stones placed thirty-nine feet beyond. These three formations line up with a V shape formed between two hills three quarters of a mile away. On the summer solstice, the sun lines up right in the V. Looking west, you can see a single standing stone (or monolith) forty-five feet from the dolmen, which lines up with the peak of a hill half a mile in the distance.

It's small wonder that people from the region call Tripod Rock the Morris Stonehenge and that they associate the place with the mystical powers of the megaliths in England that legend says were constructed by the high priests of the Celts — the Druids.

Tripod Rock is part of Pyramid Mountain Natural Historical Area, a state-maintained park. Thanks to the conservation efforts of many local residents, geologists, and archaeologists, the area has been spared from development. Put on your hiking boots for this trip. It's about two miles into the woods, on a slow incline. Maps of Tripod Rock can be found at the beginning of the trails.

West Milford's Mystery Rocks

Another similar structure can be found in the Bearfort Mountain tract in West Milford Township, Passaic County. This structure is a massive chunk of pudding stone perched upon three smaller stones. A bit remote in location, it can be found along the trail just east of Terrace Pond.

Standing stones in West Milford. The white splotches on the rocks are the result of paint-ball fire, not bird droppings.

Tripod Rock *is perched high atop Pyramid Mountain in Kinnelon.*

Also located on Bearfort Mountain is a series of mysteriously perched boulders along the parallel ridges near the fire tower on the Newark Watershed property. Some believe these formations to be nothing more than glacial erratics—odd formations that can be explained geologically—but the state has too many examples for them to be considered truly erratic. Curiously similar perched stones can be found in Norvin Green State Forest and in Ramapo, High Point, and Harriman state parks.

"They are found only on high ridges of exposed bedrock, never in valleys," explains Mark Boyer of Ogdensburg.

"They usually appear in conspicuous clusters with other large boulders, often forming equilateral triangles or three equidistant stones in a straight line, often in a true north–south alignment. Were these ancient trail markers or astronomical indicator stones? No one knows for sure, but certainly they were placed there for a reason."

Were these balanced rocks and standing stones really erected by prehistoric cultures as places of worship, or perhaps even worshiped themselves by sheer virtue of their awesome stature? It is a mystery as old as the hills on which they stand.

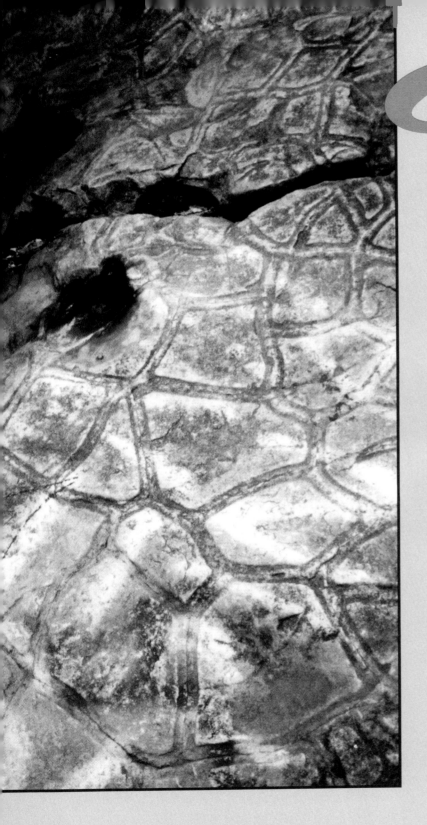

Cryptic Carvings

When the past speaks to us in the modern world, its messages are often written in stone. Sometimes these voices from long ago provide a record of a lost and forgotten civilization. In other instances, the curious markings we see in rock are the work of some geological anomaly. Trying to figure out which is which is usually the best part of the game. But sometimes, deciphering the hidden meanings is like trying to piece together a jigsaw puzzle with missing pieces, and without the benefit of a picture to work from.

Of course, scrutinizing anything prehistoric is bound to raise unanswerable questions that lead to some heated debate. The fact is that we just don't know the meaning of many cryptic inscriptions handed down to us through the misty veils of time. Some will be forever shrouded in mystery and will continue to be the subjects of speculation and conjecture for generations to come.

Turtle Back Rock of West Orange

Some strange carving might look man-made, but the artfully designed patterns are most likely in reality to be the handiwork of Mother Nature. One such stone is the Turtle Back Rock of West Orange.

As a resident of Essex County for most of my life, and one who takes pride in my knowledge of local sites, I was quite surprised when an e-mail tipster suggested that Weird NJ check out the Turtle Back Rock. Of course I was familiar with the Turtle Back Zoo (I even worked there one summer as a teenager), but I had never heard of a Turtle Back Rock. I had always assumed that the zoo had gotten its name from less enlightened times, when animal cruelty was considered harmless fun and children were encouraged to ride on the backs of the zoo's poor lumbering reptiles. According to Jim Ospenson, though, the zoo actually took its name from a strange rock formation that is found close by.

"The Turtle Back Rock," Jim writes, "refers to a bluff over Northfield Avenue that has extensive markings—grooved ovoid patterns that are textured like those on a turtle's back, except larger. As many times as I climbed on the rock, playing cowboys and Indians or cutting school and smoking, the origins of the markings were never explained to me. Indian carvings? Some sort of natural event? I don't know."

After poking around in the forest of the South Mountain Reservation for a while, I found myself perched atop a rock cliff overlooking a small stream. There were several large boulders scattered around, which I examined closely. Each one had a distinct pattern on its surface, and I'll be damned if it didn't look just like the markings on the back of a turtle. I have never seen anything quite like it before. I would guess that the seemingly arbitrary mosaic of grooved patterns was not the work of human hands, but I could not say for sure. Some geologist somewhere could probably offer a long-winded scientific explanation for the rock's reptilian relief. Perhaps it was once the bottom of a dry lake bed or the crust of cooling molten rock, but for me it's enough to know that it just looks like a turtle's shell.—*MM*

Opposite page:
Turtle Back Rock *is located in the South Mountain Reservation in West Orange, Essex County.*

The Garfield Rock *carvings are either the best examples New Jersey has of primitive art or one of the state's earliest signs of crude graffiti.*

The Garfield Rock Carvings

New Jersey's rock carvings, called petroglyphs, have never been fully documented, despite the many surveys of Indian villages and shelters that have taken place over the years. But there's one documented site in Garfield that deserves a very close look. It's a sandstone boulder located along the Passaic River, below the one-hundred-and-forty-year-old Dundee Dam in Garfield. On it are markings believed to date to the Woodland Period, which ran from 1000 B.C. to the Native Americans' first contact with Europeans in 1650. Local archaeologists believe it's a truly exciting find, since no other petroglyphs have been found in the area.

The graffiti-marred stone has four carved symbols: a bear paw with claw marks, a fish, a phallus, and a set of initials. The bear paw and fish are similar in design, suggesting the same carver. The phallus may have been chiseled by another hand, possibly at a different time.

But there's a bigger mystery to the Garfield Rock Carvings than the identity of the artist behind them and the time in which

he lived. What's more mysterious still is what they mean. The depiction of the bear paw, which is the most pronounced element, seems to be a Native American symbol. So does the phallus. But the opposite side of the stone clearly shows the letters AL and a score of five deeply etched into the boulder above the picture of a fish. The symbols may represent the fishing territory of a particular group or a warning that bears also fished in these waters. The phallus may suggest a sign to the spirits, hoping for an abundance of fish.

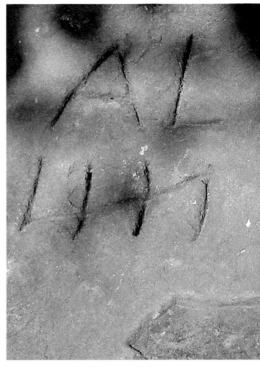

Or perhaps it indicates that someone named Al or with the initials AL had caught five fish in the river that day. The fish appears to be jumping out of the water (an image that bears a striking resemblance to the *Field & Stream* decals an outdoorsman might place on the back window of his 4X4 pickup truck). Perhaps Al also carved the bear paw while he was killing time waiting for the fish to bite, and added the phallic symbol when he was feeling a bit randy.

It is even possible that the ancient graffiti on the boulder might represent a turf war. The location was undoubtedly a popular fishing location for both the local Indians and the white settlers of the area. Perhaps the old and new cultures that shared the river for a time added their "tags" to the stone, much as modern-day gangs mark their territory with spray paint.

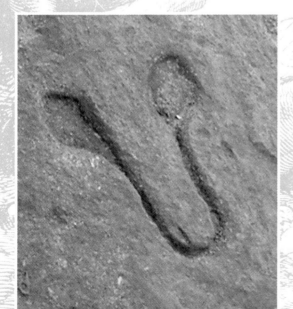

Are these carvings ancient or just a work of art crafted by a hobo or perhaps a truant schoolboy many years ago? We will probably never know the answers to this Stone Age question. The last time we visited the site, the rock was smack-dab in the middle of an encampment of homeless people. Apparently, the river and its carved stone are still a draw for those who choose to live a primitive lifestyle.

Whatever Became of the Pemberton Wedge?

Significant Native American populations have resided in Pemberton in Burlington County for more than ten thousand years. The area, located within the Rancocas Creek watershed area, has yielded artifact finds confirming the presence of indigenous people in and around Pemberton for years. One such artifact is an amazing inscribed stone found in 1859 by Dr. J. W. C. Evans. The six-by-four-inch sandstone ax was inscribed with ten characters. In 1861, archaeologist James Whittall read the published report of the artifact in a Boston library and subsequently published an interpretation of the markings in the Early Sites Research Society's bulletin. The bulletin claimed the script was Tartessian, the language was Iberian, and the inscription read, "Stand firm, on guard, parry, close in and strike."

Over the years, the Pemberton Wedge seems to have been misplaced, sent off to a museum, or simply buried among Pemberton's historic artifacts. No one knows exactly what happened to it. But with other similar stones being unearthed every few decades, it might be worth a walk along the Rancocas Creek to see if there is any more evidence of an ancient civilization that once called New Jersey its home.

The Mysterious Pemberton Wedge

An illustration of the stone, an ancient wedge-shaped ax head, was published in the *American Ethnological Proceedings* in 1861. The Pemberton Axe Pictograph has been further described in Salvatore Michael Trento's 1978 book *The Search for Lost America.* Many other inscribed stones have been found along the Delaware River in both New Jersey and Pennsylvania. Much on this subject has been further explained by the late Dr. Barry Fell of the Epigraphic Society in his book *America B.C.*

Pictographs are still being found in the Pemberton area. One such stone found near the Rancocas Creek is inscribed with ancient Celtic letters. Other stones bear inscriptions that appear to be of Viking and Saxon origin (pre-Columbian). The Pemberton Axe Pictograph is likely Phoenician, a people who sailed the Mediterranean about three thousand years ago.

In Tennessee, an ancient form of Hebrew was found inscribed on a stone that is now in the Smithsonian Institution. In other states, pictographs have been found and deciphered as Egyptian hieroglyphics, Roman Latin, and an unknown form of ogham, an ancient Celtic alphabet.

One thing is certain: Over the millennia, there have been many lost and shipwrecked visitors to our shores. The Pemberton pictographs would seem to indicate that there were some who enjoyed the natural environment of what we now know as "our Pemberton," long before Columbus got lost and our colonizing European forefathers were discovering Algonquian-speaking people.–*Harry S. Monesson*

Not-so-ancient Mysteries

Not all mysterious ancient sites are prehistoric. Though some of these sites were undoubtedly created in more recent times, their creators, meanings, and functions still cause us to wonder about them today. Here are some stone formations and carvings that are perhaps only a few hundred years old, if even that, but their mysteries still beg answers and inspire the imaginations of people throughout modern-day New Jersey.

Strange Markings Along the Lawrence Brook

On the New Brunswick embankment of Weston Mill Pond, some strange symbols can be found, carved into the red sandstone. Though they date back to 1876, nobody to date has been able to decode them. The etched symbols look like letters of some kind, but do not seem to be of any known language.

Weird NJ met up with Mark Nonestied of the Middlesex County Cultural and Heritage Commission, who took us along the path that leads to the mystery symbols and told us what he thinks they might be.

"The carvings are very fine. Obviously, they knew what they were doing," Nonestied said.

We noticed the similarity in the carving style to many of the gravestones from the era when these inscriptions were made. This, along with the fact that the riverside cliffs showed signs of having been quarried, lead us to speculate that the chiseling graffiti artists were perhaps tombstone carvers by trade.

There are other carvings along the brook that depict skulls and crossbones and graffiti from the nineteenth century, including the words "Red Rover," the name of a popular pirate novel of the time. Nonestied noted that the town of East Brunswick also got into the graffiti business.

"In 1976, the East Brunswick Bicentennial Commission added their insignia to these rocks, but they had a hard time digging into the shale."

Upon reaching the site, Nonestied said that there might be a simple explanation for the symbols, but that secret will be forever kept by the carvers.

"Maybe it says, 'Drink at Jacob's Tavern,' " we mused. "The names carved above the symbols were New Brunswick residents. They were found in some census records. But why they did this no one knows.

"The Red Rover carvings are on the New Brunswick side and rather difficult to get to. You'll see their names again, and a skull and crossbones, but not these symbols," Nonestied noted.

These ancient carvings have withstood the test of time, weather, and the re-damming of Lawrence Brook river. What the symbols signify will most likely remain a mystery for the ages.

The 300 Stone Steps of Morris Plains

The 300 Stone Steps of Morris Plains seem to be an enigma. Some believe the stairs were constructed by Washington's troops during the Revolutionary War so that lookouts could signal neighboring towns with a fire to warn them of British troop movements. Others claim that the steps are the handiwork of Native Americans and were laid long before the Continental Army used the site to spot redcoats.

One thing is certain: The steps are so mysterious that no one in the town seems to know where they are. We stopped in the Morris Plains police station one cold winter day to inquire about their location.

"I've lived here all my life," one officer told us, "but I've never heard of them." We called the local town historian from the police station, hoping that she could head us in the right direction.

"The 300 Steps?" she said. "Oh, yes, I know about them. If you'd like to stop by, I can show you where they are on a map. Where are you now?"

We told her we were in the parking lot of the police station.

"Well, if you're in the parking lot, you're looking at my house. I'm right next to it!"

We took a few giant steps and were on her porch in less than a minute. Although she said she knew where the steps were, getting to them was not so easy. With all of us looking at a map, things became a bit confused.

"Well, you turn here and turn there, but you can't get to it from here, because the road is blocked off, so you have to go around to there."

We just asked her to pinpoint the location, and we'd find our own way.

"They are way off into the woods, deep in the forest. Our group is planning a hike to them in the

spring," she said. But at that point, we were really only half listening. In our heads, we already had one foot out the door and one foot on the first of the 300 Steps.

We hit the road and made our way through the vast desolate expanse of the Greystone Psychiatric Hospital grounds, to the foot of Watnong Mountain. According to the location we were given, the 300 Steps were to be found right off Mountain Way. Since it was the middle of the winter, it was easy to peer through the trees in search of anything weird.

We pulled into a parking lot close to where we thought the steps would be found. There was a park there, and a sign enclosed in a glass case that describes the area. Part of it reads like this:

"Central to the lot is an extensive set of stone steps, reputedly laid by engineers and/or scouts for General George Washington during the Revolutionary War. They facilitated the climb to the south face of the then denuded top of Watnong Mountain. Here a massive bonfire was laid as a warning beacon to alert American troops in the Jockey Hollow area to any strategic movement undertaken by the British. There seems to be little doubt about the authenticity of the beacon site."

There were no clear directions posted on how to get to the steps, though, so we decided to just take the hike into the woods and see what we could find. Not more than two hundred feet along the trail, we came upon the mysterious 300 Stone Steps.

"Well, I wouldn't exactly call this 'deep in the forest,' " said Mark M.

"Good thing we didn't wait until the hiking expedition next spring!" said I.

"Start counting," Mark said as he began to climb. "1, 2, 3 . . ."

The flat stones ranged from one to two feet in width and ascended the mountain in a zigzag fashion. As we climbed, we could see why Washington might have wanted to use this spot for observation. You could easily see the surrounding towns from the hill. I would imagine in the 1700s the view must have been quite impressive.

As Mark got just over the summit, he yelled back down, "I only count two hundred and sixty-eight!" Satisfied with his math, I decided to take his word for it and get myself off of that freezing mountainside. My foot slipped on an ice-covered stone, and I proceeded to tumble down about twenty of the two hundred and sixty-eight steps. I finally landed on my shoulder and heard a loud crunch. Ouch! Something didn't feel right. Especially when I couldn't lift my arm.

"Are you all right?" Mark yelled from the top of the mountain.

"No!" I bellowed. "I think I broke my arm, goddammit! These are the two hundred and sixty-eight steps to hell!"

After moaning all the way to the hospital and spending three hours getting X-rayed, I was told that my arm was not broken, just badly bruised. Physical therapy was the only treatment they could offer me. The next day, about ten inches of snow fell on New Jersey, but I was too incapacitated to even shovel the three stone steps outside my front door. Luckily nobody took a fall.

The Stone Living Room

Perched high above the border of West Milford and Bloomingdale in Passaic County, one can relax and enjoy the view from the Stone Living Room. This arrangement of stone chairs and tables is the creation of a mysterious group of stonemasons who remain anonymous to this day. When and why the living room was built we cannot say for sure. Some of the rocks weigh in excess of four hundred pounds and must have been lifted and set in place with incredible determination. Complete with a fireplace and a few cozy couches, the Stone Living Room can accommodate two dozen or more weary travelers after their one-mile climb up the mountain.

When Weird NJ first visited the site back in 1997, we encountered two other hikers and inquired about the Living Room's possible decorators. "Holy shit," said one of the men when we showed him the site. "I hike this trail every day, and I never knew this was here. This is amazing!" Amazing it is, and the view isn't that bad either.

On August 26, 2001, a spiral-bound journal and pen were left among the rocks of the Living Room in a double-bagged plastic pouch. Here visitors could sign in and share their thoughts and reflections on the site. Some even offer a bit of poetry to their fellow travelers. Though we'd been informed of a

previous journal kept at the site, this new one is the only one still present. Perhaps the former book suffered a fiery fate some cold night on the mountain when kindling was in short supply.

The trail to the Stone Living Room can be found along Glenwild Avenue. Park at the roadside lot by the WELCOME TO WEST MILFORD sign. Cross the street and follow the blue trail straight up the mountain, bearing right. Don't forget to bring refreshments, because you'll need them.

Since we first published our story of the Stone Living Room, we've received several letters from our readers voicing different opinions about the possible origins of this unique stone structure—everything from Native American craftsmen to stoned-out hippy architects. The following letters speculate about the monolithic mountaintop furniture.

Mysterious Cult Lounges at Stone Living Room

I can tell you a little more about the Stone Living Room. My sister built the contemporary house on the left as you go up Glenwild Avenue, just before you get to the path. She owned ten acres of land bordering that edge of the state park. As I was growing up, I journeyed through these woods, and I know everything about them.

The stones on the top of the mountain were moved there by a cult. At night, you could hear them chanting from my sister's house. Trust me, it was very spooky. I had a friend who was in a cult that helped in making this. This was an area where they could get closer to the sky and be away from authorities.

There was another reason they chose this spot. It is said these woods are haunted, and I know they are. Mysterious things happen at this site. If you walk straight back from the path going toward the stones and then on past them, you will reach a ledge. Along this area, there are many circles of stones laid out in a pattern. You can destroy them and come back in a day, and they will be the same again.—*Brian*

Chillin' at the Stone Living Room

I live across the street from the Stone Living Room, and my friends and I have been up there before. We saw a signing book, and when we were there, weird stuff started to happen. Trees were cracking, and we thought we saw and heard someone yelling, "Come here," and screams of a girl getting beaten or something. That was just the first time. We go up there often during the summer, and weird stuff always happens.

One time we were sitting in the chairs and something pushed us and it got really cold. This was the middle of the summer, and it doesn't go from ninety-five degrees to fifty degrees that fast.—*Krystle R. and Lauren K.*

The Stone Living Room Builders Exposed?

I know one of the architects of the Stone Living Room! I can't tell you her name, since I met her through work. She was a client of an attorney I worked for several years ago, and ethical constraints and a confidentiality agreement restrain me from divulging client names. Anyway, when I mentioned to this client in passing one day about my hobby of hiking every weekend and our discovery of the Stone Living Room on one of our many hikes, she laughed at me when I speculated about ancient natives or maybe Boy Scouts possibly dragging the stones together.

She told me that when she was a hippie teenager growing up in Pompton Lakes in the late '60s or early '70s, she and a bunch of her friends would hike up the mountain most weekends to hang out and drink beer, smoke pot, etc., because it was remote and had a great view. She says they tired of sitting on the rocky, bumpy ground and decided one day to clear out the small stones and drag the really big ones together. It just happened to be coincidence that the uniquely shaped stones were there to make the "chairs."

The guys in the group got together and did all the heavy lifting. She said it took them several weekends to do it all, but it was well worth the effort. She also told me that she had recently hiked up there again and was amazed that almost nothing had changed. Even she was surprised at the size of the stones, as she didn't remember them being so big and heavy. However, she did say that they were not only drinking beer and smoking pot but doing some pretty heavy drugs, too. I wouldn't be surprised if some of her friends might have been using acid (which has a side effect of amazing displays of strength) and therefore wouldn't have had much problem moving those big stones. I didn't doubt her story since I had found her to be a very reasonable and honest person.—*Amy D.*

Architect of Stone Living Room Speaks Out

I grew up on the hill on Glenwild Avenue. The Stone Living Room was built in my youth as a place for kids to drink beer in peace. My parents purchased the property in 1987 and built their dream home on the mountain. A handful of friends and I decided to build a party spot. What began as just a few pieces of slate rock on top of each other matured into the little Flintstones area your readers have dubbed the Stone Living Room. The only thing out of the ordinary about the enclosure was the inscription of a black crow in the rock floor on the west side of the firepit.—*Ryan A.*

Holes in the Ground

Not only does New Jersey have its share of mysterious mountaintop oddities, but there are also some hallowed holes to explore.

The Brau Kettle

Located off Old Mine Road in Sandyston, Sussex County, is a local phenomenon known as the Brau Kettle. It's a hole about thirteen feet deep when dry. The name Brau comes from the German word meaning "brew." When you watch the hole filling up with water, as if by magic, you can see what the early settlers meant.

This unusual geological formation is part of the Delaware Water Gap National Recreation Area. You can climb into it when it's dry, but it is known to fill up with water quickly. Over the years, people have filled it with rocks, boards, and fence rails, which all disappear to the bottom. The bottom of the hole consists of a reddish sandy soil. Some geologists suggest that it might be some sort of quicksand but don't quite know how to get to the bottom of the mystery.

Legends of the Blue Hole

One of the most storied sites in all of southern New Jersey is a mysterious body of water known as the Blue Hole. Located deep in the Pine Barrens of Winslow, on the border of Camden and Gloucester counties, this small but legendary pool is said to not only be bottomless but also to be a frequent pit stop of the Jersey Devil.

Though its icy blue-tinged water might seem inviting, especially on a hot summer day, locals warn their children to stay away from the Blue Hole and to never go swimming there. Tales of unexplained whirlpools that suck down hapless swimmers have long been part of the hole's lore. Some who have been lucky enough to escape its clutches have claimed that they actually felt something, perhaps the Jersey Devil himself, pulling them down into the chilly depths.

The bottom of the Blue Hole, if indeed there is a bottom, is said to be made of a fine sand, sometimes referred to as sugar sand, which locals liken to quicksand. When we visited the notorious hole, we found ourselves navigating through narrow pineland trails made up of this same treacherous sand. Sure that at any moment our Jeep would get hopelessly bogged down, we decided to ditch the vehicle and continue our quest on foot.

It was a beautiful autumn day as we wandered the wooded paths of the Winslow

Wildlife Management Area. The underbrush was awash with bright cranberry red and golden-colored leaves, and the sound of birds chirping filled the sweet-smelling air. As we approached the Blue Hole, though, the atmosphere seemed to change. The birds were heard no more, and in their stead was an eerie silence. The quiet was soon shattered, however, by the echoes of shotgun blasts from a nearby firing range ringing through the tranquil forest.

The surface of the Blue Hole was as still as glass, and a thermometer that we'd brought to measure its temperature read a chilly fifty degrees Fahrenheit. Although the water was crystal-clear, we could see no signs of life in the hole whatsoever; no fish, no insects—nothing. There was something unsettling about this void, and suddenly it seemed easy to imagine why people might warn their children not to venture into these waters.

Although it might have a bad reputation now, this was not always the case with the Blue Hole. In the 1930s, the site was a popular picnic spot and swimming hole among the locals. In the 1940s, though, a storm washed out a wooden bridge over the nearby Egg Harbor River, cutting off the main access route to the Blue Hole. Ever since then it has remained isolated in a dense forest of scrub pines, accessible only by foot or off-road vehicle.

The Blue Hole is approximately one hundred and thirty feet across, almost perfectly round, and has steep banks. Its waters remain curiously cold, even in the hottest summer months, averaging about fifty-eight degrees. Its water is clear, unlike most bodies of water in the Pine Barrens, which have such a high content of iron, tannic acid, and suspended sediment that they bear a coloration similar to tea.

There are several theories as to how the Blue Hole came to be. Some say that it is the result of a meteorite striking the earth. Others claim that it is what geologists call a pingo. A pingo is a small body of water that originates during an ice age when an ice mass forms beneath permanently frozen soil. The ice mass expands for thousands of years, then breaks through the permafrost to create a depression rimmed by a hill. When the climate warms, the ice melts, forming a pool.

But what about the fabled whirlpools, or what the locals refer to as whirlypools, which are said to drag down unsuspecting swimmers to their watery graves? How could such a current exist in such a seemingly placid body of water? One explanation for this might be that the Blue Hole is fed by groundwater, not the nearby stream. This fact explains why the water is not the same murky color as the river, and might also be the reason for the mysterious surges of current.

Scientific rationale does little to lessen the mysteries of this curious body of water, though, which seem to run as deep as the Blue Hole itself.

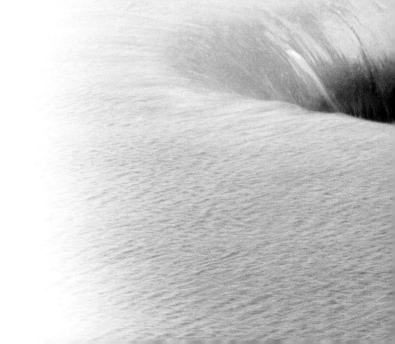

Don't Dive into the Blue Hole!

I mentioned the Blue Hole to my dad, who has lived in South Jersey all his life. Much to my surprise he knew exactly what I was talking about. When he was a kid, growing up in Blue Anchor (part of Winslow), he and his friends would go swimming in the creek about a hundred feet from the Blue Hole. My dad was told never to go swimming in the Blue Hole, because it was bottomless and freezing cold. Of course, my dad and his friends immediately had to try it. One jumped in, then climbed right out. The water was indeed freezing in the middle of summer. Another one of my father's friends who dove in did not escape as easily.

The hole looks to be about seventy feet across and roughly circular. The edges appeared to be raised, which was consistent with one of the rumors I had read: that the Blue Hole was actually a crater from an ancient meteor. The bottom, at least on the edge, was only about a foot.

An eerie calm hung over the entire spot when I visited the Blue Hole. Maybe it was the ghost of one of my father's friends, who dove in headfirst and broke his neck. *–Tony D.*

Blue Hole Too Deep to Fathom

I grew up visiting the Blue Hole often and can confirm the story. Henry Charlton Beck, a renowned, credible historian of New Jersey, devotes a chapter to the Blue Hole and its legends in his book *Forgotten Towns of Southern New Jersey.* In it, he recounts tales from old piney folk about people who died in the hole over the years, as well as the occasion when a group of scientists visited the hole to determine its depth. To accomplish this, they lowered an enormous length of twine with a heavy weight tied to the end of it into the water. After dropping a mile of twine into the center of the hole, they gave up their investigation (this was in the 1920s, I believe). *–Eric J.*

Dragged Down in the Blue Hole

The water is deep blue and ice cold. I, too, hear that there is an undercurrent that pulls swimmers to the bottom. Strange thing is, there is a murky lake nearby, but this hole is crystal-clear, while the deep part is blue. Rumor has it that it is about one hundred feet deep and that many people have drowned in it. *–Rob G.*

Fabled People and Places

Once upon a time in a land called New Jersey . . .

own through the ages, the quest for mythical lands and fabled people has circled the globe. Medieval knights searched for the Holy Grail. Spanish conquistadors sought the Fountain of Youth and El Dorado, the city of gold. Lewis and Clark tried in vain to locate the Northwest Passage. And Donovan pined in song for the lost continent of Atlantis.

Here in New Jersey, we yearn for humbler but equally elusive places. We quest for colonies of undersized or underpigmented people, for clans of Jackson Whites, Kallikaks, and Van Cleefs. We set out on our expeditions with all the fervent conviction of Don Quixote, going forth to face his windmill giants. And we keep an open mind, for we want to believe, even though we know these things we seek may only exist in the collective imagination of New Jersey's residents.

The Quest for Midgetville

Fascination with miniature versions of everyday things seems to be part of human nature. This is evident nowhere more than in the fascination with miniature people. Little people, or midgets, have always been showstoppers, from General Tom Thumb in P. T. Barnum's circus, through the Munchkins of Oz, to the Mini-Me in the Austin Powers movies.

Little people enjoy an elevated status in the minds of New Jerseyans, too. Weird NJ has heard many tales of a scaled-down town with tiny inhabitants driving downsize vehicles past diminutive traffic signs. According to legend, such houses and communities were custom built for groups of little people who had retired from a circus or the vaudeville stage. One aspect of these stories that remains fairly constant is the fact that the occupants are usually hostile toward outsiders. This is undoubtedly because the residents of these rumored Midgetvilles get annoyed at the late-night

MALINDA, DAUGHT

gawkers who plague them year after year. That's why we never give the exact locations of the supposed Midgetville communities.

Weird NJ has visited at least half a dozen locations in search of Midgetville, and in most cases, we have come up short. Many leads turn out to be cottage communities of vacation homes built in the first half of the twentieth century. They seem odd to people today because they are much smaller than your average New Jersey residence. Other sites that we've investigated have had suspiciously small doorways and windows and looked inconvenient if not impossible for an average-sized adult to live in comfortably.

Our quest for the real Midgetville is one of the main reasons why we are still out on the road after all these years. For us it is like the Holy Grail of Weird NJ, our El Dorado. If there is any truth to the rumors, we must see it with our own eyes.

Midgets Play Small Role in War Effort

When I was a kid, we used to ride our bikes down from Cliffside Park to the Midgetville on River Road in Edgewater. There were midgets living there at one time. The stop signs were also nailed low. I have driven through there once or twice in recent years, and a lot of the small houses have been replaced with newer, larger houses. The area is prime real estate.

My father told me that in the late 30s, before the war, industry along the Hudson River began contributing to the war effort. The midgets were vaudeville and circus workers who found their niche in the war industry for specific tasks, such as rivet men crawling inside the wings of planes. *–Ernest P.*

Attacked by Midgets Near the GWB

One kid told us the story of Midget Town and how he had been there and was nearly killed. We all wanted to go and see this village for ourselves. The kid was hesitant to show us, but he finally agreed. I'm not sure exactly what town we were in, but it was real close to the entrance to the George Washington Bridge. The houses were unusually small. The doors were just about five feet high, and the roads were very tight. All of a sudden we saw little midgets running after our cars throwing rocks. We didn't stay, because the kid who owned the car didn't want the car to get messed up. *–Polo Bear*

Doing the "Midget Thing" in Totowa

I just came back from Midgetville in Totowa, by Route 46. The houses were really small, and we saw a couple midgets doing their midget thing. The cars were also much smaller than normal. *–JSmallZz*

Midgetville is located about two blocks off of Annie's Road. Don't be fooled, but there are no little houses. They live in the same size houses as everyone else.

–Kristie

Four of my friends and I went to Totowa to go to Annie's Road. We didn't see Annie, but we saw Midgetville and took pictures. Then we were coming to the end of the road and we met this midget named George. We also have pictures of him. He gave us his phone number! *–Cassie G.*

Which Way to Midgetville?

We heard the stories of people getting shot at and cars being destroyed by bricks, so we parked under the Route 80 overpass and decided to walk in. We went up to a pickup truck to ask for directions. In the truck was a midget driver and a midget kid in the passenger seat. She would not give us directions. We then turned around, and another car came up to us. This car was loaded with six midgets. We asked them for directions, and the driver gave them to us, but he looked really mad.—*Fender 102*

The Right to Bear Small Arms

Recently I visited this small place, and there were many, many little people there. I was driving by, and I heard bangs as I saw a few dwarves and thought they were throwing cans at my car. When I got out to check the damage, it was much more than I had expected. I found nine bullet holes on the passenger's side of my brand new car. I went to the police. They told me that I wasn't supposed to be down there, and that any car that entered without a permit was shot at.—*Jessica M.*

O Midgetville, Midgetville! Wherefore Art Thou, Midgetville?

We took a class trip to Midgetville somewhere in northern New Jersey. The houses were tiny, yet the stop signs were normal. We were going to see *Romeo and Juliet* in an old, very tiny Victorian castle. The people who put the play on were normal-sized, however.

The houses were set back almost in the woods. There was not one normal-sized house among them. A few of the houses looked abandoned, but the rest were in good shape. We didn't see anyone but the actors there. There were no people in the streets or driving. It looked kind of spooky. The buses had a hard time getting through the tiny streets.—*Ashley*

No Midgets in Midgetville

Me and my boys went to Midgetville twice and did not see one damn midget. What's up with that?—*Jarret*

This photo *shows the cast of freaky performers employed by the Ringling Bros. circus in the early 1920s.*

RINGLING MANOR - 1916
PRE-REVOLUTIONARY PETERSBURG FORGE. LATER THE SITE OF ALFRED T. RINGLING ESTATE. CIRCUS ACTS AUDITIONED IN MANSION. ANIMALS AND CIRCUS EQUIPMENT OFTEN HOUSED IN OUTBUILDINGS.

NATIONAL REGISTER OF HISTORIC PLACES
NEW JERSEY REGISTER OF HISTORIC PLACES
MORRIS COUNTY HERITAGE COMMISSION

The Real Midgetville?

The most credible reports of Midgetville that we've investigated center on a remote enclave of houses in the woods of Jefferson Township in northern Morris County, near the St. Stanislaus Friary. That's because this monastery used to be the estate of circus mogul Alfred T. Ringling.

In 1913, Ringling purchased nearly a thousand acres of land in the area, then known as Petersburg, to build an estate and winter home for his performers (many of whom were little people). The estate proper consisted of a hundred acres, with a stately twenty-six-room stone mansion overlooking the grounds, barns, and cobblestone elephant houses. The circus would arrive at the nearby Oak Ridge train station each autumn and trek four miles down the dirt path of Berkshire Valley Road on foot or by horse-drawn wagon to the Ringling estate to spend the winter months. When Alfred died in 1919, the circus moved to Bridgeport, Connecticut, then to Sarasota, Florida, its winter quarters to this day.

When Weird NJ went in search of the Jefferson Midgetville, we stopped in to ask the monastery's Capuchin Fathers for information. Though they were gracious enough to give us a tour of the old mansion, they said they knew nothing of any nearby midget colonies.

But down a narrow dirt road leading through a pine forest, we found a group of small houses, a few of which were no larger than the prefabricated backyard sheds that you find at Home Depot. But these were actual houses, and cozy little cottages at that, some decorated with flower boxes and Pennsylvania Dutch–style ornamentation. An average-sized adult would be able to stand upright only at the very center of these houses, where the pitched roof was highest, and they would definitely have to stoop down to look out a window or get through a doorway. We knocked on the little doors and peeked through the tiny windows, but unfortunately there were no residents, midget or otherwise, to be found anywhere.

Is it merely a coincidence that a cluster of extremely small cottages is located so close to the estate where a circus that employed many little people performers once wintered? Or is it possible that Alfred T. Ringling had these homes custom built to make his tinier attractions more comfortable?

Ringling Brothers Midgets in Jefferson

I grew up in Jefferson Township, in the northern corner of Morris County. Midgetville is actually on a dirt road near the old Ringling Brothers estate. There are actually eight or nine small houses along the short stretch of dirt road that backs up to nothing but woods. I have explored the area numerous times both during the day and at night. The houses are brightly painted and have small doors and windows. I have never seen any evidence of little people, dangerous or otherwise. There is a NO TRESPASSING sign, and the police do patrol the area. –*Lauren*

Albino Village

A lack of pigmentation really freaks out some people. Even in this age of greater acceptance of people of color, many folks seem to have deep-rooted prejudices against those devoid of color. Evidence of this fear can be found in the hundreds of letters we have received at *Weird NJ* over the years from readers relating frightening encounters they have had with albinos.

One of the most fabled locations in New Jersey lore is called Albino Village. The legend of Albino Village dates back to the early 1900s. The original settlement was located in the town of Clifton, in Passaic County, also called Frogtown because of its proximity to the Passaic River. As rumors of a community of pallid people living there spread, so did its new name.

During the 1950s and early '60s, when B movies exploited all kinds of fears, many teenagers would pay a late-night visit to Albino Village hoping to scare their dates. Such trips went something like this: You would drive your car down the isolated back road leading to the old stone railroad bridge that marked the entrance to the village. At this point, your date would probably already be inching closer to you and perhaps even clutching you for comfort, if you were lucky. Then the real fun would begin. The driver of the car would kill the headlights and drive ever so slowly through the narrow darkened tunnel, inching closer to the fabled land of the albinos. Once inside the tunnel, there was no turning back.

Once you emerged from the portal, you would drive as quietly as possible, gawking at the cottages. The road was a dead end, and the only way out was back through the tunnel from whence you had come. Most drivers would turn around, turn on their headlights, honk the horn, and hang out the car's windows beating on the doors, screaming, "Albinos!" to coax some of the pale people from their shadowy lairs.

Usually folks didn't stick around long enough to see whether the aggravated residents were albinos or not. Most had already put the pedal to the metal and were through the tunnel and speeding away.

Partying Out in Albino Village

I know Albino Village very well, as it is in my old neighborhood and we used to party out on top of that bridge in the early '70s. I was best friends with a dude that lived at the end of that road after you pass under the tunnel and it turns into a dead end. To my knowledge, there were never any albinos that had lived there. It was a rumor that was started years ago by the high school gang that would drive their cars down there to scare the pants off their dates. —*Dwight*

The Albinos' Revenge

I went to Albino Village with six other cars of teens one night. The people blocked the exit after we turned around. When we got out of the car to see why, they pulled a rifle and held us until the police came and checked us all out. Of course, the rifle disappeared. It was a scary night, to say the least. —*Dennis*

Albinos Will Net You

I remember taking dates through the tunnel in the mid-'70s but with a twist. Early in the day, we'd hang pieces of string or old netting from the bridge and tell our dates that the albinos would net us if we screamed! Of course, with the windows fogged up, this trick made it even spookier! —*Cousin G.*

Albino Encounters

Clifton is not the only town said to be home to albino colonies. Here are some stories of other pale peoples found around the state.

Heed the Albinos' Warnings in Sparta

In the late '70s, I went out cruising on my motorcycle, going up to Lake Mohawk in Sparta. I went from a paved road to a dirt road that led down to what I thought was an abandoned town or village. There were lots of signs that said KEEP OUT and GO AWAY, and I recall seeing junk cars and a lot of debris spread about. The sound of my engine brought a large pack of wild dogs that eventually surrounded my bike.

Next thing I knew, a guy pulled up in an old Jeep Wrangler, wielding a shotgun, with a holstered gun and knife on his side. He yelled, "What do you want? You best turn around!" He wore mirrored sunglasses and a large hat. I also noticed he was really pale-skinned. Within moments, several other people came out, and all of them were equally fair-skinned and had pure white hair. My only concern was to get the hell out of there and hopefully in one piece. I slowly turned my bike around, apologized for causing a disturbance, and rode back down the dirt road. I dared not look back, and I only prayed that I would not be shot in the back. The dirt road led to a paved road and civilization. I spotted a state trooper parked up on the side of the road. I got off my bike and told him what had just occurred. He was not surprised by my findings, telling me he hears these stories all the time. He further told me that there are several communities of albino people in the mountainous areas. They live their own lives and make their own laws. Very rarely do they ever venture out of the mountains. The trooper further stated that even the police won't go into their areas. In retrospect, I guess I was really lucky.—*Johnnie F.*

Albino Attack

As an incurable insomniac, I have been known to hop in my car at all hours of the night and drive aimlessly to points unknown. On one of my nocturnal travels, I wound up on a deserted road in the upper regions of Passaic County. To my total horror a gang of baseball bat–wielding albinos emerged out of the woods and surrounded my car, threatening to kill me if I didn't get out of there. I hit the gas pedal and sped off into the darkness, never once looking back at these white, ghostlike people.

I am not a troublemaking wise guy. I would never bother anyone who was different. But this frightening experience in the New Jersey hinterlands has restricted my nightly drives to local diners and laundromats.—*Stephen*

Beware the Midget Albino Cannibals of Boonton

A few years back, my friend's mother was driving down a back road with her two kids in the car. A gang of midget albinos emerged from the woods and grabbed her son from the back seat of the car. She drove off, and a few months later, the boy's body was found. As my friend tells it, it appeared they had eaten him. I'm not sure how true this is, but he has promised to find me some newspaper articles from when it all happened.—*Rebecca K.*

Alpine's Albino Commune

The year was 1975. Three friends and I were driving just a few minutes north of the George Washington Bridge. As we passed a nondescript dirt road, someone brought up the old story we had all heard, namely that there was an albino commune at the end of the dirt road and that the members of the commune would kill any trespassers. Curiosity got the better of us, and we decided to see if the old rumor was true.

As we drove down the dirt road, the signs became more and more ominous: KEEP OUT—PRIVATE PROPERTY, TRESPASSERS WILL BE PROSECUTED, and NOT RESPONSIBLE FOR INJURY OR DEATH. After about a quarter of a mile, the car emerged from the wooded, dirt road into a small central town square surrounded by old houses. As we stopped and looked around, dogs began to bark. Soon, large dogs emerged from behind every house and surrounded the car, barking and snarling. Then, one by one, the doors to the houses opened and people emerged. They were all wearing mirror sunglasses and all had on big, Russian-style fur hats (this was in late April—it wasn't cold). Most of the people had white hair sticking out from under their hats.

They began to yell at us, "Hey! Who are you? What are you doing here?" then began to run toward the car. The hair stood up on my head, and the color drained from all of our faces. Needless to say, our car sped out of there in a cloud of dust, never to return.—*Ken K.*

The Albinos of Essex Road

**Tinton Falls
(Monmouth County)**

There is a strange and lonely back road in the Tinton Falls/Neptune area of Monmouth County called Essex Road. Essex Road's lore includes tales of unseen albinos lurking in the woods, lying in wait to attack any unsuspecting motorists who might wander onto their turf. The road also has an added attraction to enhance its mystique—body outlines drawn on the blacktop to mark the places where the ambushed have fallen.

The Essex Road Albinos

Ever since I was a kid, there were all kinds of stories floating around about the wooded mile-long road. Apparently there were two albinos, brothers, I believe, who lived in the woods there. People always talked about them being insane, so I stayed away from there until I was old enough to brave the road. My friend's house was nearby—walking distance—easily, and his older brother told us about his encounter with the albinos.

Actually, he only saw one. He said he was walking along the road during the day and saw the man in the woods yelling at him to leave. The man then shot his BB gun at him to scare him off. Of course, he ran away.

My friend and I drove down the road at night when we got our driver's licenses, and you couldn't see much. It was unlit and undeveloped at the time. We did stop to see a chalk outline of a body in the middle of the road. Obviously it wasn't chalk and wasn't done by the police, but it did make us wonder why someone had put it there. We were also a little afraid of standing around the area at night, so we left.—*Dave T.*

Body Outlines on Essex Road

There is a road in Tinton Falls that has a bunch of satanic stuff written on the asphalt. No matter how many times it is repaved, the symbols keep reappearing. There are stories of kids being killed by cars, and their body outlines can still be seen on the road.

I saw this stuff myself, not knowing what it was, until I stopped and looked. Then it hit me!—*Doug*

Albinoville South

While working in Freehold, my cousin and her friend told me about Essex Road in Neptune. They said that in the late 1800s, families of albinos lived along the road deep in the woods. People used to come from all over just to get a look at them. I guess they got fed up and began murdering curious onlookers and putting the bodies in a slaughterhouse. At a local gas station, we asked the attendant where Essex Road was and he said, "So, you want to see the albinos." —*Jennifer B.*

Attacked on Essex Road

Albino families supposedly lived namelessly in the woods behind Essex Road. When development started in the woods, an accidental death of one of the albinos caused a war between the workers and the albino family. Another tale tells of a romance between an albino girl and an "outsider" which was ended quickly and painfully by the girl's father. Also, satanists supposedly practice secret rites in these woods. There were pentagrams and other symbols painted on the street.

Cars have been forced off the road by unseen forces and slammed into barriers and trees. Misty forms appear in the middle of Essex Road, startling drivers into stopping or veering off the road. When I was in high school, it was common to drive down this spooky road. People were dared to get out of the car and go into the woods, but no one ever did.

Essex Road has a very strange effect on many people. In reality, the road is only about a two-minute-long drive, but when you drive down at night, the drive seems infinite, as though you'd never get off the strange road.—*Joi C.*

King Joseph Bonaparte's Reign and Ruins in Bordentown

Looking at Bordentown today, few would suspect that this quaint Delaware River community has a history of international intrigue. The modest brick buildings that line the main street hearken back to the eighteenth and nineteenth centuries, when Bordentown served as a layover between New York and Philadelphia. One particular sojourner would spend much more than just one night there, and would leave an indelible impression on—and under—the town.

In 1815, Napoleon Bonaparte saw his hopes of European domination dashed at the Battle of Waterloo. After his defeat, the French emperor and his older brother Joseph, the former King of Naples and Spain, decided to flee the country.

On July 29, 1815, Joseph Bonaparte boarded a ship bound for the New World. Napoleon, however, did not. He was captured soon thereafter and exiled to St. Helena, where he would spend the rest of his life. Or would he? Some have speculated that he ended his days right here in New Jersey.

When Joseph Bonaparte arrived in America, he set out in pursuit of a life of quiet anonymity, for Joseph was a man on the lam. When he fled, he had managed to liberate a considerable fortune from his homeland—a fortune that somebody might try to reclaim.

Two months after his arrival, Joseph purchased a large parcel of land known as Point Breeze in Bordentown, New Jersey, just south of Trenton. The estate would grow in size in the next two years to approximately seventeen hundred acres.

Joseph built a palacelike home. He also constructed a vast network of tunnels beneath the property. Some of these tunnels connected buildings, while others led from the basement of the main house out to the Delaware River and Crosswicks Creek. These subterranean waterways were said to have arched brick ceilings and be wide enough to accommodate a long-oared rowboat. What better escape route for a man ever conscious of the possibility of his own abduction?

Joseph Bonaparte entertained notable statesmen, including John Quincy Adams, Daniel Webster, and the Marquis de Lafayette. But the many visits made by his former countrymen gave rise to speculation that he was plotting to restore a Bonaparte to the French throne. Others suggested that Napoleon did not die at St. Helena in 1821 but was freed and whisked away to his brother's estate, where he was rowed into Joseph's tunnels under the cover of darkness. Here he was rumored to stay, plotting his reascension to the throne.

In 1832, things had cooled down enough in Europe for Joseph Bonaparte to return. He eventually reunited with his wife in Italy and died in Florence in 1844.

We at Weird NJ were curious about the Bonaparte estate, so we ventured down to Point Breeze with Bordentown resident Randy Ellis. Randy took us right to the site of the former estate, now owned by the Divine Word Missionaries. The grounds are still stately, but there was little evidence of the estate's regal heritage. We approached one of the single-story institutional buildings and asked the woman who answered the door for some information. She handed us a short background sheet on the property and looked as though she'd been asked the same questions a couple of hundred times before.

The missionaries purchased the estate in 1941 and used it as a seminary until 1983, when a fire destroyed the faculty house. The sheet quotes Father Emil Lesage, in a letter dated January 26, 1942, as saying, "Visitors who have heard about our secret tunnels and closets keep coming to our house. They take up a lot of time. Father Provincial wants us to de-glamorize the building and to show them only the first floor."

So what happened to Joseph Bonaparte's tunnels?

"They're definitely still there," Les Hartman, a Trenton-based attorney, told Weird NJ. "My father's friend said that he was in them years ago. He said there was still water in them, and you could even see French handwriting on the brick walls."

The information sheet said that the remnants of a tunnel entrance were located somewhere on the property. Now, we thought, we're getting somewhere! Excitedly, we proceeded to tumble down the steep, thornbush-entangled embankment toward the river, looking for tunnels all the while. George, the estate's caretaker, found us and informed us that we were on the wrong path. He kindly walked us toward the tunnel entrance.

As we crossed the lawn, George told us that a recent storm had uprooted two massive trees on the edge of the property. When a truck was brought in to cut the trees up and haul them away, a funny thing happened.

"One of the truck's wheels got stuck in a hole in the ground over there," George explained, motioning to a large piece of plywood on the grass. When we lifted the

wood, there was a hole big enough for a man to climb into. The walls were built of stone and mortar and appeared to be very old. The hole was located directly under where George had told us Bonaparte's house had once stood.

"After the tree guys left, I went down into the hole. I gotta tell you, it closes up on you real fast once you get down in there!"

George then directed our attention a few yards away to where the property begins its steep drop-off to Crosswicks Creek. There, covered with branches, was the outline of a tunnel entrance. Poking through the debris, we could clearly see the arched brickwork of the passageway's ceiling. Unfortunately, decades of dumping had made the tunnel completely impassable.

If other tunnels built by Joseph Bonaparte still exist there, wouldn't it be worthwhile for some historical organization to excavate them? They might shed some light on this all but forgotten chapter in political history. Who knows what we might find down in those dark and clammy recesses, where the only sound heard is the faint echo of dripping water on the murky canals. Perhaps the skeleton of Napoleon himself awaits us, slumped over his maps and battle plans for reclaiming France, one bony hand tucked inside the lapel of his uniform.

The Legend of the Mysterious Jackson Whites

For many years, as far back as the Revolutionary War, legends have circulated about a motley group of social outcasts living in New Jersey's Ramapo Mountains. The tales tell of a group, inbred to the point of mutation, descended from renegade Indians, escaped slaves, Hessian mercenary deserters, and refugee prostitutes. They have come to be known as the Jackson Whites.

Over two centuries, the mysterious name of Jackson Whites has become associated with the Ramapo Mountain peoples of Mahwah, Ringwood, and the southern New York State towns of Hillburn and Suffern. But exactly who the Jackson Whites are has been confused by less than scholarly historical texts that transcribe local legends as authenticated fact.

Probably the earliest written reference to the Ramapo Mountain people is in an article entitled "A Community of Outcasts" in *Appleton's Journal of Literature, Science and Art,* dated March 23, 1872. The relevant passage reads:

> In relation to this particular people, there are half a dozen legends current, all possessing more or less romance and attractiveness; but the most favored one is, for a rarity, the most reasonable.
>
> The people will tell you that this stain upon their fair country was first put there by fugitive slaves, more than a hundred years ago.
>
> There was gradually added to these fugitive slaves, fugitives of other descriptions, and the general antagonism to the world made each individual endure the others. They buried themselves deep in the fastnesses and gorges of the mountains, and reared children, wilder and more savage than themselves.

An early written reference to the Ramapo people as Jackson Whites dates back to 1900, in J. M. Van Valen's *History of Bergen County,* which states:

> The Ramapo Indians sometimes visited the settlements in the township of Franklin. They were known formerly as the Hackensack Indians, but are more properly described as the "Jackson Whites." They bear little resemblance to the Indians, yet as tradition gives it they are descendants of Hessians, Indians, and Negroes, but know nothing of their ancestry, so ignorant have they become.

Arthur S. Tompkins's *1902 History of Rockland County, New York,* told the saga of the Jackson Whites this way:

> The Jackson Whites originated when the Indians were yet living in the lowlands along the Ramapo Mountains. The first race came by a union between the Indians and half breeds on one side, and colored laborers brought from the lower part of the county to work in the Ramapo factories on the other side. The colored people were either freed slaves or their children grown up, and many of the names today may be traced as identified with some of the old Holland pioneers of Orangetown, for the slaves in old times bore the surnames of their masters. Inter-marriage among these people has caused them to degenerate intellectually if not physically.

In 1906–1907, the New Jersey historical society's annual report contained this passage explaining the Jackson Whites' curious lineage:

> The Secretary wrote that his understanding had been that they [the Jackson Whites] were a people of mixed Indian and Negro blood. . . . They are supposed to be the offspring of former Negro slaves, runaways, and free Negroes, who sought refuge in the mountains where they could eke out a living by cutting hoop-poles and wood for charcoal, in the days of charcoal iron furnaces. They have been regarded as outcasts, and hence have been allowed to sink into a degraded state . . .

In 1911, the Jackson Whites' story took on a pseudo–scientific authority when a University of Pennsylvania anthropologist named Frank Speck published an article that claimed that the Jackson Whites were Algonquian Indians, probably Minisinks of the Delaware, with some of the Tuscarora who lingered for a rest in the Ramapo Valley on their way from Carolina in 1714 to join their colleagues, the Iroquois, in New York State. To this small nucleus became added from time to time runaway Negro slaves and perhaps freed men from the Dutch colonial plantations in the adjoining counties in New Jersey. Vagabond white men of all sorts also contributed a share to the community from the early days until now. The Jackson Whites may be regarded, therefore, as a type of triple race mixture.

Also written that same year was an even less well-researched study by the head of New Jersey's Vineland Training School, Henry Herbert Goddard, entitled *The Jackson Whites: A Study in Racial Degeneracy*. Taking his liberties with the history of the Ramapo's inhabitants, Goddard gave his own slant to their lineage.

> The Indian blood found in the Jackson Whites, whether it came down through individuals held as slaves or through isolated free Indians who inter-married with the emancipated Negroes, is supposed to have belonged to a remnant of the Algonquin Tribe—to the Minsi, or Wolf Clan, who were natives of the Upper Delaware Valley in Pennsylvania, New Jersey, and New York. . . . There were also a few families of the Tuscarora Indians who remained in the Ramapo mountains after their tribe had made there a three years sojourn, from 1710 to 1713, on its way to join the five nations in New York State.

The document that solidified the Jackson Whites' legend in New Jersey folklore was a 1936 book self-published by John C. Storms, a small-town newspaper editor. *The Origins of the Jackson Whites of the Ramapo Mountains* contended that the first ingredient in the racial stew that became the Jackson Whites was a group of Tuscarora Indians, who had fled North Carolina after a war with white settlers between 1711 and 1713. But it should also be noted that Storms drew upon the day's prevailing mythology more than on any personal investigation, and that he had a well-known penchant for embellishment and romanticism. According to Storms's booklet,

> Originally the Ramapo Mountain region was a favorite resort of the Hagingashackie (Hackensack) Indians, part of the Leni Lenape family of the Iroquois [in fact, they were part of the Algonquin language group, not the Iroquois]. . . . These aborigines had practically all disappeared by the end of the seventeenth century. However, a few remained together with a scattered population that had sought the security of the mountains to evade their brother white man, his laws and customs. Thus it was a sort of No Man's Land.
>
> The first real influx of a permanent population in the Ramapo Mountains was in 1714. This was a remnant of the Tuscarora Indians . . . perhaps it was because there were to be found congenial spirits among the remaining Hagingashackies and the wild renegades who were hiding there. But the ultimate object was to unite theirs with the powerful Five Nations that ruled the country to the northward . . .

The second strain in the Jackson Whites' bloodline, according to Storms, came from Hessian mercenaries fighting for the British during America's Revolutionary War.

Reaching America under duress, placed in the forefront at every important battle in which they were engaged, beaten by their officers with the broadside of swords if they attempted to retreat, made to do the menial labor of their British companions, their fate was a particularly cruel one. With no interest in the outcome of the military struggle, unfamiliar with the theory of 'liberty' for which the Americans were fighting, it is not to be wondered at that they proved unfaithful, and deserted the army at every opportunity.

In the fighting that took place in the vicinity of New York City, from the camps scattered throughout this region, and at the marches across New Jersey, these men, known by the general name of Hessians, fled to the nearest place of safety—the

Ramapo Mountains. There was no possibility of escape, no opportunity to return to their native land, so they made for themselves homes in their retreat, mated with those they found already there, and reared families.

The third genetic element in the Jackson Whites' lineage, according to Storms, derived from English and West Indian women forcibly brought to New York to serve as concubines for British soldiers.

The British War Office had a problem on its hands—keeping New York City loyal to the Crown as a Tory city, while keeping thousands of its soldiers in the military camp that General Clinton had established there . . .

But there was a way out of the difficulty, a way that had long been in vogue by warring European nations, in fact, by England herself. A little judicious questioning and a man was found who would accept the undertaking. The man's name was Jackson—history has not preserved for us anything more about him than this, not even his given name.

A contract was entered into that Jackson was to secure thirty-five hundred young women whom England felt it could very well dispense with, and transport them to America to become the intimate property of the army quartered in New York City, thus relieving the tension now felt that at any moment these same soldiers might take to themselves such of the residents as temporarily pleased their fancy. . . .

Jackson set his agents at the task of recruiting from the inmates of brothels of London, Liverpool, Southhampton and other English cities

along the sea coast. . . . If a young woman or matron chanced to be on her way home from her occupation, or on the street on an honest mission she fared the same fate as the inmates of the houses of ill fame, and many a respectable working girl or young housewife was shanghaied, and carried off to a life of shame across the sea.

In 1783, when New York was repatriated by American Army forces, the stockade of women was evacuated and the prisoners beat a hasty retreat along with British soldiers and Tories.

By far the larger portion of the human stream that flowed out of Lispenard's Meadows on that eventful Evacuation Day of 1783 . . . reached the western shore of the Hudson . . . the horde has been estimated

at about three thousand or slightly more. . . .
To the company was added a few soldiers who
preferred to cast in their lot with the refugees, having formed a quasi-attachment for some member
of it. Tories, too, who had been unable to secure
passage to the Canadian ports considered their
bodily safety rather than their social standing. . . .

Then followed another memorable trek. Across
the Hackensack Meadows, up the Saddle River
valley, these derelicts made their way on foot. . . .
At last, with Oakland past, the crowd entered the
Ramapo Pass and soon found itself in a country
that, while wild and inhospitable in character, yet
offered the boon of peace; there was no one to
drive them away. Here the colony scattered, finding
shelters in the woods and among the rocks. Here
the individual members found companionship of
peaceful Indians, escaped outlaws, Hessians, runaway slaves — there was ample companionship and
it was readily accepted.

Storms cites a New York Tory newspaper known as
Rivington's Loyal Gazette as the first publication to
coin the name Jackson Whites.

In these columns occur references of visits paid
by various companies of soldiers to "Jackson's
Whites," and sometimes to "Jackson's Blacks."
These sly hints are made in a jocular vein, seem to
carry no stigma, reproach, or violation of military
discipline. The term "Whites" and "Blacks" following Jackson's name quite clearly show to which
group of inmates of the stockade the visitor's
attention was paid.

It would be escaped slaves, who, according to Storms,
would contribute the final piece to the Jackson Whites'
ancestral puzzle.

The Dutch settlers kept these bondsmen as servants
principally, and the bondage was not particularly
hard in most cases. Still, it frequently happened that
these escaped slaves would seek their own freedom, and the most accessible place and most secure
was the fastness of the Ramapos. . . . These people
carried with them names of former masters, white
acquaintances, or those that they had adopted.
Thus we sometimes find family names among them
that are borne by prominent and socially acceptable
white persons.

It is unclear how much of Storms's account is histori-
cally accurate and how much was merely transcribed
from oral folktales. It is certain, however, that his
"evidence" influenced people's perceptions of the
Ramapos' residents and tainted both literature and
many supposedly scholarly works. The famous canine-
story writer, Albert Payson Terhune, of Pompton

Lakes, vilified his mountain-dwelling neighbors in his 1925 book *Treasure*. And in his epic 1946 poem, *Paterson*, William Carlos Williams concocted his own version of the Jackson Whites legacy, drawing obvious inspiration from the Storms history:

> Violence broke out in Tennessee, a massacre by the Indians, hangings and exile. . . . The Tuscaroras, forced to leave their country, were invited by the Six Nations to join them in Upper New York. The bucks went on ahead but some of the women and the stragglers got no further than the valley-cleft near Suffern. They took to the mountains there where they were joined by Hessian deserters from the British Army, a number of albinos among them, escaped Negro slaves and a lot of women and their brats released in New York City after the British had been forced to leave. They had them in a pen there— picked up in Liverpool and elsewhere by a man named Jackson under contract with the British Government to provide women for the soldiers in America.
>
> The mixture ran in the woods and took the general name, Jackson's Whites. (There had been some blacks, also, mixed in, some West Indian negresses, a ship-load, to replace the whites lost when their ship, one of six coming from England, had foundered in a storm at sea. . . .)

The Ramapo Mountain people themselves will tell you a variety of stories to explain their own ancestry, intertwining elements of the Dutch, Hessian, and Tuscarora Indian sagas into their own legacy. Most insist that they are really a tribe of Indians called the Ramapough, though they bear little physical resemblance to Native Americans (most appear to be light-skinned African Americans).

They have been petitioning the federal government for twenty years to be recognized as a legitimate American Indian tribe. The state governments of New Jersey and New York have recognized them as such, but the federal Bureau of Indian Affairs has denied their petitions. Such recognition is considered crucial because it brings certain federal benefits, such as housing and health care assistance and the right to operate a casino. According to the bureau, though, the Ramapoughs are not a tribe at all, but rather descendants of settlers with African and Dutch blood who moved to the area from Manhattan in search of farmland beginning in the late 1600s.

In the end, there is not much historical evidence to support any versions of the Jackson Whites' legend. It is almost certain that many legends originally were told to create a derogatory stereotype of the mountain people among their white neighbors. While the Ramapough show a fierce pride in their unique identity, you would be hard-pressed to find a person in Mahwah, Ringwood, or Hewitt who would call him or herself a Jackson White. "Those people," it would seem, are always to be found just over the next mountain.

After our original article concerning the Jackson Whites' legend was published, we received a lot of mail. Many of the letters sounded quite angry, as though we were responsible for the existence of the legends, rather than merely documenting them. Some of the mail was actually threatening, as many residents of the region seemed to have a difficult time separating the defamatory reputation of the Jackson Whites from the historical legacy of the Ramapough Indians.

A Brief History of the Ramapoughs, by the Ramapoughs

By Dan DalCais, M.S.W., L.S.W., Director, U.S. Title IX Indian Education Program

"In 1709, the Tappan-Hackensacks Indians were unified under one chieftaincy in the Ramapo Mountains. They would remain hidden in the roughest and, to the settlers, the least desirable part of their homeland.

"The Tappan-Hackensacks are today called Ramapough Mountain Indians. They are of the northern branch of Lenape or Delaware Indians. This northern branch is known today as Munsee Delawares. The truth is, their community survived because their poverty and isolation protected them from intruders. Outsiders learned little about them. That's the way it had to be.

"The fact is, there is so much historical documentation supporting the Native American heritage of this community that it requires dozens of pages to present a fair review. Another fact is that the vast majority of the public are totally unaware of this. There are many reasons why this is so. One reason is that the decades of denigrating, slandering and mocking these people are not easily overcome. It continues today. It seems there are those who just can't let go of the notion that this group is fair game for all sorts of vicious gossip.

"Also, overwhelming political pressure has been brought to bear against the Ramapough Mountain Indians' quest for recognition. The Atlantic City gambling industry sees a recognized tribe in New Jersey as a threat to their monopoly. They have invested considerable effort to insure that the Ramapoughs never get a fair hearing. The public's ignorance of and prejudice against this community have been skillfully exploited. Prejudices and now politics have prevented the truth from being widely known.

"Like most Indians they struggle to find a balance between developing their long-suppressed identity and making a living in the modern world. All of them are human beings who deserve the same respect as the rest of us. I feel honored to work amongst and be friends with quite a few Ramapough Indians. There are still many Van Dunks, DeFreeses, Manns and DeGroots living in their ancestral mountain homeland. A few even have those blue 'Dutchman's eyes.' "

The Kallikak Family
Tracing "Hereditary Feeble-Mindedness" from Vineland Through the Pinelands

The Jackson Whites of the Ramapo Mountains were not the only group whose reputation suffered from pseudoscientific papers. Henry Herbert Goddard, whose document *The Jackson Whites: A Study in Racial Degeneracy*, set its sights on the folks of northern New Jersey's hills, also worked on the southern piney plains of Vineland, New Jersey. Instead of denigrating an ethnically diverse community for their racially mixed blood, Goddard focused on a single family and attributed their transgressions to what he termed "hereditary feeble-mindedness."

Before beginning their research at the Vineland Training School, Goddard and his assistant Elizabeth Kite worked at Ellis Island helping to filter out the good immigrants from the undesirable ones. They brought their well-honed moron-spotting skills to studying a Pinelands family he gave the pseudonym Kallikak, derived from two Greek words: "kalos," meaning good, and "kakos," meaning bad.

His theory was that around the time of the Revolutionary War, the Kallikak family had fractured into two factions. While one side of the clan led normal, productive, and even exemplary lives, the other side produced nothing but depraved, feebleminded morons. The "good" side of the family had descended from the marriage of one Martin Kallikak, Sr., to a fine upstanding Quaker woman. The "bad" side of the clan originated with the same patriarch's tryst with a "nameless feeble-minded tavern wench." The progeny of this illicit union, according to Goddard, would be a burden on the good people of New Jersey for centuries to come.

The Kallikak Family: A Study in the Heredity of Feeble-Mindedness was published in 1912 by the Macmillan Company and became a best-seller. It tapped into an influential movement in this country called eugenics, a pseudoscientific

THE KALLIKAK FAMILY

A STUDY IN THE HEREDITY OF FEEBLE–MINDEDNESS

BY

HENRY HERBERT GODDARD, Ph.D.

Director of the Research Laboratory of the Training School at Vineland, New Jersey, for Feeble-minded Girls and Boys

PANY

GREAT-GRANDSON OF "DADDY" KALLIKAK.
This boy is an imbecile of the Mongolian type.

MALINDA, DAUGHTER OF "JEMIMA."

To drive home the horror of the depraved existence that these Kallikaks led, Goddard included a number of photographs of them in his book, describing one of the children as an "imbecile of the Mongolian type." Many years after the book's publication, it came to light that Goddard himself may have actually altered the pictures to give the Kallikaks a more frightful appearance. While examining the old faded photo plates from the book, researchers discovered evidence to suggest that Goddard had painted dark circles around the children's eyes to give them a more sinister and depraved look.

method of gauging intelligence and criminal predisposition by heredity and physical appearance. Goddard's book was a big hit among eugenics "scholars," as it proposed to offer clinical proof of their beliefs—a study of three hundred families with a sixty-five-percent rate of mental defectiveness he described as "the hereditary taint."

Goddard's research into the Kallikak family began when one young girl named Deborah was enrolled at the school. He quickly determined that the poor child was feeblemind-ed, apparently without regard to her isolated existence in an economically depressed area. The standards by which he graded the young girl were undoubtedly as foreign to Deborah as her rural Pinelands culture was to the good doctor. This fact, however, did not stand in the way of Goddard summarily maligning her and her whole family. This was Goddard's expert psychological analysis of Deborah after fourteen years at his training school:

This is a typical illustration of the mentality of a high-grade feeble-minded person, the moron, the delinquent, the kind of girl or woman that fills our reformatories. They are wayward, they get into all sorts of trouble and difficulties, sexually and otherwise . . . the teacher clings to the hope, indeed insists, that such a girl will come out all right. Our work with Deborah convinces us that such hopes are delusions. . . . How do we account for this kind of individual? The answer is in a word "Heredity,"—bad stock. We must recognize that the human family shows varying stocks or strains that are as marked and that breed as true as anything in plant or animal life.

Determined to discover hereditary causes for Deborah's profound feebleminded-ness, Goddard employed field-workers to gather information on her relatives across the southern New Jersey countryside. His assistant Elizabeth Kite and other researchers observed the Kallikaks in their homes. After interviewing hundreds of relatives, the researchers could apparently ascertain not only their mental capacity but also the intelligence of their distant ancestors. Here is a description of one of Ms. Kite's visits to a typical Kallikak household:

Three children, scantily clad and with shoes that would barely hold together, stood about with drooping jaws and the unmistakable look of the feeble-minded. . . . A glance sufficed to establish his mentality, which was low. The whole family was a living demonstration of the futility of trying to make desirable citizens from defective stock through making and enforcing compulsory education laws. . . . In this house of abject poverty, only one sure prospect was ahead, that it would produce more feeble-minded children with which to clog the wheels of human progress.

In stark contrast to the degenerate side of the clan, Kite's research painted a rosy picture of the lives led by Martin Kallikak Sr.'s legitimate progeny:

On the outskirts of another New Jersey town, in a beautiful old homestead, inherited from his mother, lives a grandson of Frederick Kallikak, oldest son of Martin. He is a courteous, scholarly man of the old school. His home is rendered particularly attractive by the presence of his southern wife and two charming daughters.

When Kite's methodology was subsequently called into question, she was unable to produce any detailed information to support her findings. Still, this did little to dissuade Goddard from drawing some revolutionary scientific conclusions based on the research.

CHILDREN OF GUSS SAUNDERS, WITH THEIR GRANDMOTHER.

There are Kallikak families all about us. They are multiplying at twice the rate of the general population, and not until we recognize this fact, and work on this basis, will we begin to solve these social problems. . . . They were feeble-minded, and no amount of education or good environment can change a feeble-minded individual into a normal one, any more than it can change a red-haired stock into a black-haired stock. . . . There is every reason to conclude that criminals are made and not born.

Having discovered the cause of all of society's ills through this study of the Kallikaks, Goddard took it upon himself to suggest a few solutions—rejecting

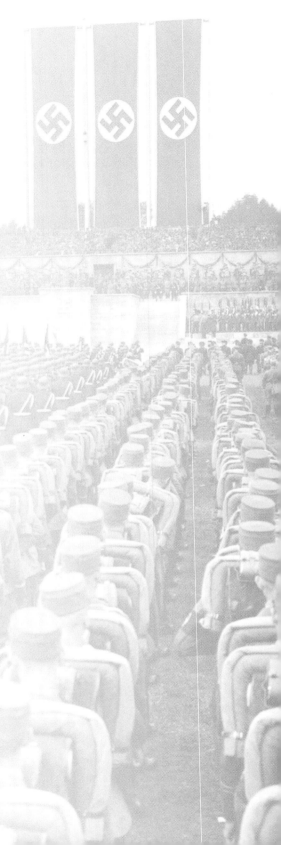

elimination in "lethal chambers" as inhumane, but considering forced sterilization, segregation, and colonization. Goddard seems to wrestle with the moral
question of wholesale sterilization of those deemed feebleminded. In the
end, though, he seems to be okay with the idea:

> Should Martin Jr. have been sterilized? We would thus have saved five feeble-
> minded individuals and their horrible progeny, but we would also have
> deprived society of two normal individuals, and, as the results show, these two
> normals married normal people and became the first of a series of generations
> of normal people. . . . It is safe to assume that two feeble-minded parents will
> never have anything but feeble-minded children.

It would be easy to dismiss Henry Goddard as a quack and his work as
merely misinformed hogwash were it not for the devastating and far-reaching
influence that his book would have in the years that followed its publication.
One telling element in Goddard's study is a term he throws into his discussion
of sterilization—"At best, sterilization is not likely to be a final solution of
this problem . . ." His book was published in German translation in 1914 and
republished in 1933, when Adolph Hitler came to power. *Die Familie Kallikak*'s
suggestions of segregation, colonization, and sterilization found their way into
the policies of Nazi Germany. And the lethal chamber that Goddard had
mentioned but rejected was readily employed for Hitler's own final solution.

Closer to home, his experience in identifying immigrant morons on sight
was instrumental in helping pave the way for the Immigration Restriction Act,
which was passed in 1924. According to his *Journal of Delinquency*, over
eighty-three percent of all Jews tested were deemed feebleminded, and many
were turned away from America's shores. This rejection would have dire
consequences as the Nazi party came to power.

Henry Herbert Goddard's study stands alone as a work unparalleled in
its tainted research methods and prejudicial assumptions. His findings were
self-serving, without empathy or compassion, and irresponsible to the point of
being criminal. The real crime, of course, was the influence that his work had
on those who put his theories into practice. Nearly one hundred years after
Goddard's study, it should be clear, even to a high-grade moron or imbecile,
who the truly feebleminded party at the Vineland Training School really was.

The Family Van Cleef of the Great Swamp

The Kallikaks are not the only New Jersey family alleged to have one good half, one bad half. In the Great Swamp region of Morris and Somerset counties resides another clan, named Van Cleef, who, like the Kallikaks, were said to have separated into two distinct factions. On this twisted family tree, though, the lesser branch doesn't just evolve into people of low intelligence and questionable morals; they actually degenerate into a race of tiny subhumans, covered with white hair.

Jack Rushing, founder of the Great Swamp Folklore Project, tells the story:

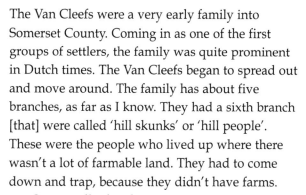

The Van Cleefs were a very early family into Somerset County. Coming in as one of the first groups of settlers, the family was quite prominent in Dutch times. The Van Cleefs began to spread out and move around. The family has about five branches, as far as I know. They had a sixth branch [that] were called 'hill skunks' or 'hill people'. These were the people who lived up where there wasn't a lot of farmable land. They had to come down and trap, because they didn't have farms.

Supposedly they began to intermarry and over time, as the local lore has it, they began to grow smaller. They began, first of all, to have white hair on top of their head. They develop white hair everywhere, although not thick white hair.

When people would come to visit them on the top of the mountain, their homes would be abandoned. Periodically they'd see them, but as time went on, they saw less and less of them. They were still shrinking. What distinguished them was not their size, nor their white hair. There's something very remarkable, which was they had one blue eye and one green eye.

Throughout this area there are excavations, like giant gopher mounds, with tunnels. People believe that this part of the Van Cleef family have now gone into those mounds and that's where they live. They seem to come out of nowhere, out of the ground.

These Van Cleefs began to steal and do other things. There's an old expression in this part of Morris County and Somerset County—if something's gone, the Van Cleefs got it. They're not referring to the regular Van Cleefs. They're referring to the little ones.

Sometimes people would have bad accidents, like a wheel would loosen and a car would crash, or perhaps on a plank bridge, the planks would be removed. And if they couldn't find anybody, they would always blame the Van Cleefs.

One of those said to be descended from the "good" side of the family was the late great actor Lee Van Cleef, whose snake-eyed gaze gained him international fame as the villain in numerous spaghetti westerns such as *The Good, the Bad, and the Ugly.* During the movie's filming, Clint Eastwood dubbed him "Angel Eyes." Van Cleef was a New Jersey farmer from Somerville before being discovered by a Clinton theater company. Though he was not little or furry, it is rumored that Lee did possess one trait of the "bad" side of the Van Cleef clan—two different-colored eyes. This telltale characteristic was corrected in the movies with colored contact lenses.

The Strange Family and Figures of the Woodbridge Clay Pits

Several peculiar wooden sculptures with a mysterious history were recently sold at a prestigious New York City art gallery. The origins of the Woodbridge Figures are unclear, although the statuettes themselves are well known among folk-art collectors. Ranging in height from three to nine inches, the carved wooden figures were found in the late 1960s near the old clay pits where Woodbridge Center Mall now stands. They closely resemble the primitive fertility idols used by prehistoric aboriginal tribes. Most are armless, and some are partially painted. The faces are very defined and well articulated, leading experts to believe they represent specific people.

In the early 1980s, an unidentified person known only as the Doll Dealer brought them to Roger Ricco of the Ricco/Maresca Gallery in New York City, which specializes in self-taught and folk artworks. He told Mr. Ricco that a construction worker had found them in a shack just before the construction of the Woodbridge Mall began. They had probably been discovered in the clay pits area, where the town's once-thriving brick industry used to gather its raw material.

Seeking more information, the gallery dispatched an intern to Woodbridge to investigate. After months of research, she came back "spooked," saying she never wanted to return. She had heard of a notebook containing names related to the figures, but never found out more. She also said she learned of a strange clan that once lived in the woods near the clay pits, who possibly had some connection to the mysterious figures.

We spoke with Roger Ricco recently about his impressions upon seeing the figures for the first time.

"Well, I was blown away," he said. "With my background in African art, I knew that I was looking at something that had an almost fetishlike quality to it. Not all of the dolls, but a majority of them, have a hole in the head and have a plug, much like a cork, and those are almost always carved in the shape of a penis and fit into the hole into the top of the skull. Some of them are actually painted red. It's my feeling that they were basically fertility-type figures, and that would be extremely unusual in a white culture. All of these people (figures) are white."

We asked Mr. Ricco if the figures were used in some ritual. "They could have been for fertility or for health in general, but the penis makes me feel that it was charging the figure with the potential for procreation. But they are not generic fertility idols; they almost have personalities, like voodoo dolls."

Local residents remember a bizarre family living near the Maple Hill dairy off Metuchen Avenue. Some people remember a woman known as the Walker, whose sons were described as inbred. Others recall squatters living in the woods surrounding the township's brickyard in what they said was a primitive miniature society. Children were afraid to venture into the woods because of their vicious dogs. Some say the family was descended from Hessian mercenaries from the Revolutionary War, who had deserted and fled into the woods.

Others recall a strange churchlike structure built in the 1940s on a hilltop off Karkus Avenue. The church was not known for any particular religion, but it is remembered as partially painted, having pews that were barely painted, with a sparse decor.

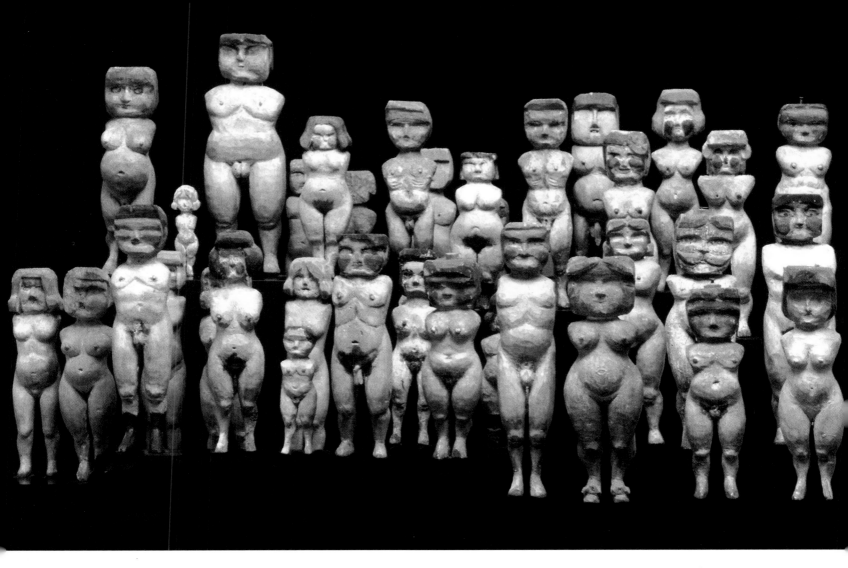

John O'Connor, a former member of the Woodbridge Historical Society, remembers stories of the church being a "healing place" where people were cured of their ills. He mentioned that the site of the church, the woods, and the former Valentine Brick Company is now the Fortunoff parking lot on Route 9.

The Woodbridge Figures are currently part of three private collections. Most belong to Gael and Michael Mendelsohn of Westchester County, New York, who are well-known collectors of self-taught, folk, and "outsider" art.

Remembers the Clay Pits and the Inbreds

In the 1940s, my grandparents, my uncle, and my aunt lived in a big farmhouse (where the Woodbridge Bowling Alley is now) and the clay pits were right behind the house. The name of the woman who lived in the shack was Eva. There were two boys who were inbred, and every time people would stare at them, the mother would yell out, "What are you staring at?"

My grandmother would forbid my father and my uncle to go to the clay pits because of the strange things she had heard about them. She said you could hear voices of the dead! She also knows a man who was in the shack when those figurines were being made, but she doesn't know why they were made.—*Kathy B., Fords*

Unexplained Phenomena

"There are more things in heaven and earth, Horatio, than are dreamt of in your philosophy."
—*William Shakespeare*, Hamlet

". . . a pair of underpants dancing and moving around like they had a life of their own."
—*R. E. Barker*, Weird NJ

Charles Fort is sometimes referred to as the Father of Strange Phenomena. Fort (1874–1932) would scour newspapers and magazines, spend hours in the New York Public Library, and travel with his wife, Anna, seeking out strange stories and what he called "weird observations." These so inspired Tiffany Thayer, a young novelist who met him in 1929, that Thayer formed a society dedicated to chronicling Fort's work and research—the Fortean Society.

Today, more than seventy years after Fort's death, there are numerous societies and publications dedicated to Forteana, a modern-day term used for anything that is classified as unexplained. These groups attract scientists, scholars, crackpots, and the occasional visitor from Mars. But as we say in *Weird NJ*, keep an open mind and anything is possible. Here is a brief summary of some of Charles Fort's findings on the state of New Jersey, taken from newspaper accounts of the day:

On Things Falling from the Sky
In 1833, lumps of jelly were observed falling from the sky in Rahway. The substance was whitish in color and resembled the coagulated white of an egg. At the same time, a mass of gelatinous substance (like soft soap) was found in Newark. It possessed little elasticity and, when heated, evaporated.

On UFOs
On July 6, 1882, there was a report of an object in the sky, similar to a comet, but moving at only ten degrees per hour, sending out quick flickering waves of light.

On Stones Falling from the Sky
On June 16, 1884, on a farm near Trenton, two young men, George and Albert Sanford, observed stones falling from the sky while hoeing the open fields. The next day, more stones fell on the cornfield while many onlookers spread out across the field to try and find the source, but none was ever found.

On Buckshot Falling from the Sky
On March 3, 1929, the town of Newton was baffled by a hail of buckshot falling in the office of the Newton Garage, a small room with one door and window. There were no marks on the walls or ceiling through which the buckshot could have entered.

On Spontaneous Combustion

On December 13, 1916, moaning sounds awakened Thomas Morphey, the proprietor of the Lake Demark Hotel. He found his housekeeper, Lillian Green, burned and dying. Apart from her clothes and a small charred spot on the floor under her body, there was no other trace of fire. The woman was brought to the hospital, but she could not explain what had happened to her. She died soon afterward.

Like Charles Fort, we have discovered unexplained phenomena by scanning newspaper articles (although sometimes they're on microfilm at local libraries).

We've found reports of mystery string hanging in the sky, mystery bullets raining down from the heavens, and mystery eyes watching you from church belfries. And we've found out another fact: New Jersey ranks fourteenth in the nation for reports of unidentified flying objects. Not bad for a state of our size! Although it's true that we have a significant Air Force presence throughout the state and one of the busiest airports in the world, reports of strange lights and formations in the night sky have fueled the notion that maybe we are not alone, and illegal immigrants are not the only aliens that call New Jersey home.

Unlike those who seek to solve or debunk these claims, we simply record the events and report our findings. We will leave you, the reader, to contemplate the possibilities and draw your own conclusions.

Caldwell's Mystery Thread

One of New Jersey's most baffling mysteries came in the form of a silvery thread that was suspended for several weeks over the house of Mr. and Mrs. A. P. Smith in the quiet suburb of Caldwell in Essex County.

The thread was first reported on Sunday, August 2, 1970, by neighbors who said it appeared to be hanging from the sky. It was rigid, with about a two-pound strength, and looked silvery when the sunlight would strike it. It was visible over the homes on Forest and Hillside avenues. Dozens of curiosity seekers converged on the area during the time that the thread dangled there. But neither they nor the police could figure out what it was or where it was coming from.

To some, the mysterious thread appeared to be a giant strand hanging from the clouds. Mrs. Smith speculated that it might be a direct line from Martians. Others theorized that it was a line dropped from a blimp that was cruising the West Essex skies.

Eventually the thread was snagged and brought down by some neighborhood boys using a fishing pole and casting line. After hooking it, the young anglers pulled enough of the anomalous line from the sky to fill several buckets.

The thread was reportedly brought to the DuPont company for analysis, but they could not determine its origins, stating only that it was a monofilament similar to fishing string, except with a hollow core. Where it had come from remains a mystery to this day.

The Society for the Investigation of the Unexplained (S.I.T.U.), another association devoted to unexplained phenomena, examined the Caldwell thread at the time. The S.I.T.U., started by famed cryptozoologist Ivan Sanderson and based in New Jersey, published its findings in the following report from the journal *Pursuit* (Vol. 4, #1, January 1971 — P. O. Box 265, Little Silver, NJ 07739. Used with permission).

Sky Lines: The Official Report by the Society for the Investigation of the Unexplained

Late last summer John A. Keel informed us that "there's been a wire hanging down from the sky over Caldwell, New Jersey, for a month, and it's never moved." We arranged a visit to Caldwell.

There was not just a single "wire" but half a dozen. It wasn't a wire but some kind of plastic that has now been identified by DuPont as "a material based on type 6 nylon (caprolactam) or perhaps a copolymer such as type 6 and type 66 nylon." Neither the upper nor the lower ends were ever seen, or located, even when they finally fell. They just came out of the sky from, apparently, down low at one end, and went up overhead and then on up into the sky to a point of invisibility.

In one case the line remained taut for a month, through electrical storms and several days of high winds. Then one "end" of the line gave way and a pile of the stuff was found in a front yard. In another case, four boys spent one hour hauling in a line, which had dropped during the night; this snagged and broke before the line could be pulled in. When the line fell it immediately curled up, just as did the nylon fishing lines on 2" spools, bought by us for comparison.

The usual reaction to this report is "little boys flying kites." But no one can produce a single kite-flyer or even someone who has seen a kite in the area. And how do you keep a line taut through all sorts of weather, without some very sturdy and visible point of attachment at each end? The police traced one of these lines over a considerable distance and had to report that the line simply went on and on, over Montclair at one end and out over a meadow at the other. They never found either end. All these lines were plotted on a map, but no pattern of any kind was discernible.

The appearance of these "sky-lines" would seem to defy a number of the basic principles of physics.

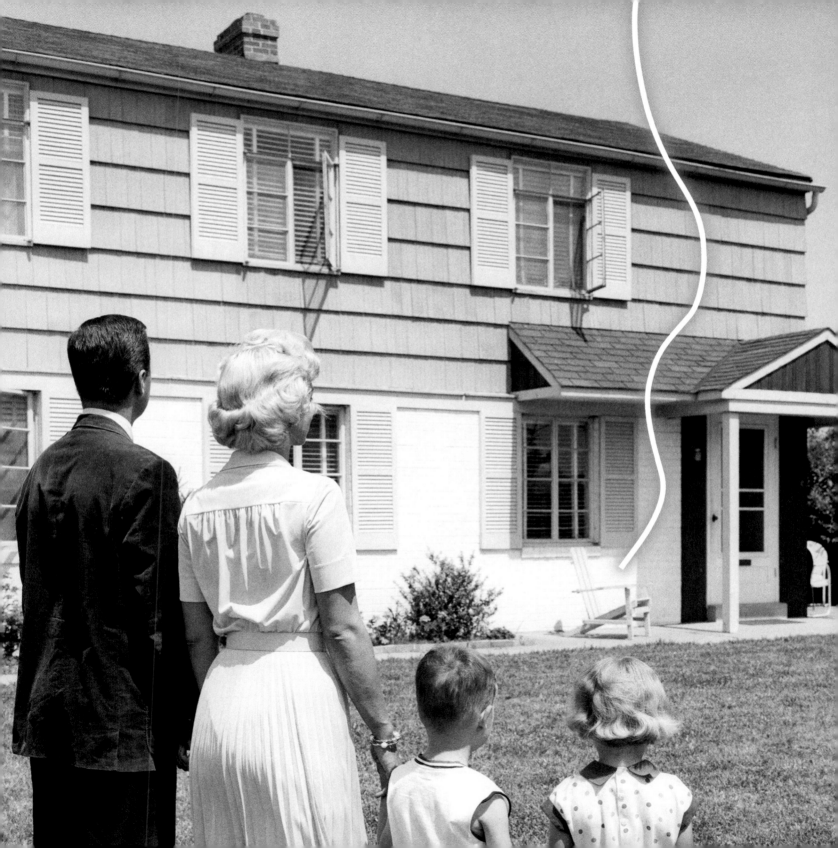

MYSTERY OF LIGHT IN CHURCH BELFRY IS STILL UNSOLVED

IS MORE TROUBLE BREWING IN MEXICO?

Five Thousand Curious People Gather in Vicinity of St. Joseph's as Priests and Police Make Efforts to Solve Remarkable Phenomena—Is Not a Reflection from Street Lights or Tube Trains—L... Sprinkled on Floor of Belfry Tower but No Footprints are Found—Light is a Pale, Phosphorescent Glimmer, at Times Showing a Bloody Red Streak.

WILL SPEND NIGHT IN BELFRY IN EFFORT TO SOLVE MYSTERY

The ghostly lights which have been gleaming from the belfry tower of St. Joseph's R. C. Church, Baldwin and Pavonia avenues, Jersey City, for the past few nights have attracted thousands of people to the church in the hope of finding some logical explanation for the apparently supernatural phenomena. Every known method of locating light rays by physical means has been tried

The Cat's Eyes of St. Joseph's Church

For more than seventy years, something strange has been going on at St. Joseph's Church on Pavonia Avenue in Jersey City. Two mysterious lights that the residents call cat's eyes have been gleaming out onto the residents of Hill House from the church's belfry. They are said to be pale, phosphorescent, glimmering, shaped like half-moons, and at times show a bloody red streak.

No one seems to know what causes the lights, also known as St. Joseph's Eyes, although they have drawn the attention of thousands of onlookers since they first appeared in July of 1921 and drew a crowd of five thousand. Though priests at the church tried every method they could think of to locate their source, including sprinkling flour about the belfry floor to record any footprints that might be left, it was evident that the lights did not originate inside the church. And if the mysterious cat's eyes came from reflected light from outside, the source could not be found.

In 1954, the lights started to appear again. For three weeks during the month of May, the lights reappeared after a church sexton was found dead in a seat of the choir loft. His last known words were "I'm going into the belfry."

These days, people passing the church still gaze up at St. Joseph's steeple in hopes of catching a glimpse of the mysterious lights. They have only appeared sporadically over the years, though, and there is no way of knowing when the eyes might shine again.

The Eyes Still Have It

I am a Jersey City police officer. The Cat Eyes in the tower of St. Joseph's steeple can be seen nightly. They are a regular occurrence. What makes this phenomenon ironic is that St. Joseph's runs a school for the blind. —*Chuck*

The Evil Eyes Just Won't Stay Shut

When I was a senior news columnist, I was sent out on assignment with our photographer to view the St. Joseph's Cat's Eyes for the first time since 1954. On February 27, 1991, standing on the northwest corner of Baldwin Avenue and Newark Avenue in front of the luncheonette, right across from the Brennan Court House, I saw the eyes again. That night, I did all I could to see if the eyes were a reflection of lights from the courthouse or anywhere else. I could find no possible reflection from anywhere. I showed my father a photograph, and he just shook his head in amazement, as these were the eyes he failed to see in 1954.

In 1954, because of the crowds, officials put a tarpaulin cover over the belfry windows to disperse the viewers. The idea worked, but something else happened. The local newspaper took a picture of the tarpaulin, and many people noted that the way the tarpaulin folded in hanging fashion, it resembled the face of a devil!

In 1991, church and city officials just let the eyes take their natural course of fading away, and no tarpaulin was used to cover the belfry windows.

—*Matthew F. Amato, Jr.*

Signs of a Close Encounter?

Weird NJ has received quite a few letters about an unusual area in Double Trouble State Park, on the border of Berkeley and Lacey townships in Ocean County. Some unknown force had apparently pushed down all the trees at the site in a strange circular pattern. Is it the landing site of a UFO or an airplane crash? Or was it perhaps ground zero for a meteor strike or the touch-down point of a freak tornado that went unobserved? Nobody seems to know for sure, but that's not going to keep us from guessing.

The next three stories are eyewitness accounts of the scene.

Strange Signs in Double Trouble State Park

Recently I went canoeing in Double Trouble Park on Cedar Creek. Our teacher told us to stop at a cleared area on the left-hand side of the creek. The park rangers, local police, state police, and such were there the day before we went. People called the police complaining that strange lights were coming from the area. The FAA thought a plane went down there, but one didn't. The weird thing is that whatever landed there pushed the trees down so flat, yet the object that pushed them did not destroy them. The dimensions are pretty big, and it's a complete circle.

It is a very creepy spot, and if you have a digital watch or take a photo, it won't show in the picture and your watch or compass will go crazy!–*Justin S.*

Tunguska Blast in Berkeley?

A few years ago my wife and I went kayaking down Cedar Creek in Ocean County. About a half a mile after you pass the Garden State Parkway, you can see that the woods off to the left look like they were cut down in a big circle. All the trees were pushed down, but not cut, cracked, or broken, just bent right down to the ground— full size pines! All of them were bent outward toward the perimeter. There was no debris from a plane crash, access roads for equipment, or anything. There was also no hole in the center from a meteor.–*John*

Cedar Creek's Mystery Spot Stole My Battery Power!

I go to Jackson Memorial High School. My school takes a canoe trip for each junior class every year. I went to Double Trouble State Park this year for the trip. The trip started off bumpy. We were hitting trees every five feet. The creek was very narrow, only fifteen feet wide. Later on, my partner and I got set back about fifteen minutes. We finally caught up to everyone else, who had pulled over on the side of the creek and were out of their canoes. I asked the teacher what everyone was doing. He told me that there was said to be a UFO landing site, and pointed over to the trees. I looked into the trees and saw a single circle of trees with complete gray sides to them.

We parked our canoe and walked into the woods. As I walked in, I took out my digital camera that I had just bought the week before. The night before, I charged the batteries for twelve straight hours. I had never once had a problem with my batteries not charging. I walked into the huge area of trees. I looked around, and it was a perfect circle. All the trees in the middle of the circle were dead, gray, and flattened, and all of them were broken. Around the circle were gray trees also, but all the trees behind them were completely alive. The trees surrounding the circle were bent outward on a slant, all at the same angle, almost as if they were fake.

I couldn't see any human machine doing this and doing it so perfectly. I turned on my camera to take a picture. As soon as I turned it on, I saw the screen indicating that it was dying, and then it shut off. I tried several more times, and it kept shutting off, until it wouldn't even turn on. I thought to myself that it was strange but just left it to the chance that my charger wasn't working the night before. I packed up my camera, and we left the area to continue our trip.

About a half hour later, we stopped once again for a rest. I took out my camera to see if I could get one more picture of my partner and I. I pressed the button and turned it on, expecting it to shut off again. This time there were no signs of a dead battery. I thought it was strange.–*Strato Chic*

Unidentified Falling Objects

Some things that fall from the sky, while much smaller than meteorites, can be even more puzzling—and just as deadly.

Stones Falling from the Sky in Hazlet

Billy Tipton seems to have a problem that follows him around. While he was living in Spokane, Washington, stones were falling on his home from August 30 through September 6, 1977. At least one hundred and fifty stones had fallen on his home and the surrounding property. The Spokane police were baffled. A few rocks fell on Tipton's roof as police officers were on the scene investigating. The conclusion was that it was impossible to determine where the rocks were coming from.

The following year, Mr. Tipton moved to Hazlet, New Jersey. In June of 1978, rocks and concrete debris fell on his home for twenty consecutive days, damaging windows and cars along Elm Street. Police took into custody a youth who was found throwing pebbles at Tipton's garage door, believing he was working with other juveniles in the rock tossing, but the boy was later let go when it was discovered that the rocks thrown upon the house were up to five pounds and appeared to be coming straight down.

Mystery Bullets Fall on Verona

On April 11, 1986, seven homes in Verona were struck with bullets that appear to have fallen from the skies. Verona police were baffled as to where the bullets had come from. One homeowner said a bullet crashed through his window as he was painting his living room. The bullets were of different calibers and fired from two or three guns, said the Verona police department.

Some have theorized that they were fired from a mile away at a pistol range in the Essex County Jail Annex. Others think that the guns could have been fired from the Essex County–owned Hilltop property in North Caldwell, with the shooter (or shooters) not knowing how far the bullets were traveling.

The police had several meetings with Verona residents to relieve their fears of flying lead. An investigation of the incidents was conducted with the help of the Picatinny Arsenal in Rockaway and the state police ballistics division. It lasted seven months without producing any evidence as to the origin of the mystery bullets.

Verona police puzzled in probe of mystery bullets falling on town

By MEG NUGENT

A seven-month probe into why seven homes in Verona were struck by bullets that appear to have been fired from a mile away in North Caldwell continues to baffle police, a detective said yesterday.

"If someone should get killed or

"We mostly want to let them know the progress of the investigation and to relieve any fears that we can," the detective said.

Wojtal said police have few leads and would appreciate any information, which will be kept confidential.

Police have been conducting "lengthy" investigation—involving Picatinny Arsenal in Rockaway T ship, the State Police ballistics div the Essex County Police Depart and North Caldwell police—sin

Please turn to Page 1

UFOs over the Wanaque Reservoir

Contrary to popular belief, calling something a UFO does not necessarily imply that it is a spacecraft piloted by little green men from another planet. It simply means that whatever was seen cannot be identified by those who saw it. That is definitely the case with one of the most highly publicized unexplained events of the 1960s—the Wanaque UFO incident. Sightings of mysterious objects in the night skies over the reservoir there made headlines throughout the entire United States.

Now, almost forty years after the event, the residents around the reservoir area still talk about it. We cannot explain what the people of Wanaque and Ringwood witnessed, nor can the authorities whose job it is to keep track of such airborne objects. The only difference is that we won't even try. Here is Weird NJ's full report.

The Roswell of the Ramapos

January 11, 1966, started like any other midwinter day in the small suburban town of Wanaque, New Jersey. The air was clear and cold, kids were enjoying the holiday vacation from school, and residents of the Passaic County borough went about their usual daily routines. Little did they know that before the day was over, something would happen, something fantastic and unexplainable that would change the lives of many of the townsfolk forever.

It all started in the early evening of that Tuesday night. It was about six thirty p.m., and the winter sun was long gone over the western horizon, past the great Wanaque reservoir, and behind the Ramapo mountain range. Wanaque patrolman Joseph Cisco was in his cruiser when a call from the Pompton Lakes dispatcher came over his police radio. It was a report of a "glowing light, possibly a fire." Then, as if right out of a sci-fi movie, Cisco heard the words, "People in Oakland, Ringwood, Paterson, Totowa, and Butler claim there's a flying saucer over the Wanaque."

"I pulled into the sandpit, an open area, to get my bearings," Cisco recalls. "There was a light that looked bigger than any of the stars, about the size of a softball or volleyball. It was a pulsating, white, stationary light changing to red. It stayed in the air; there was no noise. I was trying to figure out what it was."

Wanaque mayor Harry T. Wolfe, councilmen Warren Hagstrom and Arthur Barton, and the mayor's

fourteen-year-old son Billy were on their way to oversee the burning of the borough's Christmas trees when they heard the reports that something "very white, very bright, and much bigger than a star" was hovering over the Wanaque Reservoir. They pulled in to a sandpit near the Raymond Dam at the headworks to meet Officer Cisco and get a better look at the thing. The mayor's son Billy spotted the object at once, flying low and gliding "oddly" over the vast frozen lake "like a huge star," Billy told reporters the next day. "But it didn't flicker. It was just a continuous light that changed from white to red to green and back to white."

"The phenomenon was terribly strange," Mayor Wolfe would later recall. He described the shape of the unidentified object as oval, and estimated it to be between two and nine feet in diameter.

The next thing that Officer Cisco remembers is his patrol car's radio "going bananas" as calls from all over a twenty-mile radius flooded into the police headquarters. Cisco radioed Officer George Dykman, who was on patrol nearby. Just as Dykman received Cisco's message, two teenagers came running up to his patrol car, frantically pointing at the sky and shouting, "Look, look!"

At that moment, Wanaque civil defense director Bentley Spencer drove up with CD member Richard Vrooman. "The police radios are all jammed up!" Spencer said excitedly. Dykman and Spencer gaped at the sky along with Michael Sloat, sixteen, and Peter Melegrae, fifteen. "What the heck is it?" Dykman wondered out loud. "Never seen anything like it in my life."

Back at the sandpit, Joseph Cisco's radio crackled as another unbelievable message came across the airwaves: "Something's burning a hole in the ice! Something with a bright light on it, going up and down!" Then another transmission fought its way through the din: "Oh, boy! Something just landed in front of the dam!"

Spencer and reservoir employee Fred Steines raced to the top of the fifteen-hundred-foot-long Raymond Dam, where they described seeing "a bolt of light shoot down, as if attracted to the water . . . like a beam emitted from a porthole."

Patrolman Cisco, Mayor Wolfe, and town councilmen Hagstrom and Barton climbed to the top of the dam to get a better look.

"There was something up there that was awful bright," Hagstrom recalls. "We don't know what it was. We thought it was a helicopter, but we didn't hear a motor. It looked like a helicopter with big landing lights on. We got goose bumps all over when we saw where the hole was."

According to John Shuttle, another councilman who witnessed the UFO, there was no doubt about it: "It was there," he said. "I saw it, a brilliant white object, two to three feet across, and its color—no, not color, shade—it kept changing."

Curious residents who had been listening to their police scanners began to congregate around the entrance to the reservoir hoping to catch a glimpse of the mysterious flying object. Traffic slowed to a crawl and then stopped altogether as motorists watched agape from their vehicles' windows. Reservoir police lieutenant George Destito was forced to close the main gate of the reservoir to keep out swarms of onlookers who converged from the north and south on Ringwood Avenue. "People were coming out of the woodwork," Cisco recalls. He and the other town officials stood on top of the dam in the freezing January night air for half an hour watching the strange light. Then, without warning, it sped off to the southeast. It hovered briefly over Lakeland Regional High School in the Midvale section of town, then reappeared over the Houdaille sandpit in Haskell. From there, the UFO continued southeast in the direction of Pines Lakes in Wayne.

Before the sun came up the next day, Joseph Cisco would see the bright light once more. At about four a.m. on the morning of January 12, he saw the object moving from north to south along the horizon over the town of Wyckoff. He and Wanaque police sergeant David Sisco would take turns looking at it through a pair of binoculars. The next day Sisco's wife told him that she, too, had witnessed what she described as a "silver, cigar-shaped object moving south from their home, about a thousand feet from the reservoir."

January 12, 1966

One day after the initial sightings of the UFO, Patrolman Jack Wardlaw reported seeing a "bright white disk" floating in the vicinity of his home in the Stonetown section of Wanaque, just west of the reservoir. "It seemed like only a block away, above Lilly Mountain, maybe a thousand feet up," Wardlaw said. "Don't ask me what it was. But I do know it wasn't any helicopter, plane, or comet. It shot laterally right and left. It stopped. It moved up straight. And then it moved down and disappeared in the direction of Ringwood, to the north." Wardlaw described the object as "definitely disk-shaped, and at certain angles, egg-shaped."

Sergeant David Sisco said that he was on patrol at about six thirty that evening when the UFO noiselessly hovered into view. "It glided, then streaked faster than a jet," he told reporters, "and when it rose, it went straight up." Reservoir guard and former Wanaque policeman Charles Theodora and Sisco went to the top of the dam to take a look at the bright light. "We looked across the water and saw a cylinder-shaped object," Theodora remembers. "It was moving back and forth like a rocking chair motion. We were astonished." A few minutes later the object shot straight up into the night sky, until it was indistinguishable from the stars. Theodora said that he didn't hear a sound while the light show was going on. "I didn't believe in UFOs; I thought they were a lot of bull. And then I saw it. It was a breathtaking sight, something I'll never forget." After the January 1966 sightings, radar was installed atop the reservoir dam.

October 10, 1966

Whatever it was that visited the skies over the Wanaque Reservoir in January reappeared in October for its most fantastic showing to date. The first reported sighting of it came shortly after nine p.m. on the evening of Monday the tenth, when Robert J. Gordon, of Pompton Lakes, and his wife, Betty, saw a single saucer-shaped object about the size of an automobile glowing with a white brilliance. "At first I thought it was a star," Betty Gordon recalled, "but it seemed to be moving. It had a definite pattern. It would move to the left of the tower, and then move back directly over it. I'm quite sure it was not a star or planet." Bob Gordon, an officer on the Pompton Lakes police force, called police headquarters and requested that a patrolman be dispatched to their home. Officer Lynn Wetback responded, but was told that the "saucer" was already gone. The Gordons and their neighbor Lorraine Varga, who had also witnessed the UFO, told Wetback that the object was headed in the direction of the Wanaque Reservoir. The officer radioed Sergeant Ben Thompson, a six-year veteran of night duty with the Wanaque Reservoir police department, who was driving south along the reservoir at the time.

Thompson looked out and to his astonishment saw the UFO heading right toward him. He pulled his cruiser over at Cooper's Swamp, near the Dead Man's Curve stretch of Westbrook Road. "I saw the object coming at me," he said. "There was a bright white light. It was very low. It appeared to be about seventy-five feet over Windbeam Mountain. It was traveling very quickly and in a definite pattern; first right, then up and down, then repeating the pattern. Distances are deceiving, but it might have covered an area of a half a mile. It went straight over my head, stopped in midair, and backed right up. It then started zigzagging from left to right. It was doing tricks.

Making acute angular turns instead of gradual curved ones. It looked as big as a parachute. I got out of my car and continued to watch it for almost five minutes. It was about two hundred to two hundred and fifty yards away. It was the shape of a basketball, with the center scooped out and a football thrust through it. Sometimes the football appeared to be perpendicular to the basketball and sometimes standing up on end. It didn't make much noise, but as it was moving, it stirred up brush and water in the reservoir. It was about a hundred and fifty feet up. I had difficulty seeing because the light was so bright it blinded me."

At this point, other motorists along Westbrook Road also began to notice the strange light hovering in the sky and slowed their cars to get a better look at it. Fearing a collision, Thompson went back to his patrol car to turn on the red dome light as a warning. "The instant it started to flash," he remembers, "the object sped away over the reservoir and, without passing over the horizon, disappeared. It seemed as if it had gone right into the mountain. It was more than a little frightening."

Back at the Wanaque police station, "the switchboards were completely jammed," recalled an officer. "So was Pompton Lakes. There must have been a hundred and fifty calls." Some witnesses may have their doubts about just what they saw that night, but Ben Thompson is convinced he saw a UFO.

Denial and Cover-up

No report of a UFO sighting would be complete without the element of an official cover-up (either actual or perceived) by the U.S. government. This case is no different. Shortly after midnight on the first night of sightings over Wanaque, word came from Stewart Air Force Base in Newburgh, New York, that an Air Force helicopter with a powerful beacon had been on a mission over the area at about the same time the UFO was spotted. At six fifteen the following morning, however, an official spokesman for Stewart AFB, Major Donald Sherman, denied any such aircraft had been on any such mission that night. The next day, the Pentagon said that the mystery object was indeed a helicopter with a powerful beacon.

McGuire Air Force Base in Wrightstown said that the object was a weather balloon that had been launched from Kennedy International Airport. Shortly afterward, the base called local police to tell them the balloon explanation was just a lot of hot air.

Officials at Stewart Air Force Base and at McGuire denied any interest in the UFO. However, Wanaque police reported seeing a pair of jets fly over the reservoir shortly after the UFO was first reported, and Patrolman Joe Cisco said that he recalled seeing helicopters in the Wanaque skies that night.

Improbable Explanations

Thirteen years after the 1966 UFO sightings at the Wanaque Reservoir, the nonprofit organization Vestigia, which was based in Byram, prepared a detailed study of the strange lights that were witnessed. Vestigia, an organization that seeks to provide plausible scientific explanations for unexplained phenomena, came to the conclusion that the glowing lights were the result of seismic pressure from the nearby Ramapo fault. According to Vestigia founder Robert Jones, the fault in the earth's crust creates an electrical energy field within the quartz-bearing rocks underground. At times of extreme pressure, this highly charged field will supposedly escape into the atmosphere. Jones asserts that under just the right climatic conditions, air particles that are exposed to this energy field will ionize, and the result is a glowing sphere of light.

Vestigia's theories, however, did little to dissuade eyewitnesses. Jack Wardlaw and Charles Theodora rejected the explanations of the mysterious lights as swamp gas, a helicopter, or a seismic anomaly.

"I've ridden these streets at midnight for years," Wardlaw said, "and I know a strange light when I see one. The Army tried to tell me it was marsh gas—that's ridiculous! Then they said it was a helicopter. Well, if you can't discern a helicopter or hear one you have to be pretty bad off."

One week after Stewart AFB sent down its inexplicable explanation for the Wanaque sightings, the Pentagon offered its own scenario. What hundreds of people had witnessed in the skies over the reservoir that January and described as a brilliant white light that floated, hovered, shot up, down, and side to side, was in actuality, according to the great military minds of Washington, nothing more than the planets Venus and Jupiter in a rare celestial alignment.

Quotations in this report were taken from reports of the Wanaque UFO sightings published in the Newark News, *the* Herald-News, The New York Times, The Star-Ledger, *and the* Record. *Some quotes have been edited for the sake of continuity.*

UFOs Still Buzzing Wanaque Reservoir in '79

In late 1978 or 1979, there was a major drought in the Wanaque area, and the reservoir was really low. I had bought a truck up in West Milford, and a friend and I went to pick it up. I was following him home to Oakland past the reservoir. It was just past dark when all of a sudden he slammed on the brakes and threw his car over to the shoulder.

By the time I got out of the truck to see what he was doing, he was standing on the hood of his car and pointing to the sky. I looked out over the reservoir and saw a group of three or four lights in the sky, and they were doing some pretty wild maneuvers. They looked like fireflies in the sky zigging and zagging, but they were much larger. We couldn't make out anything other than the lights.

We watched for about five minutes or so and couldn't for the life of us come up with any logical explanation. We decided to investigate a little further. We drove the vehicles down into the old Stonetown quarry. The reservoir was so low that we could walk into most of it. We started walking toward the lights. We walked for about an hour, and we were definitely getting closer when all of the sudden the lights just stopped and hung in the air. A split second later, they all shot straight up in the air and disappeared.

We just stood there for a while and looked at the spot. After a while, my partner pointed out that there was no noise. We started looking around and realized there were no crickets, no owls, no noise at all. Very weird.

I'm hard-pressed to find any kind of logical explanation for what went on up there that night.—*Brian R.*

Vouching for Joe Cisco

I lived in Wanaque, right next to the reservoir, in the 1960s during the UFO sightings period. No one ever did find out what created the lights. I personally knew Joe Cisco, the police chief at that time. He lived a block away from me. He was always an honest, truthful, and straightforward guy who told it like it is. I never got to see the lights, but many of my friends did. There WAS something out there.—*DLC*

A Skeptic Sees the Light in 1974

I served on an aircraft carrier and heavy cruiser during my time in the Navy and am familiar with most types of aircraft. I have seen various helicopters and high-performance aircraft during day and night hours. While I would not pass myself off as an expert, I do feel that I've seen more things in the sky than most folks.

I consider myself to be a skeptic on the question of UFOs. I do not subscribe to any particular theory, but I do believe that many incidents are deserving of further study. In the case of the Wanaque sightings, which apparently have been going on for a long time, there may be some phenomena in the area which is of interest—although I'm not sure that it involves space aliens.

I personally saw one set of lights that you might find interesting. This incident occurred in 1974 during the winter months—I'd guess at January or February. It was about ten o'clock on a clear night. I was on a weekend pass from the military and was returning to my parent's house after visiting my sister, who lived directly west of the reservoir. My usual route was to follow Westbrook Road east across the reservoir and then turn south on Ringwood Avenue. I was just east of Townsend Road when I observed a set of lights in the sky. The lights were very bright and appeared to be one large light in the center with a smaller light on either side.

The lights did not appear to be a "point source"—they definitely had a circular shape and a hard edge. The relationship of the lights to each other remained constant throughout the incident, which might indicate that there was a solid object behind the illumination. The color was an intense blue-white. Probably the best way I can describe it would be similar to looking directly into the tail cone of a high-performance jet like an F-4 Phantom with the afterburners lit off.

I observed the object above the hills which border the west side of the reservoir through the windshield of my car. The evening was very quiet, and I could not hear any engine or helicopter noise, which would have been significant at what appeared to be the low altitude of the object.—*Dave*

More UFOs

The Wanaque incident **is only one of many well-documented UFO events to have unfolded in the skies above New Jersey. Here are some other close encounters of the weird kind that have been reported throughout the state.**

The Mysterious Carteret Lights and the Morris Booms of July 2001

An article appeared in a Morris County newspaper on July 14, 2001, about mysterious booms that were heard throughout the area. Denville police said about twenty calls came in shortly after four p.m., while Rockaway Township police received two dozen calls. Montville police stated that there were "too many [calls] to count." Some reports stated that the disturbance shook some houses.

Police officials still have not determined what caused the thunderous sounds. There were no explosions in the area, and the National Weather Service in Mount Holly reported no record of atmospheric disturbances. The U.S. Geological Survey Earthquake Information Center in Boulder, Colorado, was called, but they reported that there was no indication of any seismic activity in the area.

Two days later, on July 16, the media blitz was all over mysterious lights that had appeared in the skies above Carteret (Middlesex County) around twelve forty a.m. Carteret police dispatchers said that at least fifteen calls came in to the station reporting orange flares floating above the Arthur Kill. The lights, more than a dozen of them, all in a V-shaped formation, had at least seventy-five cars pulled over on the New Jersey Turnpike to witness the strange spectacle.

Some witnesses claimed that the lights were not in formation at first, but rather were floating freely, only later to form a V-shaped pattern and move off in formation. The lights were clearly visible for over ten minutes, were witnessed by police officers, residents, and highway travelers, and were even captured on home videotape.

Police could not identify the source of the lights. Newark International Airport, which is located not far from the area, reported no unusual flight patterns, and the National Weather Service claimed nothing in the atmosphere could have caused the bright lights. When contacted, McGuire Air Force Base officials said none of their military planes were in the vicinity at the time of the sighting.

"We've ruled out meteors and balloons," UFO expert Pat Marcattilio told the *Courier Post* of Cherry Hill after the incident. "The lights moved too slowly, and balloons don't float in formation."

Might there be some kind of connection between the mysterious Morris County booms and the sighting of the Carteret Lights? Could the UFOs have been breaking the sound barrier over Morris County two days earlier? Has something otherworldly invaded New Jersey? Or was it just that same old "weather balloon" that people have been seeing for the past fifty years now? So far, the strange lights continue to be a mystery and will probably always remain "unidentified."

Close Encounters over Denville (Morris County), 1979

In the summer of 1979, my then girlfriend Barbara and I were returning from visiting friends at one a.m. We were on Route 80 heading to Denville. As we were climbing the hill just before Denville, we heard a woman on my CB radio hysterical and screaming, asking for help. I immediately got on the radio and asked her what the problem was. She screamed that she was being chased by lights over her car. I asked where she was, and she stated she was driving on Route 80 West in Rockaway. I thought she was drunk or pulling a prank.

When we reached the top of the hill, we saw her car on the other side of 80. Above her car was a globe of white light the size of a basketball. My eyes then were drawn to the dozen or so lights that were flying behind the car or standing stationary along the side of the highway about twenty feet or so off the ground. The globes lined up and flew away.

It was at this time my car died. As I pulled to the shoulder, my girlfriend pointed out her window and began to scream. I opened my door and looked over my car to the north. Perhaps a mile away and a thousand feet up was a ship, moving west slowly. It was the size of a stadium, oblong in shape. There were white lights all along the sides of the ship that were moving in a circle counterclockwise in a pattern, and on the bottom was another circle of colored lights moving very fast, also counterclockwise. In this bottom circle were globes of light entering from different parts of the sky, and others were leaving from this circle and taking off at speeds only seen in science fiction movies.

We saw lights come and go, stop on a dime in midair, and make forty-five-degree turns while flying. We watched this mother ship for at least five minutes as it headed east. When it was out of sight, my headlights came back on. I was able to start the car, and we drove into Denville.

We went directly to the police station and reported what we had seen. The officer on duty stated to us that there had been a lot of calls and that they had cars on the highway checking it out.

Now here's the oddest part: I worked for a large retail store at the time in one of the larger malls. Several months after the incident, I was informed by my supervisor that someone was at the courtesy desk to speak with me. At the desk was a man in a dark suit. He was very pleasant, and he stated he had a few questions regarding what I had seen on the highway that night. I told him what had occurred. He stated that it was routine for these things to be looked into and stated that with Picatinny Arsenal so nearby, perhaps it was military aircraft on maneuvers. He was polite and soon left.

When I returned to my desk, I realized, What the hell? I never told anyone about the incident other than close family members, and how the hell did anyone connected with this know where I worked? Furthermore, I never gave my name to the police when we reported it—they never asked.—*Kirk*

On Duty in Denville the Night of the UFOs

For the past twenty-nine years, I have been telling friends and rookie cops about a UFO that appeared over Mountain Lakes/Denville. Just today I was looking at my daughter's desk and came across your magazine. Flipping through the pages, I came across the article about the UFO over Denville— and by God, I think I found them! "Them" would be the two individuals that stopped in headquarters to report it, exactly as it was mentioned in the article.

I went out to the area where this was witnessed, took the report, made an investigation report, and called the UFO hot line. After the call was placed, I received a call from an investigator about my report.

I can't believe seeing this in print after all these years. It does bring back memories of that night. About a week after the incident, myself and another officer saw lights in the sky in the area of Split Rock Reservoir. Not wanting to be laughed at, we never reported it. Several days later, the county newspaper ran a story about witnesses seeing lights in that same exact area, which has a history of UFOs.—*Lt. Jack Nicholais*

Flying saucers sigl reported in Hudso1

By Greg Wilson
Journal staff writer

NORTH BERGEN — Robert Herzig is sure he saw a UFO over Tonnelle Avenue Wednesday night. So are the other four passengers who were in his car.

Although their descriptions of a brightly lit flying saucer match an independant account given by another area resident

of bright lights moving very fas

No blimps w Teterboro Airp The Blockbust moored at Lind yesterday morni in flight at the t alleged sighting.

There were blips on the ra

Also Remembers Denville UFOs

I've heard many stories about the 1979 UFO sighting in Denville. I remember my fifth-grade teacher telling our class about it. She had been sitting in her car with her boyfriend (a Denville cop) in the Burger King parking lot. All of a sudden, the lights of the cars going by started flickering. Many people had car trouble. She didn't see anything, but her boyfriend told her what his coworkers had told him about the reports that night. Her best friend had seen a small UFO, but much like the one Kirk described as the mother ship. Apparently, there were many of those ships above Denville that night.

Another incident happened about eight years ago. I was walking from my bedroom to my bathroom when I was about eleven. We have skylights along the upstairs hallway, and my cat often climbs into the house through them when he gets stuck outside on a cold night. I heard a noise as I passed the second one in the hallway and looked up to see if my cat needed help getting in. When I looked up, he scrambled through the window and took off down the hall with a look of terror. I ran downstairs and out the front door. I heard a soft hum from the sky and looked up. Above me was a very large, slow-moving circle with one white light in the center and multicolored spinning lights along the outside of it. I told my father, but he wouldn't get out of bed to look. The next day, I overheard my mom telling my dad that a few neighbors had called to ask if we had seen anything.

While most people don't believe me, I'm still certain I didn't dream it.

—faerieprincess684

The Toms River UFO Sighting

On a summer evening of 1998, the sky had just grown dark, but a full moon backlit the sky to a deep blue over our apartment. I was inside watching a movie while my roommate stepped out onto the terrace. About ten minutes later, my roommate excitedly said, "Get out here! Hurry up! Come look at this!" I did. Flying in the distance was an object of a kind I have never seen before, nor have I ever seen since. It was flying at about two thousand feet from the ground.

I would describe it this way: A small neonlike intense blue object with a red light circling the object in a diagonal fashion. The light seemed to disappear as it reached the lower portion of the object, resembling a pulsing effect. I strained my eyes to see if I could make out wings or a sound as it passed closer, and I assure you, it had neither.

To prove what we were seeing, my roommate ran out our door to get our neighbor to see it. He also watched in pure amazement.—Russ and Gail

The Nutley UFO Incident (Essex County)

valette,
ends. I
with
pinning
ed. For
I of my
ad traffic
aight at
blue
tory of

ear

oward
r, West
o go past
tear
enough
is about
rns. It
e there

a slow
trees to
n the
nard to
ut

ped
ad. It had
se it
object
me was

vas gone,
it was
Kerry

Around Christmas or New Year's of 1970/71, I was visiting my cousin in Nutley. I had gotten out of the Air Force the previous April, where I served as a multiengine jet mechanic. The incident at Nutley occurred at around six p.m. We were just going up the walk to his house when two hysterical girls came racing down the street in a car and screeched to a halt in front of the house. Both were screaming, "What's that? What's that?"

I saw an object with a series of lights rotating around a round or oval shape. The object was about a thousand to fifteen hundred yards away, twenty to thirty feet in diameter, and cruising around one hundred miles an hour. Now, I'm sure you may be wondering how I can make these estimates, but remember that I was an aircraft mechanic for four years and I spent many hours near the runways. I was using my experience to try to make some identification of standard markings such as navigation lights, but there were none.

The damnedest thing about it was that there was absolutely no noise! You can always hear an airplane that close. In fact, you can hear them miles away, but not this one. The last thing my eyes zeroed in on was a dome, lit up by some lights that were on the top of the fuselage. The craft remained visible for quite a while, heading in a northerly direction, and I guessed that it was probably near or over the parkway. We were not the only people watching this, because the neighbors had heard the noise the girls made and came out to see what was up. My cousin kept urging us to go chase it in the car, and I asked him who was going to drive and keep his eyes on the road. He got the hint.

So I did what anyone would do who wants to be ridiculed. First I called the police and asked if any reports of a UFO had been called in. That got a warm reception. Then I called the locally prominent Nutley newspaper and asked the same question of the receptionist who answered. She put me on hold and came back about twenty seconds later and said, "About that flying saucer—it landed!" Click! Trust me—never try to report a UFO.—*Allen C.*

Unidentified Flying Orbs

Not all unidentified flying objects reported look like something you might envision as a spaceship. A great number of sightings are described by eye-witnesses as balls of light, or orbs.

A UFO Occurrence on Route 78

I have driven Route 78, a river of asphalt connecting New Jersey and Pennsylvania, many times. By day, it is a busy commuter artery. Those who have driven it at night, however, know that it can be a dark, desolate stretch of highway. It was on this road that I encountered a UFO in 1992.

It was past midnight, and I was cruising eastbound, in the vicinity of Millburn. Suddenly I saw a flash of light in the black sky. I looked up and saw what appeared to be a shimmering metallic orb streaking from out of the north directly over my car. It was very low, merely several hundred yards up, and moving very quickly. It looked to be a seething ball of liquid metal, its glow almost painful to behold, not unlike the brightness of a welder's torch. It made no sound. Then it disappeared as it passed over my vehicle. I looked around, expecting an impact of some sort, but the thing had vanished.

I have always been a UFO skeptic. As a stargazer, I am familiar with meteors, or so-called shooting stars. I have witnessed comets, such as the Hale-Bopp in 1997, and have seen satellites traverse the sky. This was not a meteor or comet or disintegrating satellite. If it were something burning up in the atmosphere, it was so low that some remnant of it would have managed to strike the ground. I have also seen many low-flying aircraft approaching nearby Newark airport, and this was no aircraft.

I continued on my way, shaken and exhilarated by what I had seen. I was sure I could not have been its only witness. When I got home, I switched on the news and waited to see a story on the strange object. There was no reference to it on any of the channels. The next day there was nothing in the paper. I phoned the state police and asked if there had been any reports of a strange light or peculiar aerial craft on Route 78, and they said there had not. I am not speculating that it was an alien spacecraft, only that after years of thought, I am unable to explain what it was.—*Edward K.*

The Metedeconk Ball of Light

I had many sightings over the Metedeconk River during my childhood. Once, as a young teen, my brother and cousin and I were sitting in the yard just talking. We were not experimenting with drugs at this age, so you can write that off. All of a sudden, this orange globe, about basketball-size, came over a big pine tree from the eastern sky on a slow downward curve. When it got about ten feet from us, it stopped. It had a rhythmic pulse of light and color. It would go bright yellow and then dull orange. It had a very faint sound or hum.

We all just sat and stared at it for about a minute. Then it corkscrewed up to the southwest, slow at first and then very fast. You would think we'd all get up and go, "Did you see that?" or maybe run inside and tell our parents. Instead, we sat there like we saw it every day. We never spoke of it, not even at the moment.

Once I got to my late thirties, I finally asked my older brother, "Do you remember that orange thing in the yard?" He said back to me, "I think it had a shade of green also." I asked, "What was it?" He said, "I don't know." And to this day we don't speak of it, and to tell you the truth, I had a hard time writing it down.—*Steve P.*

The River Vale Orange Lights (Bergen County)

The first time I saw "my" orange light was when I was seventeen and coming home with my date. We were driving on Kinderkamack Road and turned east on Woodcliff Lake Road to head toward River Vale. As we started down the hill, we noticed quite a few cars pulled over and the drivers all looking and pointing east. I immediately thought there was an accident ahead until we drove a little bit further down the hill and saw what they were looking at—the biggest, orange full moon that I have ever seen, rising up in the eastern sky. I also noticed that the real moon was already up in the southern part of the sky.

That's when I noticed that the orange moon had no features and seemed to be glowing from within. My date floored the gas pedal to race up the other side of the hill to get a better look. When we reached the top of the hill, the light vanished.

About a year later, I moved to Colorado, where I met and married my husband. One night, we started talking about the strangest things that we had ever seen, and I told him about my orange light. While I was telling him about the way it looked, I noticed his strange expression. I asked him what was wrong, and he told me that he, too, had seen that weird orange light. Only his sighting took place while flying a search-and-rescue mission through the Rockies.

While he and his pilot were headed due west, my husband noticed a light flying beside their plane. After they inquired over the radio whether there were any other aircraft in the area, their radio controller told them that he was just about to call them and ask them the same thing.

Apparently, the light registered on radar but did not transmit any identification codes. The light flew along with them for about three or four minutes, until it moved directly overhead, then out in front of their aircraft before shooting straight up into the sky. Their controller asked if they wanted to report a UFO, and they both said no, knowing that they could possibly be grounded.

When I asked my husband what his light looked like, he described my light in perfect detail—round and orange like a rising moon, no features and in the wrong part of the sky. Neither of us have seen our orange moons since our sightings, but there's always tomorrow night.—*DAS*

Unidentified Weird Objects

Some stories defy categorization. **We put such accounts in our "Unidentified Weirdness" folder for future reference. Here are a few stories that prove that sometimes the weirdness is** *really* **out there.**

The Dancing Underpants

I hail from Rahway and can remember many things weird as a kid. One such story comes from going to a nudist camp when I was nine. I remember playing with some kids at the camp, and there was this old converted barn with an apartment on top. We always dared each other to go up to the top of the staircase on the side of the barn. Of course, I was elected and went first.

The door wasn't open, but there was a gap between the floor and the bottom of the door. I swear that when I looked under that door and looked up I got the scare of my life! Inside, straight ahead, with sunshine coming through an opposite window, was a pair of underpants dancing and moving around like they had a life of their own. White Fruit of the Loom–type underpants prancing around. Well, I just bolted down the stairs as fast as I could.—*R. E. Barker*

The White Speedy Mattress of Mist, and Leave the Last S Off for "Spooky"

One night in early November 2001, I was taking a friend home from my daughter's house. I was headed north to Highway 36. There was a light mist but no moon.

Suddenly, and at a very high speed, something flew across the road very close to and in front of the car and was gone. It was wider than my car. It was about two feet thick and three feet above the road. It passed us so swiftly I had trouble believing I saw it—a flying mattress of mist? I finally asked my friend if she saw it.

"Square? White? Fast?"

"Yup."

"Yup!"

Oddly enough, it upset us enough that we did not discuss it again that night.—*Judy R.*

The Mysterious Lights of Slabtown Road

In Salem County off of Route 40 in Woodstown is Slabtown Road. The road starts out between two fields before cutting through a small section of woods. Then it runs over a small stream, and if you walk from this bridge toward Route 40 at night, it will sound as if you are being followed on both sides by footsteps in the woods. When the footsteps stop, the lights begin. Small white lights appear in the trees, on the road, and on the grass, but not in midair. You can touch the lights, but you can't get rid of them.

We have walked the road on various nights under various conditions. Full moon, new moon, winter, summer, things like that, and always the same thing—first the footsteps, then the lights. We have taken people there without telling them what we experienced, and they experience it, too.—*Joe R.*

Bizarre Beasts

Do *mysterious creatures* roam the New Jersey countryside?

Does it seem possible that strange animals or demons could walk among the pinelands or mountainous regions without ever being captured or photographed? Despite the state's widespread development, there are still remote areas where sightings of unusual beasts are reported every year. Stranger still are the reports of mysterious animals that appear in the heart of urban areas, where the population is shoulder to shoulder.

Legends have circulated for years about New Jersey's famous Pinelands Devil, the cloven-hoofed, winged creature that roams the isolated flatlands of southern New Jersey. But few have written about the creatures that have been witnessed in the state's northern reaches, like the Big Red Eye, who resembles a Bigfoot-type primate, as well as lizardlike bipeds, monkey men, water monsters, and feral red-eyed dogs. But do they exist, or are they merely a product of our own imaginations and fears? Many times the only proof we have to go on is people's firsthand accounts.

Researchers suspect that only one sighting in ten is ever reported because most witnesses fear ridicule. In 1975 and 1976 alone, more than sixty separate reports of Bigfoot sightings were recorded in Morris, Warren, Hunterdon, and Sussex counties. So there may have been up to six hundred sightings during that time, most of which will never be known by the public.

If an eyewitness is courageous enough to report a sighting to us or to the local police, we believe they are relating what they believe to be the truth. The reader will have to make his own decision as to whether to believe the stories or not. After reading some of these tales, though, we'll bet that even the most die-hard skeptics might find themselves thinking twice before entering the woods alone on a dark New Jersey night.

The New Jersey Bigfoot

Reports of encounters with the legendary creature known as Bigfoot, Sasquatch, and the Abominable Snowman are common in the Pacific Northwest as well as in rural areas in Illinois, Ohio, and Pennsylvania. When traveling the *Weird NJ* route, though, you may encounter this creature, too, especially if you live in the northwest section of the state, where most of these sightings have occurred.

Lake Owassa Sighting

A Sussex County newspaper reported that in 1975, five people spotted a creature nine feet tall near the Bear Swamp, south of Lake Owassa, in the farthest reaches of Sussex County. The creature walked upright and was covered with shaggy gray hair. Locals who hunt and fish in the surrounding forest said that it's possible that something like that could exist because of the remoteness of the area.

Encounter in a Northwest Swamp

According to *The New York Times* (9/19/76), Irving Raser of Layton and Charles Ames of Flatbrookville encountered Bigfoot while examining a beaver dam twelve miles northwest of Newton. The two men claimed they found their dogs surrounding a creature half submerged in the swamp water. Thinking it was a bear, they called the dogs off, only to see the creature climb out of the water and stand on two feet.

"It was about six feet tall," Mr. Raser told *The Times*. "It weighed two hundred and fifty to three hundred pounds and was covered with long brown hair. It had a flat face with deep-set eyes, and the palms of its hands were hairless. If I didn't know better, I'd have said it was a man dressed up in a monkey suit."

But Mr. Raser does know a monkey suit when he sees one—he had been the state deputy game warden for over twenty-one years at the time. The creature started to scream at the dogs, whacking its hand loudly on a nearby tree, and all the time keeping an eye on the two men. The two men witnessed this for more than half an hour before jumping into their pickup and driving to the state police in Hainesville.

They returned with two state troopers and shotguns, but neither the dogs nor the creature were anywhere to be found. The spot where the creature had been standing was inaccessible because of the deep water, but the state troopers found a deer carcass close by. In the state troopers' report, they said that apparently the dogs had been fighting the deer and that the earlier report must have been a mistake.

Bigfoot Wears the Pants in Sussex

Another deer-slaying hairy beast showed up in the early 1970s. One New Jersey resident, who asked not to be identified, encountered the hostile beast while camping with his friends in Sussex County in the early '70s.

"We all heard the growling, spine-chilling noise at the same time," he claimed. "About twenty feet off our path, crouched by the brook, was this creature holding a carcass of a half-eaten deer. I ran the flashlight from head to toe. It had hair completely covering its body and was about seven feet tall and at least three hundred and seventy-five pounds. It had on a ripped-up pair of dungarees that were probably the largest human size available. It was covered with matted blood and smelled awful.

"Our first instinct was to shoot it. We got out our .22 guns, bows, and arrows. We started shooting at it when it let out a bloodcurdling scream and charged us. It tackled my friend, biting and clawing him. I stopped and shot at it with my .22. It let out a howl, then ran off into the woods.

"We went to the hospital, and the police were notified. I called the police after a couple of weeks, but they claimed there was no report or record of us ever being there. They were obviously covering up for some reason."

Bigfoot Kills Bunnies in Wantage

In May of 1977, a Sussex County farmer in the town of Wantage reported that a large brown hairy creature had broken down a one-inch-thick oak door and killed his rabbits. Some of the bunnies' heads were torn off, while other hares were crushed and twisted. The man said there was an unusual absence of blood at the scene. Four men waited with loaded guns the following night for the creature to return. The Bigfoot-like creature with no neck and glowing red eyes reappeared at dusk, was shot at, and was reportedly hit at least three or four times before running away growling. Although there was an account of the wounded beast reemerging a few days later, no carcass was ever found.

Bigfoot and the Hunter

About seven a.m. on a brisk October morning, I was hunting in Passaic County with my two older brothers. I saw some woodland creatures scurrying about. Then it got awfully quiet, when all of a sudden I heard what sounded like two massive tree trunks colliding with great force. THUD! THUD! THUD! I heard three times. Each sound was about ten seconds apart. Then again—THUD! THUD! THUD! THUD! This time I heard it four times, so close that the ground was shaking, and accompanying each thud was the sound of breaking branches. After about three minutes of this eerie sound, it ceased. I never actually saw anything, but I'm convinced it was some kind of Bigfoot creature.

After our unsuccessful day of deer hunting, I went to the spot where I thought the sounds were coming from. I saw no footprints or any kind of trace of anything, but what I did see scared the hell out of me. There were broken branches and small trees broken and another tree torn out by its roots! It was all fresh damage because the breaks in the trees had not turned brown yet. There is no way in hell a black bear could have done this. I would say that there were about five broken trees and they were anywhere from three to six inches in diameter, and the tree that was torn out by its roots was about ten inches in diameter at the base. When I saw this, I got the hell out of there in an awful hurry! I really regret not staying and examining things. Maybe I could have found something to give me a clue as to what exactly it was.—*Jeff S.*

The Big Hairy Man of Somerset County

A *Bigfoot-like entity* has been seen in the regions of Somerset County, from the Great Swamp area and the Somerset Hills to as far away as Hillside. According to eyewitness reports, he stands about eight feet tall and is covered with hair the color of a deer's. The locals call it the Big Hairy Man.

He walks upright like a human, according to a bone specialist and a physical therapist who encountered the Big Hairy Man while taking a short-cut through the Great Swamp on Lord Stirling Road in a hurry to reach the airport.

They claimed the Big Hairy Man walked in front of their car and hopped the fence alongside the road. They could not see his face, because he (or it) was looking down. These sightings, according to the Folklore Project in Bernardsville, have occurred for many years.

Something Hairy This Way Comes

My husband and I still don't know what the heck we saw in 1976. If I had to guess, it was a half man, half ape, we spotted in the Bernardsville section of New Jersey. We've only told a handful of people about our encounter. Some feel we must have seen a bear, but we've never seen a bear swing his arms like a monkey or take strides like this thing did.—*MS and RS*

The Big Red Eye

The Big Red Eye in the northwest corner of the state seems to resemble Bigfoot and the Big Hairy Man of the Great Swamp. Witnesses describe a large bipedal creature covered with long hair from head to toe. But what witnesses in Sussex County remember most are the creature's glowing red eyes. Here, some of our readers recount their run-ins with Big Red.

Two Decades of Big Red Eye

Over a period of two weeks back in 1977, strange moaning sounds and eerie haunting screams filled the night along Wolfpit Road in Sussex County. They started around two a.m. and went on until almost dawn. The wailing noises were constant, and they lasted for hours. It sounded like some kind of huge primate, and it woke me out of a sound sleep. It made the hair on the back of my neck stand straight up and my eyes water. I had the windows open, so I could hear it really well, but I couldn't tell which direction it was coming from. I called my friends to see if they could hear it at their house, which is about a quarter mile away.

"It went on for such a long time," said a neighbor, J. D. Grant. "It was this horrible, bloodcurdling, wailing sound. I have heard coyotes, bears, and foxes, and I've never heard anything like it before. This low, guttural sound, it went right through you."

Another witness to the night of Big Red Eye serenades was my friend Chris, who recalled, "It was around two thirty a.m., and I just got home from work. I heard this low moaning noise, kind of a cry. It definitely wasn't a person. Anything that could make screams that loud definitely had to be big."

Grant recalls a night back in 1996 when she and a friend were walking along Layton Road, when they encountered the creature nearing the side of the road.

"I knew it wasn't a bear—it was too lean and upright. It was humanoid. It had been there the whole time, watching our approach. It was tall and shaggy, with red eyes," she said. "The eyes were glowing red from reflected light, not glowing like LED lights. It just stood there motionless, arms hanging limply at its sides. It didn't seem to have any bad intentions; it was just creepy. Then, of course, we ran, and we did not look back."

I have lived in Sussex County for nearly my whole life and never heard people talk about Bigfoot, but you mention the name Big Red Eye, and you would be surprised how many people have seen him or heard of someone who has.—*Vashni De Schepper*

Big Red Eye Hates Condos

After reading about the Big Red Eye in a recent issue, I got the chills. One night, early last summer, we were walking our dog in our condo development (Paddington Square in Mahwah) and heard this guttural sound. It wasn't a dog or bear, but it was big and angry and had red eyes. It was roughly thirty yards from us. I told my wife to pick up the dog and go into the street and walk home slowly. I was shaking in my boots as I slowly backed up, keeping my eyes on the brush. We made it home and called the police, not once, but twice, to find out what the hell that thing was. They investigated but found nothing. To this day my wife and I wonder what it was.—*Mike V.*

Big Red Eye Chases Girl Right Outta New Jersey

I am originally from Hamburg, New Jersey, born and bred in Sussex County. I now live in Savannah, Georgia. About eight years ago, I had a very vivid encounter with the Big Red Eye. I was driving along Route 517 and decided to take the shortcut into Scenic Lakes, where I lived. The road was simply referred to as the Dirt Road, though later I found out its official name was Shady Lane. I was halfway to the end of the road when I saw this awkward looking bear (?) saunter across the road. Naturally, I stopped the car, and the creature stopped, too. He looked at me for a few seconds (probably the longest few seconds of my life!) and lumbered off into the thick of the woods. The strange thing was that his eyes were red, and I could see the whites in the corners of them.—*Amanda G.*

The Jersey Devil

Without a doubt, New Jersey's most enduring piece of folklore is the tale of the infamous Jersey Devil. For close to three hundred years now, Jerseyans have told tales of a beast that stalks the Pine Barrens. Most reports concern strange tracks in the sandy soil in that desolate area. The tracks resemble the claw prints of a strange bird or hoofprints made by a two-legged creature. Actual sightings are less common, but those who catch a glimpse describe a weird collection of animal parts: the body of a kangaroo, the head of a dog, the face of a horse, large leathery wings, antlers like a deer's, a forked reptilian tail, and intimidating claws. A typical description appeared in the *Asbury Park Press* of October 1988, in which a Howell Township man described a 1981 encounter with a six-foot-tall creature with a furry body, huge three-toed feet, and large teeth.

Any story this persistent raises a few questions. Why have New Jerseyans embraced this legend so steadfastly? Is there actually some sort of creature roaming southern New Jersey? And if so, what in God's name is it?

Legend has it that in 1735, a Pines resident known as Mother Leeds found herself pregnant for the thirteenth time. The Leeds family was among New Jersey's earliest settlers, but Mother Leeds was not living a wealthy lifestyle, by any means. Her husband was a drunkard who made few efforts to provide for his wife and twelve children. Reaching the point of exasperation upon learning of her thirteenth child, she raised her hands to the heavens and proclaimed, "Let this one be a devil!"

On a tumultuously stormy night months later, Mother Leeds went into labor. Her children and husband huddled together in one room of their Leeds Point home while local midwives gathered to deliver the baby in another. By all accounts, the birth went routinely, and the thirteenth Leeds child appeared to be a normal baby boy. Within minutes, however, the unholy wish came true and the wailing infant began to grow at an incredible rate and metamorphose into something hideous.

It sprouted horns from the top of its head, and talonlike claws tore through the tips of its fingers. Leathery batlike wings unfurled from its back, and hair and feathers sprouted all over the child's body. Its eyes began glowing bright red as they grew larger in the monster's gnarled and snarling face. The creature savagely attacked and killed its own mother, then turned its attention to the rest of the horrified onlookers. It flew at them, clawing and biting, voicing unearthly shrieks. It tore the midwives limb from limb, maiming some and killing others.

The monster then knocked down the door to the next room to attack its father and siblings, killing as many as it could. Those who survived saw it fly up the chimney, destroying it on the way and leaving

9TH AND ARCH MUSEUM

T. F. HOPKINS............Manager

CAUGHT!!!
AND HERE!!!
ALIVE!!!

THE

LEEDS DEVIL
Captured Friday After a Terrific Struggle

EXHIBITED EXCLUSIVELY HERE AT
$1000.00 A WEEK.

The Fearful, Frightful,
Ferocious Monster Which
Has Been Terrorizing
Two States.

Swims! Flys! Gallops!

Exhibited Securely Chained
In a Massive Steel Cage.

---

a pile of rubble in its wake. The creature then made good its escape into the darkness and desolation of the Pine Barrens, where it has lived ever since.

In the years that followed, the creature became known as the Leeds Devil, the Jersey Devil, or the Phantom of the Pines. In the eighteenth and nineteenth centuries, it appeared sporadically throughout the Pine Barrens region, frightening residents and anyone brave enough to traverse the undeveloped expanses of New Jersey's southern reaches. Unearthly wails from the dark forests and swampy bogs and the slaughter of domesticated animals would invariably be attributed to the Phantom of the Pines.

As the legends grew, so did the devil's stamping ground. During the week of January 16 through 23, 1909, he apparently traveled far afield. Early in the week, reports emerged from all across the Delaware Valley telling of strange tracks in the snow. The mysterious footprints went over and under fences, through fields and backyards, and across the rooftops of houses. They were even reported in the large cities of Camden and Philadelphia. Panic spread, and grew even greater when reports came through that bloodhounds refused to follow the trail in Hammonton. In lower New Jersey and Philadelphia, schools closed or suffered low attendance. Mills in the Pine Barrens were forced to close when workers refused to leave their homes and travel through the woods to get to their jobs.

Eyewitnesses spotted the beast in Camden and in Bristol, Pennsylvania. Police in both cities fired on it but did not bring it down. A few days later, it reappeared in Camden, attacking a late-night meeting of a social club and then flying away. Earlier that day, it had appeared in Haddon Heights, terrorizing a trolley-car full of passengers before flying away. Witnesses claimed that it looked like a large flying kangaroo. Another trolley-car full of people saw it in Burlington when it scurried across the tracks in front of their car. In West Collingswood, it appeared on the roof of a house and was described as an ostrichlike creature. Firemen turned their hoses upon it, but it attacked them and then flew away. All that week, townsfolk in Bridgeton, Millville, and elsewhere reported that their chickens and other livestock were being slaughtered. In Camden, a local woman found the beast attempting to eat her dog. She hit it with a broomstick and it flew away.

While there has not since been another week to match the frequency, fervor, and intensity of the January 1909 rampage, Jersey Devil sightings continue to this day. The tale of the devil has spread beyond the Pine Barrens and has been embraced by all of New Jersey, even to the point where it has been largely commercialized. The devil is portrayed in toys, on T-shirts, and is even the subject of a 2002 feature film, *13th Child,* starring Cliff Robertson and Lesley-Anne Down. Most famously, the devil has lent its name to New Jersey's NHL hockey team.

While some Jerseyans embrace their devil as nothing more than quaint folklore, others find that a moonlit night in the Pine Barrens changes their opinion. There, where a ghostly mist drifts across the cedar swamps and the unearthly cry of some unseen creature can be heard piercing the stillness of the dark forest, few disbelievers can be found. Whether it's deep in the Pine Barrens or deep in our collective unconscious, one thing is certain—the devil still lurks in New Jersey, and most likely always will.

Driving by the Devil in the Pale Moonlight

This has haunted me since it happened in 1972. One winter night, as I was driving on Greentree Road from Blackwood to Glassboro, I caught a glimpse of something in my rearview mirror. Curious as to what it could have been, I slowed down to take a gander. It was dark out, but the moon lit enough that I had no trouble at all discerning the upright figure of a creature crossing the road roughly twenty-five feet behind my car. The figure stood taller than a man by far, and had thick haunches (similar to a goat's) supporting its nearly human-looking torso and huge wooly head. It moved heavily and didn't seem at all disturbed by my being there. I didn't linger long enough to see much more. I hit the gas and flew to the Mansion Park apartments in the 'Boro. I slept in the car, unwilling to get out in the same darkness that had introduced me to the Jersey Devil.—*Mary Ritzer Christianson*

Field Trips to the Jersey Devil's Turf

Cape May County Technical High School sponsored trips to the Pine Barrens for good grades in certain classes. I was one of the fortunate students to go three times during my four-year career at CMCT. Each time I went on this trip, a heavy-footed "thing" followed my canoe. I heard branches snap under its feet (hooves?). Every ten minutes or so I could hear deep beastly growls that to this very day give me the creeps. Being in a canoe and on a class trip didn't afford me much opportunity to flee in terror, so I stuck it out—for three years. Every year it was the same.

During my sophomore year, I was pretty confident about my canoeing skills, so I didn't look over my shoulder much. I went canoeing with a friend of mine, when we came across a bag that had been torn open and gone through. Around it were prints on the ground that looked something like a horse's hoof, only bigger. Then I heard it, the cry that still haunts my dreams: part human, part beast, and full of anger, pregnant with pure hate. I nearly flipped the canoe!

We left, leaving whatever it was out there behind—or so I thought. It seemed to follow us. Every time we stopped or paused, it got closer to the river. We pushed on. Then we tipped the canoe. I heard the thing running behind us and thought for sure we were dead. Then we righted our canoe and got into it as fast as humanly possible. We finally made it out to safety, sun-fried to a crisp, missing all of our valuables and most of our clothes, but never happier to be on shore.—*Kellie*

The Devil on Route 9

Let me tell you of a sighting of the Jersey Devil. I was driving up Route 9 in Bayville at around ten p.m. There were two cars in front of me, and we were traveling about thirty-five miles per hour. To the right of Route 9 is a mini-mall–type building with woods behind it. All of a sudden, I saw this big thing running across Route 9! It looked like one of the classic pictures of the Jersey Devil. It had no tail, no fur, its ribs showed, and it had a long, odd head with short ears that laid flat. It looked almost ten feet tall! I noticed it because the first car stepped on its brakes, as did the second car. When I looked ahead, I saw this thing galloping across Route 9 and straight into the woods.

I was certain that I had seen the Jersey Devil. No one believes me. They say it was a deer. I have never seen a "deer" that big, that fast, or that weird-looking in my life.—*Sonny Z.*

The Screams of the Jersey Devil

A few years ago, I was talking to my uncle, who is from Pamona. He said that when he was growing up, he had this dog that would stay by him all the time as he played out in the woods and fields around his house. One day while he was on his porch, he could hear screams coming from deep in the woods, and his dog ran out of sight after the noise. Apparently, the screams got louder, and the dog scrambled back to the porch with his tail between his legs and never left the porch again. As hard as he tried, my uncle could not get his once faithful dog to follow him into those woods. So maybe this isn't any hard evidence, but it sure as hell is weird! There is no doubt in my mind that something exists out there.—*Megan*

The Jersey Devil in the Backyard

I think the Jersey Devil has left the Pine Barrens for a vacation up in Kinnelon. Last summer, I was in the living room with my husband when an inhuman sound pierced the quiet. I couldn't imagine anything capable of producing such a noise, which was like that of a puppy being murdered. I'd grown up surrounded by woods and heard a lot of strange animal noises, but this was entirely novel to me. My husband and I ran outside to see what it was. We saw tree branches over our garage shaking violently for about five minutes, after which the leaves grew still and all was quiet. The next day in the light we found no evidence of anything weird.

As if that wasn't bad enough, in May of this year it happened again. I was upstairs getting ready for bed, but this time I was nine months pregnant. All of a sudden, that same unearthly noise ripped through the night: a long, continuous, inhuman scream-ing. I ran downstairs and out into my yard with flashlight in hand. When I shined it across the street around where I thought the shriek was coming from, the light caught two yellow eyes that seemed to be advancing toward me. I could hear the thing they belonged to running through my yard. I couldn't move—it was like being in a night-mare. Finally I turned to run and fell over my own feet. I was lying there for what seemed like an eternity, thinking I was about to die. Finally I regained the strength to scream, get up, and run in the house. I looked outside and saw nothing. I heard my screaming cease along with the bloodcurdling screaming of the monster outside.

Had the Jersey Devil come to Kinnelon? What else could this unusual creature have been?—*Lisa H.*

Camping with the Jersey Devil

In the late 1980s, a couple of my friends and I took a camping trip to the Pine Barrens. I was unaware that we were headed to the home of the Jersey Devil. While everyone was asleep, three of us decided to hit the trails a bit earlier than usual. We were about one hundred yards away in the woods when my bike stalled out. I looked and found that my friends had stalled also. At first I thought it had something to do with the terrain or maybe something to do with the nearby power plants. We tried to start up our bikes, when suddenly from the woods we heard the most horrible pier-cing scream. It sounded inhuman, like something being tortured.

Once back at camp, they asked us if we had heard screams earlier. They had heard them, too, four miles away. That night we headed into the local town. We went into a bar and the bartender asked, "Hey kid, whad'dya see, a ghost or somethin'?" After I told him the story, he smiled and said, "It looks like you met our little friend." He then asked us to come out back. He showed us a tin garbage can that was shredded to bits. It looked like the shreds were made from something with three claws.

I have never returned to the Pine Barrens since, and I do not plan to go back.

—*Frank T.*

Children of a Lesser Devil

The Greenwich Devil Dog

A newspaper article in the *Daily Times* of Woodbury dated December 15, 1925, described a strange ani-mal shot while stealing chickens from a farm in Greenwich. The farmer showed the animal to hun-dreds of visitors, but no one could identify it. The creature was the size of a grown Airedale and hopped like a kangaroo. Its forequarters were higher than its rear, and it crouched. Its hind feet had four webbed toes. Its eyes were yellow, and the jaw was neither dog, wolf, nor coyote.

The Hopping Devil of West Orange

According to a report in the *New York Herald*'s July 3, 1924, issue, several people saw a strange animal in the vicinity of West Orange. A local resident, Mrs. Clyde Vincent, described her encounter: "We were picnicking along the road a while ago when an animal that had a head like a deer, that ran like a rabbit, and had fiery eyes came along and jumped all over us." A patrolman on duty also reported sighting the creature, and a farmer in nearby Livingston had seen it jumping about his fields. The police thought the creature might be a kangaroo escaped from a circus, but found no evidence when they searched.

Darker Worlds Down Below

Not all the weird creatures that inhabit our home state walk on dry land. From Cape May to Lake Hopatcong, creatures from the deep occasionally rear their ugly (and sometimes antler-toting) heads from underwater.

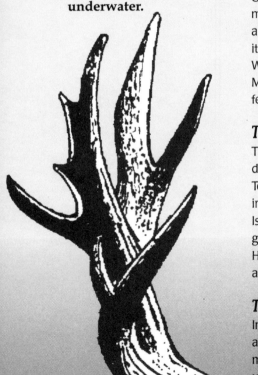

The Beast of Lake Hopatcong

Two hundred years ago, a monstrous beast in the area of Lake Hopatcong threw the region's early settlers into a state of panic. The creature would thrust its huge horselike head above the water's surface with a titanic splash. Its head sported an expansive rack of antlers, and its elephantlike body was reportedly so large that beside it an ox would look like a fawn. After the leviathan's disappearance, the Lenape Indians told area residents the creature had plunged to its death through thin ice while crossing the lake in winter. When some of the settlers rowed a boat out to the spot that the Indians had described, they reported seeing the creature's carcass in its watery grave. Its gigantic skull and ten-foot-long antlers were clearly visible beneath the lake's surface.

The Beast Grabs from Beneath the Surface of Hopatcong

On November 11, 1999, my friend and I went to Lake Hopatcong to pull my boat out of the water, and you wouldn't believe what we saw! It was a pitch-black wave that was six or seven feet tall. When it hit our dock, it almost knocked us off it! Then we saw something go up and down. We thought it was a buoy, but my neighbor said it was too big for a buoy. My friend fell off the deck and into the lake. He popped up about ten feet away and said he felt something grab him. *–Pete*

Tommy in the Toms River

The legend of Tommy, an underwater creature, goes back to precolonial days with the founding of Toms River in the early 1720s by Indian Tom. Sightings are numerous, and rumor has it that Tom sank a boat in the 1920s. Tommy can sometimes be viewed from the gazebo in Island Heights when the full moon is directly overhead. Residents gather in the summer to light a bonfire on Summit Beach in Island Heights to send Tommy a message. They only hope he doesn't claim another victim. *–David K.*

The Sea Monster of Cape May

In November of 1921, the remains of a tremendous mammal washed ashore at Cape May. The animal weighed an estimated fifteen tons or more—the same as five full-grown elephants. Visiting scientists were unable to identify it and stated that nothing yet known to science could compare with it. Eventually the smell from the rotting carcass got so bad, the creature was towed back out to sea.

The Hoboken Monkey-Man

Weird NJ has heard many tales of monkeylike men lurking around our state. Some of them turn out to be real people, apparently mentally challenged and rumored to be inbred, but hardly the bizarre beasts we've come to expect. But the Hoboken Monkey-Man is a different story. In October of 1982, rumors circulated throughout the Hoboken school system about a mysterious apelike creature terrorizing schools, attacking children walking home, throwing students out of windows, and even killing a teacher. After the rumors had circulated for more than two weeks, the Hoboken police department set up a task force to quell the mounting hysteria with help from the Public Safety Council.

"There is no Monkey-Man, no students or children are missing," said one official from the Public Safety Council. "We went looking for him—he wasn't even in the streets. How do you stop a rumor that's growing like wildfire?"

Hoboken Monkey-Man Cleans Up in Jersey City

I read the story on the Hoboken Monkey-Man, which triggered a memory of mine. This event happened one summer in Jersey City when I was ten years old. It was very quiet in the apartment, and I was reading. For some reason, I started getting a little spooked. I looked out the window at an apartment across the way, and I saw this man dressed in a janitor's uniform, sweeping. But the weird thing was that he had a monkey's face with a human body! I yelled and woke up my father, but when we checked to see if he was still there, he was gone. So could it have been the Hoboken Monkey-Man or what?—*Evelyn*

The Lizard Men of Wayne and Great Meadows

Lizard men have often been spotted crossing low-lying roads through the swamps of many southern Atlantic states—especially South Carolina, where eyewitness accounts have made headlines in the local papers as recently as 1994. New Jersey has its own share of reptilian bipeds. In the 1970s, a motorist driving through Wayne reported seeing a green scaly "Lizard Man," with bulging eyes and a lipless mouth. Another motorist, traveling west on Route 80 near Great Meadows in 1974, witnessed a towering humanoid creature covered with green scales standing beside the road. As the driver sped past the animal, he could see its reptilian face, bulging froglike eyes, and broad lipless mouth illuminated in his headlights.

The Half-Human Scream of the Essex Phantom

I have some insight that the residents of Essex County might find disturbing. I have heard half-human screams—a bone-chilling and mysterious wail. The scream suddenly silences conversations, music, and even the TV. For about fifteen years now, we have come to know this annual vocalization as the cry of the Essex Phantom.

Straddling the border of Cedar Grove and Upper Montclair is an area known as the Mills Reservation. The down slope has a number of open sewer pipes that empty out into streams and flow back into the ground. Here there exists a being whose whereabouts are a mystery for ten months out of the year. This creature, it is said, was once a man, but for whatever reason was transformed into a four-legged being. His body resembles that of a large sewer rat, while retaining his own head. During summer nights, the beast just walks around and screams in agony at its own existence.—*Justin F.*

Strange Animal Roams West Orange

When I was younger, I would often stay at a friend's house until late at night and then walk through a series of trails to return to my house. Toward the end of the walk, there was a small patch of waist-high bracken. One night, I saw something out of the corner of my eye disturbing the weeds and carefully took a look at it. It was about five feet long and walked on all fours. It looked like a cross between a cat and a wolf, and had black fur. I was scared as hell and picked up a tree branch and crouched behind a tree waiting for it to pass. It lingered for a while and then jumped a six-foot fence into a gully and disappeared from sight.—*Adam W.*

The Chicken with the Human Face

This report appeared in *The Pioneer* newspaper, dated January 22, 1880: Ex-Freeholder John Lillis, of Jersey City, owns one of the most peculiar freaks of nature ever seen. It is a chicken with a human face, and with feet so misshapen as to be more like lumps of dirt than pedal extremities. The face is almost perfect. Instead of a beak, a common nose shows itself, underneath which is a mouth, regularly proportioned, the upper jaw of which is armed with a set of teeth. The face is bare of feathers, but light whiskers adorn either side of the face, while attached to the chin is a heavy beard. The fowl at present is at the corner of Hoboken and Oakland Avenues, but will probably be secured by some museum.

—Contributed by James Gandy

The Gremlins of the Highlands

My first encounter with a gremlin was when two friends and I were taking a shortcut home through the woods in the evening. I refer to it as a gremlin for the lack of a better word. We noticed some sporadic movement behind us. At that point, we attempted to move faster. We then noticed the movement following us. We began walking down a grade after a fork in the trail that eventually led to a small development. At this time, a shadowy figure darted onto the trail about fifteen or twenty feet in front of us. It was dark, so we couldn't make out much. I sought a better glimpse and began approaching it. As I got closer, I noticed it was probably about three feet tall, with a small, stocky body and a fairly long neck with a large head. I got as close as about ten feet; then, as I tried to close more distance, the gremlin darted back into the woods faster than the fastest deer I have ever seen. We quickly continued moving toward the development, all the while hearing faint and distant bursts of rustling far behind us.—*Damien*

Birdlike Creature Roams New Jersey Same Week as the Devil in 1909

The following excerpt is from *The Asbury Park Evening Press* from January 22, 1909, page 2:

The Jersey Devil was also not the only strange being to appear this Friday. Dan Possack of Millville had a struggle with "one of the strangest freaks of nature, or a monster straight from the bad place." While Dan was doing his chores he heard someone in the backyard walking around, calling out to him.

When he turned around, he beheld a "monster beast-bird" about 18 feet high. The visitor demanded to know where the garbage can was, asking in perfectly good English. Dan, terrified, ran towards the barn, but the bird caught up with him.

It wrapped its sinewy and red beak around Dan's body. Dan began hitting it with a hatchet that he kept in his belt. He was astonished to see that he could chop splinters out of the body, much like he could out of wood. While he was chopping, the beast whispered something in Dan's ear, and with a mighty blow, Dan set the hatchet square into the monster's face. "Out popped an eyeball, and with a scream of pain, the assailant took in a long breath, filled its body like a balloon, and floated into space . . . " Mass hysteria was certainly gripping the area.

—Contributed by Ben Ruset

Strange Birdlike Creature of Wanaque

During the seventh grade, I had a science project to identify and categorize as many insects as I could find. As any local person would tell you, Wanaque was the insect capitol of New Jersey. I decided to go to Dead Man's Pond, a piece of swampland accessible by a tiny dirt path. With my trusty net and killing jar, I traveled to my destination and got down to business. Not ten minutes into my endeavor, I notice this huge shadow moving back and forth across the pond. I looked up and saw the biggest, scariest birdlike creature with glaring eyes gliding silently across the pond. It looked like it had fur rather than feathers, and its wingspan was about twenty feet. I beat a hasty retreat.

Since the Route 287 project came to Wanaque, most of the swamplands have been developed, destroying any research that could be done to find out if, indeed, anything strange was living there.

—*Fred A.*

The Cyclops Snake of Woodbury

One day walking home from high school, I saw some kind of snakelike creature wiggling but not going in any direction. It was about four inches in length and the thickness of a pinky finger. It was brown and rough like a tree branch, though it seemed to have scales. It had a large eye nearly taking up its whole head, except for a small mouth from which it hissed. We ran home to get a jar, but by the time I got back, it was gone.

—*Christoph and Mia*

Local Heroes and Villains

Colorful characters and local loonies—every town has at least one. Their exploits may garner fame outside their communities, even earn them a place in the history books, but most of them achieve celebrity only in their own hometowns.

We feel that the people featured in this chapter have done something to set themselves apart from the crowd, and that makes them worthy of attention. In many instances, these folks are probably better known to the residents of their own communities than their own town's mayor!

It is our sincerest hope that everyone reading this will understand that we mean no disrespect to the people represented in these pages—quite the contrary! With a few obvious exceptions, such as John List, we truly hold these unique individuals in the highest regard. We appreciate their presence here and the fact that they help make our home state a more interesting place.

A League of Their Own

Let's hear it for the ladies! Never let it be said that *Weird NJ* isn't an equal opportunity publication or that the women of New Jersey aren't every bit as weird as the guys (if not more so). Whether they're walking the streets covered in mud or fighting evildoers in costume, the gals of this state have really got some kind of weird girl power.

Underdog vs. the Evil Howard Stern

Most local heroes gain celebrity only within the borders of their own hometown. One New Jersey legend, though, attained national celebrity after appearing on the Howard Stern show in 1992. She is choreographer and dancer Suzanne Muldowney, better known as Underdog.

Ms. Muldowney has been a South Jersey celebrity since the 1970s, thanks to her elaborate homemade outfits and her frequent appearances in South Jersey parades. Muldowney portrays pop culture icons, such as the 1960s cartoon superhero Underdog, which she regards as performance pieces.

After twelve years of public appearances as Underdog, Muldowney was contacted by the producers of the Howard Stern television show in 1992 and asked to appear in character on a segment called "Howie-wood Squares." She had never heard of Stern, but agreed to appear in the segment, which satirized the game show *Hollywood Squares.* However, when she discovered the other participants were fortune-tellers, scantily clad women, and members of the K.K.K., and that the show's subject matter focused on sex, vulgarity, and the bizarre, she regretted the decision. She couldn't leave her square, because she was seated in the top row of the three-story set, and the ladder had been removed. Muldowney was visibly angry with Stern, and launched into aggressive arguments with him on the show.

Needless to say, this performance satisfied Howard's rabid fans and has haunted Muldowney for the past decade. "I became a laughingstock and an outcast," Muldowney said. At parades and other public appearances, she has been

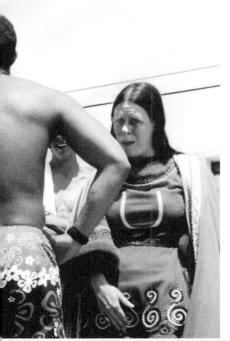

bombarded with taunts, often using Stern's name for her—Underdog Lady.

Muldowney worries that this infamy affects the integrity of the Underdog character. Most present-day youth know Underdog only as the eccentric, angry person on Stern's program.

"They think Underdog is Howard's invention," says Muldowney, "and that the character and I are lustful cads."

So Muldowney has set about correcting these injustices, promoting Underdog's superheroic nature and casting Stern as the adversary. "Howard Stern and his minions have committed very real deeds of super-villainry," she proclaims. "How many countries over the world could have gotten brainwashed via Stern? Underdog has to be detoxified worldwide!"

She May Be Underdog, but She Ain't No "Lady"

I'm writing in reference to the article about Suzanne Muldowney. She performs as the cartoon superhero Underdog and responds kindly only to being called Underdog, and not Underdog Lady, as some folks have attempted to call out to her.—*Anonymous*

Rooting for the Underdog

Miss Suzanne, as I called her growing up in Delran, is a very unusual woman. Highly educated and from an affluent Boston family, Miss Suzanne still lives in the same sparsely furnished apartment that she originally rented in the early '70s. A former dancer who makes all of her own clothing, including a winter selection of eighteenth century–style capes and long skirts, she does not drive and can be seen most mornings walking along Route 130 looking to catch the bus to her job in Philly. Her eccentric trait of playing dress-up first materialized in the mid-'70s, when she appeared in the *Burlington County Times* as an avant-garde Dracula, complete with an aluminum foil sword and fruit punch on her mouth to simulate blood. She would coyly make references to herself as an authentic Dracula, if only in an artistic sense. She takes these characters very seriously. If you see her on the boardwalk in her costume or walking along the highways in her cape, show some respect for a true South Jersey icon.—*Monica St. Clair*

Don't Mention Howard Stern to Underdog

I saw her on a corner in Ocean City waiting for a ride or something, and I approached her, telling her how I had just seen her on the Howard Stern show. She yelled at me. She loudly began telling me to get lost or shut up. She is truly a bizarre person.—*Anonymous*

Let Them Entertain You

Some folks want nothing more out of life than the opportunity to share a song, a dance, or a joke. Some go on to stardom; others toil in obscurity waiting for their big break. But whether they are being cheered or ignored, they give of themselves for the enjoyment of their public. So won't you please lend them an ear and give them a big hand?

The Fall and Rise of Sam Patch— the Jersey Jumper

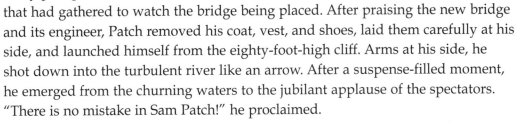

Although Samuel Patch was born in Rhode Island in 1807, it was right here in New Jersey that he would jump his way into America's consciousness. In 1827, when Sam worked at the Hamilton Mills Cotton Works in Paterson, he announced that he would jump over the Great Passaic Falls. He set the date for September 29, the day that the new Chasm Bridge was to be opened across the span.

That Saturday, he appeared high atop the rocky precipice and addressed the large crowd that had gathered to watch the bridge being placed. After praising the new bridge and its engineer, Patch removed his coat, vest, and shoes, laid them carefully at his side, and launched himself from the eighty-foot-high cliff. Arms at his side, he shot down into the turbulent river like an arrow. After a suspense-filled moment, he emerged from the churning waters to the jubilant applause of the spectators. "There is no mistake in Sam Patch!" he proclaimed.

The daring feat was reported in newspapers and magazines across the country, including *The Saturday Evening Post*. The legend of the Jersey Jumper was born. Patch would repeat his jump several times in Paterson, often passing a hat among the crowd to collect money before embarking on his Jumping Tour. In Hoboken, he jumped from a ninety-foot ship's mast into the Hudson River before a crowd of five hundred. He jumped from bridges, cliffs, and anything else on the East Coast that was high enough to look life-threatening. Somewhere along the way, he acquired a trained bear that would occasionally jump with him.

In October of 1829, Patch was invited by a group of Buffalo hotel owners to leap over Niagara Falls. Standing on an island in the middle of the river, Patch waved to the crowds assembled on both the American and Canadian sides. He then kissed the American flag and hurled himself a hundred and thirty feet down into the turbulent river. The Jersey Jumper became the first person ever to survive a trip over Niagara Falls. For good measure, he did it again ten days later.

For his next daredevil stunt, Patch announced that he "was determined to astonish the natives of the West before returning to the Jerseys." Patch leaped over the Genesee Falls in Rochester, New York, on November 6, "gracefully and fearlessly," according to the account of one local paper. Sam planned one more jump in Rochester before returning home. On Friday, November 13, 1828, ten thousand spectators from the U.S. and Canada watched Patch make the one-hundred-and-twenty-five-foot jump into the Genesee River. Patch began his trademark arrowlike descent, but part of the way down, something went very wrong. According to a witness, Patch "descended about one third of the distance as handsomely as ever," then suddenly went limp, arms and legs akimbo. Patch hit the water at an angle with a loud smack, and sank.

His body was recovered two days later. An autopsy revealed the Jersey Jumper had suffered the "rupture of a blood vessel, caused by the sudden chill of the atmosphere through which he passed to the water." On his grave, a crude wooden marker was placed bearing the inscription SAM PATCH—SUCH IS FAME.

But fame sometimes has a way of living beyond the grave. After his last fateful leap, the Jersey Jumper became something of a national folk hero. Two wildly popular plays—*Sam Patch, or the Daring Yankee*, and *Sam Patch in France*—toured the United States for years, with Danforth Marble in the title role.

The Great Falls area in Paterson where Patch made his first leap still looks today much as it did that September day in 1827. The Passaic still crashes mightily beneath the Chasm Bridge, then winds its way past the factory mills where the Jersey Jumper once worked. Gazing down into the swirling water, you can almost hear a faint echo over the roar of the falls. It rises up through the spray and seems to whisper in your ear, "There is no mistake in Sam Patch."

BARNUM'S GALLERY OF WONDERS. Nº 13.

LITHOGR. BY CURRIER & IVES.

152 NASSAU ST. NEW YORK.

"WHAT IS IT"?

Is it a lower order of MAN! Or is it a higher order of MONKEY! None can tell! Perhaps it is a combination of both. It is beyond dispute THE MOST MARVELLOUS CREATURE LIVING. It was captured in a savage state in Central Africa, is probably about 20 years old, 4 feet high, intelligent, docile, active, sportive, and PLAYFUL AS A KITTEN. It has the skull, limbs and general anatomy of an ORANG OUTANG and the COUNTENANCE of a HUMAN BEING.

TO BE SEEN AT ALL HOURS AT BARNUM'S MUSEUM.

Zip the What Is It?

Circus freaks seldom enjoy the glamorous show business lifestyle. But one curious little fellow enjoyed a long and fruitful career with an audience estimated at one hundred million people. The man P. T. Barnum billed as Zip the What Is It? had a normal body but an underdeveloped head described at the time as "like the slim end of an egg, with a long broad nose and a prognathous jaw." Supposedly the survivor of a lost Amazon tribe discovered during the exploration of the River Gamba and a missing link between the apes and men, Zip appeared at various stages of his career in a monkey outfit, playing the fiddle and dancing and, on special occasions, dressed in a tux.

But Zip was no missing link. He was born William Henry Johnson in Liberty Corners, New Jersey, in 1857, one of six children born to former slaves William and Mahalia Johnson. He became Zip only after P. T. Barnum plucked young William from a stint in Van Emburgh's Circus. Barnum had already billed one of his exhibits as What Is It? — an English actor named Harvey Leech who had been exposed as a fraud (instead of the feral man-beast in the advertising). When Barnum saw Johnson, he knew he'd found the ultimate What Is It?

Barnum gave William a makeover — shaving his cranium, except for a little tuft of shaggy hair on the back of his head, and fitting him with a furry monkey outfit. Dressed in it, Zip was billed as a nondescript — somewhere between monkey and man.

But despite his billing, his odd appearance, and the undecipherable dialect he used in front of an audience, Zip was smarter than he seemed. His sister, Mrs. Sarah Van Duyne, claimed in a 1926 interview that her brother would "converse like the average

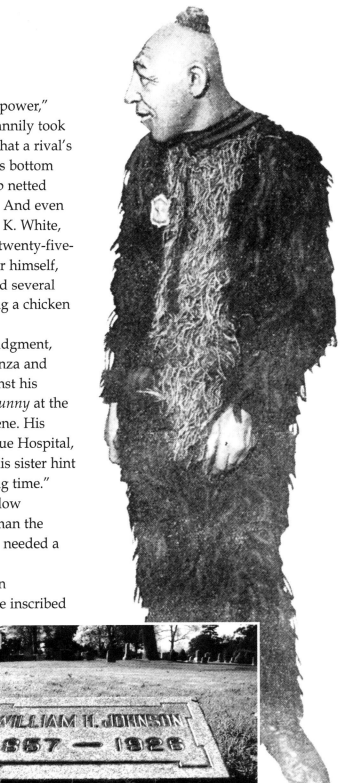

person, and with fair reasoning power," when he came to visit her. He cannily took up the fiddle when he realized that a rival's ukulele playing was boosting his bottom line—and by some accounts, Zip netted $14,000 in six years by doing so. And even though his manager, Captain O. K. White, probably did better out of their twenty-five-year association, Zip did well for himself, with a home in Bound Brook and several successful investments, including a chicken farm in Nutley.

He did make one fatal misjudgment, though. After contracting influenza and bronchitis in 1926, he went against his doctor's wishes and closed out the run of the musical comedy *Sunny* at the New Amsterdam Theater, in which he appeared in the circus scene. His condition deteriorated, and he was moved to New York's Bellevue Hospital, where he contracted pneumonia and died. His dying words to his sister hint at Zip's hidden depths: "Well," he said, "we fooled 'em for a long time."

His brief and simple funeral played to a packed house of fellow performers, including Alphonso the Human Ostrich, Gus Birchman the Human Claw Hammer, and the morbidly obese Jolly Irene, who needed a whole pew to herself.

Zip's remains were interred in the Bound Brook Cemetery on April 28, 1926. Few people today who walk past the simple stone inscribed WILLIAM H. JOHNSON 1857-1926 realize who lies there—a little-noggined fellow who led a life larger than most.

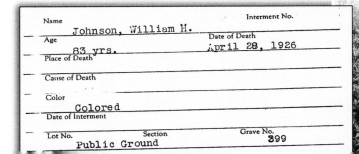

Name		Interment No.	
Johnson, William H.			
Age		Date of Death	
83 yrs.		April 28, 1926	
Place of Death			
Cause of Death			
Color			
Colored			
Date of Interment			
Lot No.	Section	Grave No.	
	Public Ground	399	

Hackensack's Singing, Dancing Man

James Roberson has been singing and dancing at the intersection of Anderson and River streets in Hackensack for more than three years now. Every day he arrives early in the morning and spends the entire day dancing and shouting out the lyrics to songs only he can hear through his headphones. On an average day, he does this for twelve to fourteen hours nonstop.

Hackensack natives call him the Dancing Man, and to those who travel to see him, he's the Hackensack Dancer. He believes commuting is incredibly stressful, and claims his goal is to lessen that stress. It makes him happy for motorists to stare or honk, and for busloads of people to crane their necks to see him better.

Some people call him crazy, and by some definitions they're right. Roberson lives off federal disability checks for mental illness—what he calls "strange behavior"—and a local clinic provides him with medication. But town officials have stated that they have no plans to stop the music.

"He doesn't hurt anybody," Hackensack mayor John Zisa told the *Bergen Record*. "What can you do?"

The community has generally responded to this quirky kindness with wonder and amusement. Roberson does have medical care and family in the area, as well as the watchful eyes of a community that has embraced him. As long as he's safe and willing to grace us with his songs and gyrations, there's no reason this one-man dance party should ever end.

He Danced Till a Quarter to Three!

I spotted the Dancing Man at the corner, dancing away with a big grin on his face. He was going all out. I got tired just looking at him. As I pulled away, someone honked, and Dancing Man waved. On my way back from lunch, he was still there.

Four hours later, on my way to happy hour, he was still there dancing, but he had changed clothes! He's wearing a Walkman, so no one else can hear the music he's dancing to, but if you put your car radio on, no matter what song it is, he seems to be dancing to your tune.—*Christopher K.*

Why Did the Dancer Cross the Road? To Get to the Other Side!

He's not the greatest dancer (he only has one dance move), and seems completely oblivious to cars and people. I've seen him dance at all different hours of the day. He'll even cross the street when the light changes from green to red and dance on the other side of the street, returning to his original side after the light changes back!—*Steve*

The Hackensack Dancer's on a Mission from God

The heat wave this past summer did not stop him. He just keeps going. The Dancer thinks God put him on this earth to dance for the people in their cars in order to help stop road rage and other tantrums. He is an entertainer for God.—*Lola M.*

The Devil Made Them Do It

Different people kill for different reasons. There are crimes of passion and anger. There are murders for profit. And then there are those who kill for their own impenetrable reasons—it almost seems as though some outside force eggs these troubled souls on to commit heinous crimes. New Jersey has seen just about every kind of killing. From the cold and calculated crimes of Antoine Le Blanc to the religiously motivated slayings of John List, our fair state has seen more than its fair share of gruesome homicides.

Seeking the Hide of Antoine Le Blanc, The Morristown Murderer

Although Antoine Le Blanc's triple murder of one of Morristown's most respected families was horrendous, his public hanging was just the beginning of a tale so gruesome that we still recoil at it a hundred and sixty years later. For it is said that the remains of Antoine Le Blanc may rest in pieces as heirlooms in some of the finest homes of New Jersey.

Le Blanc, a French immigrant, arrived in New York in April of 1833. Three days later, he was hired to work the family farm of Samuel Sayre of Morristown, New Jersey. He took his work orders from Mr. Sayre; his wife, Sarah; and the Sayres'

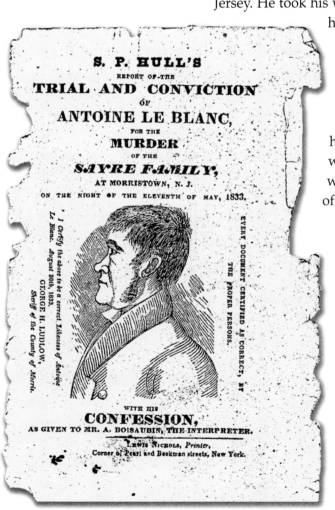

household servant, Phoebe. For his labors, thirty-one-year-old Le Blanc earned a small room in a dank basement, but no wages.

After a few weeks of this indignity, Le Blanc exacted a grim revenge. On the night of May 11, he returned to the Sayre house at about ten thirty p.m. from a night at a local tavern. Faking distress, he lured Samuel Sayre out to the stable, where he killed him with a shovel. Then he did the same with Sayre's wife. After hiding the two bodies, he killed Phoebe in her sleep with a single blow from a club and escaped into the night on one of Sayre's horses, with stolen household valuables at his side.

The next day, some of Sayre's effects were found on the road. Then the bodies were discovered and the chase was on. Sheriff George Ludlow apprehended Le Blanc in the Mosquito Tavern in the Hackensack Meadows with a pouch of Sayre's possessions by his side.

Antoine Le Blanc's trial for the murder of the Sayre family took place in the Morris County Courthouse on August 13, 1833. The jury took just twenty minutes to find him guilty, and Judge Gabriel Ford handed down the sentence. Le Blanc was to "be hanged by the neck until dead" and then "be delivered to Dr. Isaac Canfield, a surgeon, for dissection."

On the afternoon of September 6, Le Blanc stood atop the gallows erected on the village green for the occasion. The jeering mob made its way into tall trees and onto nearby rooftops for a better view.

Le Blanc's body twitched for about two minutes at the end of the rope and then was still. But the true horrors of the story began after his lifeless body was cut down from the gallows.

The corpse was whisked across the street to Doctor Canfield's office, where he and Dr. Joseph Henry hooked it up to a primitive battery to see the effects of electrical current on muscular motor impulses. The scientists reportedly got Le Blanc's eyes to roll around in his head, caused his limbs to tense, and even elicited a slight grin from his dead lips. They then took a death mask likeness of Le Blanc's face, skinned him, and delivered the hide to the Atno Tannery on Washington Street to be fashioned into a variety of "charming little keepsakes." A large number of wallets, purses, and other artifacts were produced and sold, with Sheriff Ludlow's signature to prove their authenticity.

The story might have been forgotten but for a startling discovery made in 1995. While liquidating the estate of the late Carl Scherzer, a retired surveyor and unofficial town historian, workers from Dawson's Auctioneers and Appraisers of Morris Plains found the glazed plaster death mask of Antoine Le Blanc and a suspicious-looking change purse.

Douglas Scherzer, Carl's son and the chief of police of Morris Plains, invited Weird NJ to see these artifacts. He brought out a cardboard box and laid it on the table before us. Folding back the corrugated flaps of the package, he revealed the peaceful face of Antoine Le Blanc. Looking as though Le Blanc was merely sleeping, the death mask's delicate plaster eyelids closed gently over gracefully intertwining lashes. The pronounced cheekbones sloped down to the broad, smooth lips. Then we noticed that both ears had been hacked off before the cast was made, perhaps to ensure the easy removal of the mold. A small paper tag stated in nineteenth-century script, "Antoine Le Blanc, a Frenchman—murdered Judge Sayre and family—hanged in Morristown, NJ 1833."

Chief Scherzer pulled out a dusty old picture frame that contained a small rectangular wallet about four and a half inches long and greenish brown in color. It folded over, and a tongue flap fit neatly into a slot on top to close it, labeled with a typewritten strip of paper: "A wallet made of human skin allegedly that of Antoine Le Blanc."

Today the Sayre house on Morristown's South Street is the home of Jimmie's, a restaurant and bar. What other reminders does our state have of this horrific story? We don't know. But Antoine Le Blanc will no doubt rest in pieces throughout that town for years to come, and an old wallet at a garage sale there could turn out to be a truly weird find.

John Emil List

You'd never think that a person could kill his whole family, disappear, and reappear under a new identity to live a completely unassuming suburban life. But this is exactly what happened in the case of one of New Jersey's most infamous murderers, John List.

John Emil List was an accountant who lived with his mother, wife, and three children in a large home off Hillside Avenue in the tranquil bedroom community of Westfield. In addition to material wealth, List attempted to enrich his family spiritually as a devout pillar of the local Lutheran church.

While this might seem like quite the suburban dream life, the List family had some dark secrets. His marriage to Helen List was an unhappy one that had begun with a pregnancy scare that turned out to be a false alarm. Furthermore, she was nearly blind and unable to walk, from a bout with syphilis left over from a previous marriage.

The Lists were living beyond their means, with three teenagers at home, when John's career began to waver. He had to leave his vice presidency at the accounting firm and began selling insurance to pay the bills. As John saw his life unraveling, he decided to save his family's souls by removing them from the earth. As John recently told an interviewer on the TV program *20/20,* he thought that if his home was foreclosed upon, the family would split up and turn away from the church.

"The only way to save them from that was to kill them. I thought about [killing myself] but my belief is that if you do that your soul can't go to heaven. . . . Later I could confess my sins and get into heaven myself."

On November 9, 1971, John put a carefully calculated plan into action. In the days before, he had mailed notes to his family's friends, coworkers, and teachers with cover stories to explain why they wouldn't be seen in coming weeks. John started off that fateful day by dropping the kids off at school. When he returned around nine a.m., Helen greeted him with a "Good morning" as she was having breakfast in their kitchen, and her husband shot her in the back of the head with a .22-caliber pistol. He ran up to his eighty-four-year-old mother Alma's living quarters in the attic. "Like Judas, I gave her a kiss," he explained later, then shot her the same way.

Later in the day he picked up his sixteen-year-old daughter, Patricia, from school, and as they entered the house together, killed her the same way. His younger son, thirteen-year-old Freddie, met a similar fate, but his fifteen-year-old son, John, did not die so easily. After the first shot, he was still alive, so John senior stood over his son and repeatedly shot him in the heart with the .22 and a 9-millimeter he was carrying. "I didn't want him to suffer," he confessed in a court transcript.

List meticulously arranged his wife's and children's bodies in the estate's large ballroom, laying them out on sleeping bags in the shape of a cross with their faces covered. With each body, he left a note explaining why he had killed. His mother's body remained in the attic, with a note explaining she was "too heavy to move." Other notes were addressed to his pastor and employer. One note reflected on the actual act of killing. "I'm sure some will ask, 'How could anyone do such a horrible thing?' My answer is that it wasn't easy."

The bodies lay undiscovered for nearly a month until December 7, when Patricia's drama teacher, Ed Illiano, paid a visit to check on his absentee student. He discovered the bodies on the floor of the ballroom, with church music playing over the home's intercom.

A full-scale manhunt began, but List's trail was lost. Over the next seventeen years, police turned up List's car, some papers, and a lot of dead ends. Then, on May 21, 1989, the story of John List appeared on the popular television show *America's Most Wanted*. The program showed a reenactment of the murders, a photograph of John List, and a sculpture of List as he might look after two decades on the lam.

That night, as a quiet man named Robert P. Clark attended a church function in Midlothian, Virginia, several of his acquaintances dialed the hot line at *America's Most Wanted* to report how much he resembled List. Other calls from Golden, Colorado, pointed the finger at a local french-fry cook, Robert Clark, who had recently relocated to Virginia.

The FBI swiftly moved in and apprehended List. At his trial, defense attorneys tried to portray him as a man whose parents forced religion upon him, pushing him into insanity. But the coldness of List's notes, his carefully planned escape, and his lack of remorse led to conviction. On April 12, 1990, a New Jersey judge proclaimed John List a "man without honor" and sentenced him to life in prison.

List still hopes that he will go to heaven and hopes to meet his family there. "I'm sure that if we recognize each other," he said, "we'll like each other's company just like we did here, when times were better."

Ninety-nine Percent Perspiration

The Stuff They Didn't Teach You in Grade School About Thomas Alva Edison

Few people would disagree that Thomas Edison was among the most influential figures of the past hundred years. Just try to imagine the twentieth century without Edison's contribution of recorded sound, motion pictures, and electric light—all of which were developed right here in New Jersey, first at Edison's Menlo Park laboratory, then later at his West Orange factory. But for all of his greatness, Edison had his foibles. He once said, "I learn just as much from my failures as I do from my successes." He must have learned quite a bit from the episodes you're about to read. If invention really is ninety-nine percent perspiration (as he also said), we can only imagine how much he must have sweated over some of these inspired failures.

How Competition Killed the Elephant:
The Shocking Truth Behind Thomas Edison's Most Electrifying Invention

Thomas Edison loved competition. Actually, he loved *crushing* his competition. Throughout his long career, he tried to dominate any field he ventured into, and he was pretty good at it—until George Westinghouse came along.

Westinghouse challenged Edison's dominance in the electricity market. He purchased the patents of Nikola Tesla for a system of alternating current (AC) that rivaled Edison's direct current (DC) systems. Because AC required far fewer generators and transformers and transported electricity much farther than DC, it quickly overtook the market. Not one to swallow his pride, Edison tried to influence public opinion with dire warnings of the dangers of alternating current. "Just as certain as death," Edison proclaimed, "Westinghouse will kill a customer within six months after he puts in a system of any size." Westinghouse had little choice but to agree. "Yes, the alternating current will kill people," he replied. "So will dynamite and whiskey."

To win ground in the War of the Currents, Edison used AC to electrocute small animals such as dogs and cats before the public at his West Orange laboratory. He could kill a decent-sized dog in about ten seconds. But instead of scaring people away from Westinghouse's service, the system appealed to certain people precisely because of its killing potential. New York State had been looking for a humane way to execute condemned prisoners, and approached Edison for assistance. After some initial reluctance, he decided to help out—and help his own cause against the Westinghouse system.

To prove AC electricity's killing potential on larger animals, Edison "Westinghoused" a cow and then a horse at his West Orange lab. Then he saw his chance to really prove his point when an elephant at Coney Island's Luna Park assaulted a patron (who, in the animal's defense, had fed the poor beast a lighted cigarette). The park's owners decided to destroy Topsy the elephant, and Edison's workers wired the three-ton pachyderm—and filmed the event with Edison movie cameras. When the switch was thrown, Topsy's body stiffened, smoldered, and lurched, then stood rigid as plumes of white smoke billowed from beneath her massive feet. After just ten seconds, the mighty beast pitched forward, lifeless. Edison made sure that film of the electrifying event was distributed around the country to further his cause.

Of course, the propaganda campaign was not

successful. Alternating current is in almost every house today. And beginning in 1890, the electric chair was widely used to execute humans. By all accounts, the first human execution was much less successful than Edison's earlier experiments. Convicted murderer William Kemmler got a seventeen-second charge and began smoking—but

was still moving and bleeding afterward. A second jolt lasting seventy-two seconds finished the job, during which Kemmler smoldered and, according to some reports, burst into flames. It took four minutes for the body to cool down enough for it to be moved. George Westinghouse had the last word in the War of the Currents. "They could have done it better with an axe," he quipped.

Edison Hears Dead People

In 1878, Edison briefly associated with an organization of mystics known as the Aryan Theosophic Society. Though he left the group and denied ever associating with them, his discussions with the group's leader, Madame Elene Blavatsky, turned his thoughts to Eastern religious ideas, particularly reincarnation.

He developed a theory that human intelligence and personality were based on memory, and memory was composed of small physical particles. These particles, which Edison called "little people," came from

outer space. Each particle had its own consciousness, and they swarmed together to form human minds. Death occurred when the "little people" disagreed and parted ways.

"They fight out their differences," he said, "and then the stronger group takes charge. If the minority is willing to be disciplined and to conform, there is harmony. But minorities sometimes say 'to hell with this place; let's get out of it.' They refuse to do their appointed work in the man's body, he sickens and dies . . . and they are all free to seek new experience somewhere else."

With typical bravado, Edison saw no reason why he couldn't find a practical way to communicate with the dead—and even reanimate them. He theorized that if the exact same group of particles could be put back together, then a dead person's personality would return. He tried to chart swarms of little people with photographic plates but never succeeded, and his experiments dropped off severely when Henry Ford introduced Edison to a new hobby—attempting telepathy. After visiting a parapsychologist at Ford's invitation, Edison conducted experiments in telepathic communication by wrapping electrified coils around his own head and those of his guests.

Who knows what would have happened if Edison had lived longer? Perhaps instead of going to summer action flicks, we could entertain ourselves with electroshock telepathy to chat with our departed loved ones.

Hate in the Garden State
Alma White's Fiery Cross to Bear

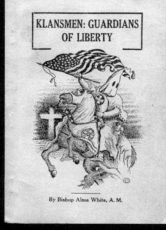

In 1901, a Methodist parishioner in Colorado named Alma White split with her church and formed a small group known as the Pentecostal Union. By 1907, the group had relocated to a settlement three miles outside Bound Brook, New Jersey, and acquired the nickname the Pillar of Fire. Their new town, Zarephath, would become the international center for this religion, complete with its own radio station and college, Alma White College. Thousands would flock to hear Bishop White's outdoor sermons every Sunday.

While this seems par for the course in terms of religious activity, Alma White herself had some strange and contradictory attitudes. An ardent proponent of feminism, she also favored a group known for racial and religious intolerance.

Among the dozens of books she published were *The Ku Klux Klan in Prophecy, Klansmen: Guardians of Liberty,* and *Heroes of the Fiery Cross.* The Klan's Grand Dragon, Arthur H. Bell, the K.K.K.'s official Imperial Representative of the Realm of New Jersey at the time, wrote favorable introductions to more than one of White's books. Bishop White saw no contradiction in her liberal and more suspect causes—in fact, she wrote, "We are looking to the Knights of the Ku Klux Klan to champion the cause of woman and to protect her rights." Her fulsome praise of these "heroes of a new reformation . . . robed in white, emblematic of the purity of the principles for which they stand" often spilled into inaccuracy. Few at the time or since could support her statement, "The Klan is opposed to mob violence and lynchings, and has succeeded in abolishing them in places where they were of frequent occurrence." As for another of her statements, only half of it is believable: "The Klan believes that America is a white man's country and should be governed by white men. Yet the Klan is not anti-negro; it is the negro's friend."

Alma White seemed equally ill informed about the Klan's history. In *Klansmen: Guardians of Liberty,* she claimed that the founding fathers of the United States were full-fledged members of the K.K.K. and that Paul Revere made his famous ride in Klan robes and hood. She refuted the well-documented fact that Confederate general Nathan Bedford Forrest founded the Klan after the Civil War, and defended her revisionist history by likening her critics to "blind Samson grinding in the mill of the Philistines."

Today Zarephath is still a thriving town and still the international headquarters for the Pillar of Fire. Their colleges aimed at educating people in Bible study are still running at full steam, and their radio broadcast can still be heard on WAWZ 99.1 FM. While they may not espouse racist views today, it cannot be denied that in earlier days their founder certainly seemed to be guilty by association.

Traveling to the Beat of a Different Drummer

Some people just seem to move through this world slightly out of step with the rest of society. Their distinction may be as simple as when they choose to take their daily walk—at midnight, for example, when most of their neighbors are home in their beds. Perhaps it's the pace at which they move or the mannerisms they employ while in motion that sets them apart from other pedestrians.

Whatever it is, though, there is something out of sync about these folks that makes the rest of us notice them and wonder what might explain their curious behavior. Stories are invented, told and retold, and embellished with each retelling. Some stories have proved to be far-reaching and also endowed with a surprising longevity. In this chapter we will be taking a look at how in some instances the simplest gestures have, deservedly or not, transformed certain more or less ordinary people into the stuff of legend.

The Midnight Walker of Wyckoff

From one street up from the famous Gravity Road in Franklin Lakes comes this story of a local legend. There is a man in this area that walks every night from midnight to three a.m. Supposedly the man has cataracts, and he always looks kind of creepy, with his eyes always looking white. Whenever you ride by this man, he would immediately stop and look at your car. He never speaks or waves. The local kids are scared to death of this guy. The man is always there walking along the road—at night—alone.–*Anonymous*

The Midnight Walker Took His Own Eyes

There is a man that walks along a road off Route 208 in Wyckoff. There is a story behind him. His daughter was walking home one late night. She wandered aimlessly into the middle of the road for some reason. She was struck by a truck and was killed. Her father found her that night and couldn't stand the sight of his dead daughter, so he gouged out his own eyes. After that, they sewed his eyelids shut. He now walks up and down the road every night, at midnight, hoping to see his daughter once again.–*Sal*

The Blackest Eyes

There was a tale going around in the late '80s that a girl was walking home from a party, and she was severely beaten and raped and dragged down the road. I don't know if this is true or not, but my friends had kept telling me about it. Then my friend brought up the Midnight Walker. So we left at about eleven fifteen to find him. At about twelve seven, we were coming around the bend when all of a sudden, we saw a man walking the road. The legend tells you that it is the girl's father, who is looking for her, and every night he will walk the road at exactly midnight.

Sure enough, he was exactly as people had described—hunched over, walking slowly. My friend said to him, "Excuse me sir, do you know how to get back on 17?" The man looked up, and I will never forget his face. He had the blackest eyes. He just pointed, and my friend drove away as fast as he could. I still have never been back there but plan to go again.–*Jeff*

Watching the Walker in Wyckoff

The first time you see him, you would think that you were dreaming. Here, walking by himself in the middle of the night, was an enormous white-haired man. He would walk up and down the side of the street, looking as if he had lost something. The man is simply huge. An unsuspecting tourist might get the living hell scared out of them. His head is always down, until the time you pass. As you do pass, he slowly lifts his head and turns to look at you. The first time I saw him, it gave me the chills. Then the inevitable words left my mouth: "What in the hell was that?" There are a couple of stories floating around the area about him. One story says that he lost his wife and child on the turn where he wanders. So every night, when there is nobody around, he walks the streets to the section where his family died.–*Neal S.*

He Walks by Night

We think that maybe his daughter didn't die. Maybe she is missing and her curfew was midnight, so every night he goes to look for her at midnight. We think this because he looks into every car that passes by.—*RoxyQSlvr*

Midnight Walker Is a Ghost

There is a ghost who walks around in Wyckoff at around midnight. We saw him really close-up. He was wearing a plaid or flannel shirt. He is an old guy just walking around on the sidewalk. We asked him where Grandview Avenue was to see if he could talk, and he turned sideways and pointed. It looked like he had no eyes, as they were closed the whole time. It looked like he couldn't open them.—*Alison*

The Midnight Walker Becomes the Green Man

The town of Wyckoff seems to be a normal, quiet town, but lurking around the corner of the road may be the dim figure of the Green Man, wearing his flashing, protective vest and gripping a small box in one hand. The caution and alertness in the man's movement are evident. It is believed that years ago, when he was walking down the street with his young daughter, a car spun out of control and hit both of them, killing her and blinding him. To this day, he wanders up and down the same street, waiting for that same car to reappear so that he can avenge his daughter's death. He appears each night on those streets for those same hours, in rain or snow. Where he disappears to afterward is unknown. The only thing that is known is the fact that he has never been seen during any other time of the day or in any other place.

—*Wei H.*

Green Man Not Green at All

After circling his territorial two streets, we saw the outline of a zombielike figure and made a U-turn so as to observe him more clearly. His eyes reflected a perfect stream of headlight brilliance as his shoes slowly caressed the sidewalk. His sloth-like moves sent a chill up my spine, down my back, and out to my limbs. My toes curled up inside my sneakers as his head slightly lifted from a heavy stare toward his feet, and I held my breath, although I knew he couldn't hear my insignificant inhalations. But there was that small chance—perhaps, somehow, he knew I was there, even though he couldn't see me. His skin was pale and faintly wrinkled—not green in the slightest. He was an average mid–sixty-year-old. What frightened me most was being stopped by two police cars. A policewoman demanded my friend's license, registration, and insurance card, and explained to us that "The Walker is not a freak—he's just a blind man, too sensitive to sunlight to walk during the day."—*Kristen W.*

A Cop Checks in on the Midnight Walker

When I first started on the Wyckoff Police Department, we were warned about a local man who would walk late at night and would appear to be somewhat strange. To protect the harmless, I won't tell you his name. Believe me, however, he exists. His physical description is somewhat strange also. He was very tall, about six foot three inches, and somewhat scary-looking. He suffered from some eye disease that caused him to be about ninety-five-percent blind. He could barely even see bright lights. He gave many people the heebie-jeebies, especially in the late-night hours.

He never bothered anyone, but was quite unfriendly. If you tried to talk to him, he would just ignore you as if you weren't there and keep on walking. Because of his very limited sight, whenever cars would be driving toward him at night, he would appear to stare and lean in toward them. He wanted to be sure he was not out in the street, and this was the only way he could see the position of the headlights.—*Heidi M.*

The Weird Twins of Cedar Grove

If you ever want to see double, take a ride through Cedar Grove and glance at the twins enjoying their daily stroll. These are identical twin brothers in their sixties who dress alike, walk alike, and, I have been told, even talk alike, sometimes in unison. One day, out of curiosity, I followed them down a treelined street in Cedar Grove. "Tweedledee and Tweedledum" live in a little box-shaped cottage, festooned with pretty flowers. I felt like Alice in Wonderland when I discovered this.—*Denny*

Mike and Ike of Little Falls

I wanted to mention a pair of colorful characters from my youth. I'm from Little Falls, where there was a pair of identical twins who we would always see walking through town—we called them Mike and Ike, also Pete and Re-Pete (corny, I know). Anyway, these two always kept in perfect step with one another, turned their heads at exactly the same time, and dressed in contrasting colors (blue shirt, green pants—green shirt, blue pants).—*Michele S.*

The Twins Married Sisters and Live in Twin Houses

I grew up in Little Falls, right next to the railroad tracks. Every day at the same time, two male twins would walk past my house going to and from work. They looked identical, had the same haircuts and glasses, and wore matching clothes every day. We would wave and say, "Hi, twins," and they would wave with the same arm at the same time. Turns out, they married two sisters and bought similar houses right next door to each other on the border of Cedar Grove. I still see the twins when I visit Little Falls, and they still wave in unison.—*Janet M.*

Twins of Little Falls a Scientific Experiment?

A native told me about the Little Falls Twins, but it wasn't until I'd lived here for about a year that I saw them. They dress identically. They usually wear plain white T-shirts and dark blue or green work pants. I think they carry chain wallets and wear plain black leather belts, and I know they both wear glasses, which are identical. Their clothes are neat, their shirts are always tucked in, and their gray to white short hair is always combed and parted the same way.

They walk in step, but it's not a march. Their walk is casual and natural, which makes seeing two people walking exactly that same way a little unnerving. Their arms swing in unison. It all looks practiced and purposeful, but if you would see just one person walking that way you wouldn't find it remarkable at all.

They always look directly ahead. The one time I saw their heads turn, it was in unison, and they looked down and to the side, but there was nothing there! They turned their heads slowly back to front and kept walking. I've never seen them talk to each other or anyone else. They have blank expressions on their faces.

The impression I get from them is that they are two of the same person. That's how alike they look, like you would expect clones from a science fiction story of the '50s to look. Their lack of expression and synchronicity of movement makes you think of robots. My theory is that they are retired soldiers that have lived together for the majority of their lives.—*Sean*

Idle Hands with Bad Habits

Most folks have a hobby or two that they like to engage in to while away their free time. Some go fishing or bike riding. Others collect stamps or coins. For some, though, run-of-the-mill doodad collections just don't float their boat. These people invent strange new pastimes that make even the most fanatical collector of train paraphernalia seem normal and well balanced. Perhaps it's a fine line between wholesome hobbyist and flagrant fetishist. And that's a line that some people in our state have chosen to cross in strange new ways.

The Sock Man of Middletown

I went to school in Red Bank. There used to be a coach that taught at the school. After he left, we started hearing stories about him living in Middletown with his mother. We found out that if you drove by his house and flashed your headlights, he would come out with his dog, approach the car, and ask if you had any socks to sell. A few of my friends actually would go to his house and sell the socks right off their feet to get some money. I think it used to be $5 for socks and $10 for sweaty, smelly ones. The two times I went with a bunch of friends, I couldn't stop laughing. I thought the whole thing was too damn weird.—*Ted W.*

I Sold My Soul . . . Er, Socks

My first sale was about nine thirty on a Friday night in June. Now, you have to realize that you can't just walk up to his house and knock on his door. You had to drive by his house very slowly so he would notice you from his window, and either wave a sock or stick a foot out the window and wriggle it about. The next step was to park in a dark, secluded area around the corner and wait. He would come out walking his dog. He was very straight and to the point about the transaction. There was no small talk as we went right into detailed descriptions about every sweaty activity we did that day. His favorite socks were the long Wigwams. After he decided which socks he wanted, he would pull out a wad of $5 bills. He was very quick and deliberate in the exchange and would always quickly shove the socks down his pants when he received them. We didn't know what he did with them, and we didn't want to know. The Sockman was basically my allowance for the remainder of my youth until I went to college.—*Scott*

Personalized Properties

Home, Home on the Strange!

A *man's home is his castle,* they say, but in New Jersey, that home could just as easily be a cookie jar or gigantic sheet-metal tepee. Some of our state's eccentric abodes are the work of artists who do not confine themselves to a studio space. But more often these unique homebuilders have little or no connection to the mainstream art world—or any other world for that matter. They are usually self-taught, self-styled, and draw on their own personal vision for inspiration.

Of course, not all the results are appealing. The enhancements to some homes just seem to creep out the average person. We can only wonder what the owner might have been thinking—and think that perhaps it's best not to know. In any case, the creators of these uniquely decorated dwellings seem to live outside mainstream culture and society. Their properties are extensions of their personalities, and in them, we

see a reflection of the owner's soul. These homeowners have a singular vision, and have created their own slightly off-center place in which to spend their lives.

PALACE DEPRESSION
George Daynor, Originator, Designer & Builder
VINELAND, N. J. U.S.A.

A Little Bit of Naples in Nutley: Angelo Nardone's Statue House

"I'm trying to bring back the Renaissance," Angelo Nardone told Weird NJ six years ago as he stood in front of his home on Franklin Avenue in Nutley surrounded by Romanesque ruins.

In 1960, when Nardone took over the single-story building from his father, its lot was being used to sell reconditioned cars. He turned the building into the Villa Capri, a coffeehouse that catered to local beatniks and bohemians, with Italian operas playing over the loudspeakers and one-act plays performed by local students. Velvet drapes and Pompeian-red plaster covered the walls. At times, there were lines of people waiting outside to get into the place. But building inspectors cited the café for violating codes that limited occupancy, and banned candlelit tables. The substantial list of citations forced Nardone to close it down.

It was then that he began transforming the place into an artist's workshop. He began to adorn the property with rescued stones, architecture retrieved from demolished buildings in Newark, including two angels from the Prudential building's executive boardroom, and plaster castings he made from church statuary.

He would leave his casts outside to get weathered, and the thousands of pieces would sit on the roof, along paths, and beneath a huge weeping willow that a storm had felled (but not killed) in his front yard. He filled just about every crevice with plaster casts of his Renaissance vision. Visitors were welcome to wander through the labyrinth of cherubs, Madonnas, and demonic gargoyles that were piled in four-foot-high walls buttressed up against the house and fences along the property's perimeter.

But the authorities still slapped violations on him.

Complaints from the neighboring landowners about the condition of Nardone's property never seemed to cease. They saw it as an eyesore and a threat to property values. Angelo retaliated with his own lawsuits charging town employees with illegal search and inspection. He insisted that if he were to win a judgment against the town, he would rebuild the place as a real monument to high art and culture.

"Nutley says it's junk, but it's art; it's beauty," Nardone told *The Hometown News.* "They don't appreciate the culture."

In July of 2002, after twenty years of battling the township to preserve his vision for the Franklin Avenue property, Nardone's home burned to the ground in a mysterious fire, allegedly started by two kids playing with matches. At the time, Angelo was living at a veterans home and heard about the fire only after it was over, leaving him no time to rescue any of his artifacts or personal belongings. It took firefighters

four hours to contain the blaze, which destroyed everything.

Though the city of Nutley had brought Nardone to court many times over the years, citing his property as an eyesore, Angelo could see only the beauty in his Renaissance rubble. Today, the property remains empty and devoid of any of the cultural significance that once was, and perhaps could have been again.

Pinky's Secret Hideaway

Pink Austin Bellamy is a private man. So private, in fact, that he wouldn't open his door when Weird NJ came calling at the squatters' paradise in a swampy wood in Woodbridge. The side windows of his little home are made of wood to keep the curious from looking in. The cement foundation around the Hansel-and-Gretel cottage collects stagnant water in a moatlike pool. And the plastic flowers and fencing complete the effect, making this abode a testament to one man's ingenuity and his desire for a tax-free home sweet home.

Bellamy is a mason by trade and has lived in the area for over thirty years. Although other individualists searching for tax-free housing have built boxlike shacks throughout the woods, none are nearly as charming as Pinky's chalet. However, it's best to pay attention to signs like KEEP AWAY, STAY OUT, and BEWARE OF DOGS, and bones nailed to the trees. If you plan to view these squatters' dwellings, do it from afar.

The Palace Depression

One of Vineland's many contributions to the state's weirdness quotient was a landmark built of old car parts and other junk during the Depression years of the early 1930s by a wild-looking man called George Daynor.

The Palace Depression, as the site was called, stood on a mosquito-infested automobile graveyard on Mill Road, just south of Landis Avenue. The eighteen-spired storybook castle was a hodgepodge of unusual building materials. Odd pieces of cement and rocks formed the walls, the chassis of old cars acted as floor beams, and the gables were fashioned from old fenders. Old bedframes were made into swinging doors. To paint the house, Daynor pulverized old red bricks and mixed them with crankcase motor oil. A large kettle formed the dome on top of the house, and discarded wagon wheels formed the bases for cone-shaped towers and revolving doors. The Palace's dining table was a huge cypress log with knee slots cut into it, with smaller stumps for seats.

The castle itself had no real windows, but displayed shards of glass that created a colorful sunrise and sunset mosaic. The property was neatly laid out with ponds and gardens that Daynor would guide tourists around, all for twenty-five cents a head.

Among the darkened corners where Daynor regaled visitors with tales was a crawl-through Jersey Devil's den and the Knockout Room, where a heavy boulder suspended above a chair would help you forget your troubles by giving you a bonk on the head. Reportedly, no one ever took him up on this offer.

Daynor's talent for self-promotion made sure the Palace received attention from the media. He claimed he started out with only $4 in his pocket, having lost half of his fortune in the San Francisco earthquake of 1906 and the other half in the 1929 Wall Street crash. "The Palace Depression stands as a proof," he stated, "that education by thought can lift all the depressed

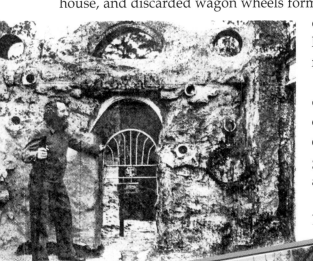

"Turtle Shell Door"
Palace Depression
Vineland, New Jersey, U.S.A.

peoples out of any depression, calamity or catastrophe; if mankind would use it. The proof stands before you my friends. Seeing is believing."

Robert "Believe It or Not" Ripley devoted one of his syndicated cartoons to the Palace, and Daynor appeared on the TV program *You Asked for It.* In 1938, Universal Pictures released *The Fantastic Palace,* a documentary featuring Daynor giving a tour of the property. The Palace Depression became so well known that by the 1940s it was featured on road maps distributed by Esso gas stations and was the subject of comic books, print, newsreels, and a series of postcards.

Eventually, Daynor's efforts to keep his name in the headlines would prove his undoing. During the Weinberger kidnapping case in 1957, he claimed the kidnappers contacted him about hiding their victim in the dungeons of his Palace. After confessing his story was made up for the publicity, he was sentenced to one year in federal prison for giving false information to United States officials.

During that time, the Palace was left to souvenir hunters and vandals, who looted and partially burned the place down. When he was released from jail, Daynor was nearly a hundred years old, and unable to restore the Palace. He died penniless on October 20, 1964, at the Cumberland County Hospital at age one hundred and four and was laid to rest in a pauper's grave in the Oak Hill Cemetery.

For five years, Daynor's architectural wonder gradually returned to its former incarnation as run-of-the-mill junk, before the city of Vineland finally demolished it in 1969. All that remained of its former glory were a few artifacts, pictures, some fifteen-minute films, and the memories of the Palace's five hundred thousand visitors. But that was not the final chapter in this story. Thirty years later, a nonprofit group called the Palace of Depression Restoration Association began raising grants and donations to rebuild the Palace, using mostly donated labor and materials. The city, which owns the property, donated it for this project. Local artists and college students have offered to help, and so has grassroots artist Isaiah Zagar, whose mosaics use bottles, mirror shards, bicycle wheels, and tires to decorate buildings along South Street in Philadelphia. Even the local Home Depot is chipping in for the effort.

We recently toured the all but vacant Palace site to check the progress of the reconstruction effort. The land has become a free-for-all dump for every contractor in Cumberland County, but the gatehouse where Daynor sold admission tickets still stands. Along the path, you can see Daynor's handiwork—broken shards of pottery and bottles wedged into crumbling retaining walls. A foundation has been set in odd-shaped stones, but there's no sign of the planned visitors center, with its look borrowed from the 1983 movie *Eddie and the Cruisers*, which featured a Hollywood version of the Palace.

Amazingly, bits and pieces of the original Palace are still resurfacing from local basements and mantels and are being offered to support the reconstruction. It will be tough to pull this feat off, since no architectural plans of the original structure exist. But whether the group re-creates it faithfully or not, it will be an interesting and weird second coming.

The Rocking Horse House of Kendall Park (and the Battle of the Balls)

Richie and Leila Zorzi of Kendall Park are collectors, but they don't collect normal things like fine art. The treasures displayed through the Zorzis' home came from garage sales and flea markets. Elvis collectibles and souvenir plates from all of the fifty states adorn the walls. One room contains nothing but dolls. And another is devoted entirely to baseball caps. For nearly forty years, the township and residents had no issues with the Zorzis, but that changed when Richie decided to display a new collection on his front lawn.

"I just started acquiring bowling balls," says Richie, a retired bricklayer and

volunteer fireman.

"I placed them around my trees, and up and down the driveway. After a while, people would just leave them at my doorstep. What was I supposed to do?"

Before long, the multicolored spheres were adorning flower beds, edging the front-yard walkways, and dotting his back and side yards, along with bowling pins, trophies, and other bowling alley paraphernalia.

Not everyone liked the change.

"All of my neighbors were fine with my bowling balls," Richie exclaimed, "except one. She started spying on me. Then one day, when I was up on my roof doing some repairs, this guy comes by and asks if he can buy a bowling ball. 'Just take one,' I told him. So he does. The next thing I know, my spying neighbor calls the cops on me and tells them that I'm selling bowling balls! So she takes me to court. I can't prove it, but I think that she sent that guy over to buy a ball so that she could frame me!"

After a bitter dispute with local authorities, and a court case that dragged on for more than two years, Zorzi was forced to remove the balls from his property and pay a fine of $500. So he rented a Dumpster, and with the help of some volunteer firemen friends, disposed of the more than four hundred balls.

Zorzi's litigious neighbor might have scored the first strike, but as any bowler will tell you, the frame is not over until the last pin drops. Not long afterward, Zorzi began to decorate his property once again—this time with children's ride-on rocking horses. Before

long, the comparatively drab ball collection had been replaced by a brightly colored spring-loaded plastic menagerie.

"I've been written up in a lot of newspapers," boasted Richie, proudly displaying a boxful of clippings. "It was a gift to my wife. As a young girl, she used to ride horses on her family's estate, which wasn't far from here."

Zorzi commented that after the battle of the balls, the judge paid a visit to his home to see that Richie was in compliance with his court order.

"When the judge saw that my wife and I were collectors and not just piling my house full of junk, he said that maybe I shouldn't have been fined, but what are you gonna do?" he said. "As long as I didn't sell them, the judge said I could put them wherever I wanted.

"While the judge was here, this guy comes over and asks if he can buy a rocking horse for his niece," Richie added. "I figure that my neighbor is try-ing to set me up again. 'No way!' I told the guy. 'They ain't for sale!' "

The Insulator House of Galloway

"Do you think we'll be able to spot the Insulator House?" I asked Mark M. as we pulled off the road in Atlantic County. We parked in front of what looked to be thousands of glass jars lining the fence posts along Jimmy Leeds Road.

"It looks like some sort of power station," Mark observed. "I think we found it."

Stanley Hammell's collection of vintage glass telegraph wire insulators is the largest in New Jersey, probably the largest on the East Coast. He gathered most of them while walking along old railroad tracks, poking around the fallen telegraph poles. Strolling around Mr. Hammell's property, you can see the intense labor and thought he has put into his "crown jewels." The insulators are mounted on posts that look like telephone poles with crossbeams. The yard looks like a lineman's version of a Christmas wonderland.

So what are insulators, anyway? "In the days of Morse code, the 'dot-dash' ran along the wires," said Mr. Hammell. "They had to insulate the wire from the wood. That was the insulator's main purpose."

Mr. Hammell started his collection fifteen years ago, when he retired. "Some of the insulators are so rare, they can fetch about $20,000. Believe it or not, there are guys who have many more than I do. I just show them more."

Thank you, Stanley. We're glad that you do!—*M.S.*

South Jersey's Statue of Liberty

Most people don't know that in New Jersey you can see not one, but two Statues of Liberty. One stands proudly in New York harbor. The other has been looking out over the former Vineland home of George Arbuckel for seventy years.

Arbuckel, who created the statue in the 1930s, was a plumber and an eccentric. It was said he dabbled in spiritualism and astrology and held seances. He often debated psychology with scholars from the Vineland Training School.

The Great Depression left Arbuckel with a lot of time on his hands to indulge his whims, and he rebuilt the 1883 frame house and five-acre parcel of land he bought in 1919 into a remarkable landmark.

He covered the house with concrete blocks, initialing and dating each section. Unlike his neighbor George Daynor, who assembled the Palace Depression out of junk, Arbuckel adorned his grounds with beautiful things—lion statuary, winding trails, sculpted archways, and of course, a scaled-down Lady Liberty. He also built a greenhouse where he grew prizewinning amaryllis plants.

Like Daynor, Arbuckel was an ambitious self-promoter. When he built a new statue, he would have an unveiling at his property, which he called Gempokus Farms. Messages were inscribed into the cement walkways behind the house that read "Indian Park," and "Chief Rolling Water Black Feet Trail 1490." Nobody knows the origins of the quotes or why they were written.

After Arbuckel's death in 1948, the house, property, and statuary were sold. The family of the current owner, Raymond Sotnychuk, has owned the property since 1950. Thanks to Sotnychuk, the Cumberland County planning board has placed the property on its register of historic buildings. The Sotnychuk family remains loyal to the vision of George Arbuckel. Other

tural museum on the grounds to display Arbuckel's antique farm equipment.

When we visited, we were amazed at the pristine condition of most of the statuary, some of which looked as though it could have been cast seven years ago rather than seventy. And without a doubt, the most impressive work is the thirty-foot-tall version of the Statue of Liberty. We asked Mr. Sotnychuk about a black metal gas grill in the statue's gazebolike interior. "It makes the perfect place for Fourth of July barbecues!" he said.

Although Lady Liberty's torch is no longer electrified, this odd bit of South Jersey eccentricity still shines brightly, like a beacon to proud property owners everywhere.

than restoration, they have made no changes to the building or property.

But time has taken its toll on the water pipes and electrical systems. Most no longer work. At the back of the property are some artifacts that were deliberately destroyed by Arbuckel. The molds he used to cast his concrete creations lie there, smashed so that no more pieces could be cast from them.

Currently, Sotnychuk is thinking of ways to generate revenue to help maintain the property. He's contacted schools that he hopes will give students thesis credits for landscaping the grounds. Another option is setting up an agricul-

Steven Paul Sotnychuk, *whose family now owns George Arbuckel's property*

The Pebble Palace of Joseph Laux

On a recent tour of Camden County with our Camden/Burlington correspondent, Kurt, he remembered a weird roadside attraction from years ago: a group of tiny stone houses built on a lawn on Hurffville Road in Deptford.

"How tiny?" we asked, skeptical that they might be run-of-the-mill lawn ornaments.

"Well," said Kurt, "there's about a dozen of them, and they're maybe two or three feet tall."

Knowing our fondness for all things of small stature in New Jersey, he agreed to guide us to this long forgotten minicity. Just four feet from the road as we pulled off Route 41, we found what we can only describe as the Pebble Palace, a concrete-and-stone utopia of tiny bridges, houses, walls, canals, and other strange structures of diminutive stature.

The property is just as impressive as Vineland's Palace Depression was in its heyday, but on a much, much smaller scale. Like George Daynor's eccentric creation, the Pebble Palace is a free-form arrangement of stones, broken shards of pottery, chunks of multicolored glass, and other material pressed into concrete.

Upon closer inspection, you can see small metal pre–World War II army figures inserted into the turrets of the tiny towers. There are large hunks of raw blue glass strewn about the property, some the size of a human head, which makes the place sparkle. The centerpiece of the creation is a huge birdhouse made of thousands of pebbles in the shape of an urn.

We knocked on the door of the house to see if we could get any more information. The woman who appeared at the door told us that all she knew was that a man had built the tiny fantasyland over forty-five years ago. She called her landlord to help us.

"I don't know the name of the man," he said, "but I've been told that he was inspired by the Coral Castle in Florida." He told us that the sculpture's creator was a real bird fanatic, and showed us the many birdhouses, feeders, and baths that can be still be found throughout the yard.

After some research, we learned that the garden was the creation of a man named Joseph Laux in 1945. He started collecting colored stones, shells, and bits of glass from around the country while traveling with his wife, Eva. The larger rocks lining the driveway were taken from the Skyline Drive in Virginia. Although he never had a name for his creation, he often described it as a fairy garden, which delighted his four adopted children.

People would come by, and Laux would give them guided tours of his garden, often noting where each of the special stones came from. At one time, Laux had a pad and pencil attached to his nearby house, and invited people to leave their comments on the garden. He estimated that he had over a thousand responses written on the pads.

Laux, a carpenter by trade, also filled his home and property with wooden birdhouses—some shaped like work boots, some like churches, which would draw native and migrating birds to his garden. Inside his home, he also had a wooden four-foot tugboat he had carved out of white pine, a reminder of the carpenter's time spent at a Philadelphia shipyard.

The current owner of the property said he would like to restore the Pebble Palace to its original grandeur.

"It used to light up and have water running through it," he told us, but he admits its maintenance is a huge undertaking.

"It needs to be cleaned up. I just mowed the lawn last week, and it's overgrown already," he said. "If they do visit, maybe we could convince them to take a weed from it with them when they go."

Split Rock Road Artist Digs Rocks

Recently, while driving down Split Rock Road in Morris County, we found something extraordinary. On the south side of the road, near the Rockaway/Boonton border, was a beautiful home on a well-manicured piece of property.

Nothing strange about that, right? But a closer look revealed some very odd gravity-defying sculptures. The first was a huge ball of stones, perhaps seven feet tall, which seemed to levitate a few inches over the lawn to the left of the house. With no visible means of support, the ball looked as if it might roll away at any moment. The next form we noticed was a six-foot-tall stone pyramid behind the house. To the right were two more stone structures—an arch and a twisting spiral column about ten feet tall.

The sculptures are the work of artist Vicki Diamond, who as luck would have it was in the backyard when we stopped by. She told us that her first structure was a stone house in the woods at the edge of her land, which she built in 1993. The craftsmanship of the cottage is undeniable.

"I laid every stone myself," she said with pride, "including digging and laying the foundations." Vicki completes one new stone struc-

ture each year, though she is starting to run out of space.

"I'm also running out of stones," she admitted. "I've made all of these pieces with rocks I've dug up on the property, and now it's getting harder to find them. A few neighbors bring by theirs, but they're getting harder to come by. I'm currently working on a manger to house our two llamas, and that's going to require a lot of rocks."

"Llamas?" we asked. "What do you do with llamas?"

"Well, they can pull a cart," Vicki told us.

"A cart full of rocks, perhaps?" we wondered.

Vicki is also an accomplished sculptor of other media, and she showed us some less rigid work that she was preparing for her one-woman show at the Paterson Museum.

"So why the fascination with rocks?" we asked her.

"Well," she said, "when my husband decided to use our barn for storage, instead of the studio he promised me, I decided to build this stone house. I told him, 'Let's see which one will still be standing in two hundred years!'"

Then she added, "I live on Split *Rock* Road, in the township of *Rock*away, and my name is *Diamond*. I just think that it all makes sense."

The logic seemed rock solid to us.

Welcome to the Dollhouse

Dolls really freak some people out.
I'm one of those people. They are such cold-skinned, lifeless little things. The worst have beady little eyes that blink, unsee-ing, when you tip them up and down, back and forth. This is why I've never understood people who collect dolls. Do they really enjoy having all those lifeless little eyes staring at them all of the time? I guess some people do. And some people like to share that experience!

Salem Street in Dover connects the downtown area with Route 10; a lot of commuters use it as a convenient short-cut. A community of small homes neatly lines the street. Although one of these homes looks normal today, this was not always the case. Once it was the Dollhouse of Salem Street.

I first saw this house when I was a kid, riding shotgun with my Mom on the way to Kmart. The entire front porch was covered with the kind of dolls that you win at carnivals, with beady blinking eyes, tacky dresses, and a plastic sheet covering their faces. Somebody had nailed, stapled, or bolted them right onto the siding so that they could silently watch the street with their dead little stares. The dolls were never brought in, so over the years they slowly deteriorated from exposure to extremes of heat, cold, rain, and snow. This just added to the overall effect. Decrepit-looking dolls stuck to the side of a house are a whole lot creepier than new dolls stuck to the side of a house.

I was afraid that if I looked into the eyes of the dolls, I'd see the captured souls of lost UPS drivers and meter-readers softly howling "join usss . . . join usss on the walllll." Then I'd feel a blow to the back of my head, and I'd wake up nailed to the wall, too, dressed in poufy taffeta and left to stare with lifeless eyes at the cars going by on Salem Street as the rain poured down on me. Or maybe I was just afraid of getting yelled at for trespassing.

One day a few years ago, I drove by and noticed that the dolls were gone. The Dollhouse of Salem Street now looks like every other house in the community. I wonder how many commuters passed the Dollhouse, unaware of its existence. Maybe they felt that they were being watched, not knowing that it was by hundreds of little plastic eyes. It's too late for picture proof, but I'm sure somebody else can back me up on this story.–*Joanne Austin*

The Boiardo Estate: Transylvanian Traditional

On a shady lane near the outskirts of Livingston lies the former residence of one of New Jersey's most notorious crime families. But it doesn't take a G-man to locate the Beauford Avenue estate. The entrance is adorned with iron gates, lion's head statuary, and is emblazoned with the family name—Boiardo.

When I was young and living in the area, my mother told me a story about one of her friends, a den mother who took a wrong turn in her station wagon while driving a troop of Cub Scouts on a field trip. Some recently unearthed dinosaur fossils were on display at nearby Livingston's Riker Hill Park, and seeing the impressive gateway at the Boiardo residence, she assumed that she had found the museum. She proceeded up the wooded drive to the hilltop mansion. Upon entering the compound, the hapless platoon was immediately set upon by two well-dressed, tommy gun–toting guards who informed the woman that she had made a navigational error. More than a little shaken, she turned around and retreated back down the long driveway with her scouts in tow and a story to tell.

The story of the Boiardo clan in New Jersey's history starts with Ruggiero "Richie the Boot" Boiardo. Rising to prominence in Newark during the Prohibition era, Richie was well connected to other Jersey underworld kingpins of the day, including Charles "Lucky" Luciano and Abner "Longy" Zwillman. This group established the first Italian-Jewish bootlegging cartel to control Newark's beer trade. After the repeal of Prohibition, Richie the Boot shifted the focus of his operations to the numbers racket.

One of the best descriptions of the Boiardo residence in its heyday appeared in *The Boys from New Jersey* by Robert C. Rudolph. The following is an excerpt from the book.

"The Estate was featured in a double-page spread in *Life* magazine, which described the home, aptly enough, as designed in 'Transylvanian traditional.' For

along the dark drive leading up to the main house was a bizarre collection of statuary: likenesses of the entire Boiardo family, their busts and name-plates arrayed on pilasters surrounding the padrone of the dynasty, a youthful Richie the Boot, outfitted in formal riding wear, sitting astride a prancing white stallion.

A less familial, but grisly feature of the estate was a private crematorium. It was here, underworld rumor had it, that Boiardo disposed of his enemies, burning them on a huge iron grate after they had been murdered.

'Oh he just did it to show everybody what a great guy he is, that he got guts,' one mobster explained.

In his declining years, Boiardo had become something of a recluse, rarely venturing from the cloistered confines of his sprawling baronial mansion, which was located just over the crest of the West

Orange Mountains in Livingston. Guarded by wrought-iron gates and stone pillars topped with bronze swans, the house was located at the head of a winding drive, hidden from the road by a forest of tall trees and shrubbery. The main house was constructed of imported Italian stone, resembling the dark, brooding fortress of a feudal lord . . .

   There, behind the walls of his private sanctuary, the once-robust Boiardo had passed his time puttering in a vegetable spread that, in a final glimmer of his once-characteristic humor, he had marked with the sign GODFATHER'S GARDEN."

After Boiardo passed away at the age of ninety-three, the extensive grounds around the estate were sold off. They are now part of the exclusive Rainbow Ridge development, consisting of pricey, angular-looking modern homes. But the new roads, such as Drummond Terrace and Twilight Court, allow for a closer look at the old Boiardo compound. One can

FRANKIE
BARILE

JENNIANN
BARILE

ROGER
HANOS

LILLIAN
HANOS

clearly see through the back gate to the mansion and the surrounding villas, designed in the Mediterranean style, with red terra-cotta roofs. Also visible is the labyrinth of flowering gardens, bizarre statuary, and gurgling fountains. It's a setting from a bygone era, frozen in time, like an overexposed still from a Coppola movie. It really must be seen to be believed. Just don't tell anyone that you heard about it from me!–*M.M.*

Uncle Sam's House: Anarchy in Piscataway

In the North Stelton section of Piscataway sits a house that was the brainchild of a Russian-born artist, musician, paperhanger, and anarchist named Sam Goldman. Goldman built 143 School Street in 1915 in a utopian commune called Fellowship Farms. Most of the street names in the commune reflected the ideals and heroes of the cooperative—International Avenue, Brotherhood Street, Voltaire Street, Justice Street, and Karl Marx Street (which the capitalist bourgeoisie later renamed Arlington Place). Sam's School Street address takes its name from the cooperative's Modern School, which was conducted along progressive lines by followers of the Spanish martyr-anarchist Francisco Ferrer.

Sam's house was constructed of wood with a plaster façade. The windows were made from shards of glass Sam had lying around the house. Rather than buy square panes, he constructed the frames to fit the glass, making each a one-of-a-kind work of art.

"Sam was a hippie, a free spirit, a bohemian of the times," said Sam's seventy-three-year-old niece. "What Sam wasn't was an architect. The house was built without a level, and you could roll a marble from one end of the house to the other." That rejection of the established order somehow fits a member of a group that, in 1934, formed the Anarchist Federation of America. Sam's niece recalled other memories of her eccentric uncle for us.

"He had the uncanny ability to paint wood grain. He would spend hours painting the knots of the wood and the lines that go around it. They

rented out to students of Rutgers University. Although the flat-roofed building has seen better days, the anarchist reliefs Sam had sculpted still inspire free-spirited thinkers when they ride through the now bourgeois neighborhood. Seeing this house is well worth the ride down School Street. You have nothing to lose, comrades, but your chains.

still remain on the trim inside the house."

But Sam didn't lavish such attention on all his decorating duties. "Sam and his brother were wallpaper hangers, and his brother was a master at it. Sam was sloppy, he had little interest in proletarian pursuits, and only did it to help make ends meet for his family. They would call him a 'schmearer' because of the way he sloppily hung the paper. He and his brother papered some buildings at the University [Rutgers]."

Although the collective's Modern School is now nothing more than weeds and an old foundation, 143 School Street remains. The Uncle Sam House, as the family calls it, is still in the family—it's owned by Sam's son and

Signers of Independence

In this great land of ours, we are privileged to say and think freely whatever we wish. If you have a particular political candidate you want to endorse, you can put a sign on your lawn. If you want to advertise items for sale, you put a sign in your storefront window.

If you think the government is corrupt or someone's out to get you, you have every right to air your grievances. Here now are some free-thinking New Jerseyans who took these rights very seriously.

Shore Signs: Rumson's War of Words

To nostalgia lovers, the thought of an early-twentieth-century ice cream parlor evokes images of a simpler, more genteel time. However, even something as innocent as that ice cream shop can become a focal point of strange activity. At the turn of the last century, in the well-to-do hamlet of Rumson, lived a man named James M. Allgor. He lived along Rumson Road, an elegant street just over the bridge from Sea Bright that was a popular strolling path. Realizing that his property was ideally situated to attract passersby, Allgor had the bright idea to open an ice cream parlor and bowling alley on this spot.

Unfortunately, town officials didn't see Allgor's vision as clearly as he did and refused him permission. Like any true visionary struggling against oppression by the Man, Allgor built signs—big signs, as tall as his house—on what came to be known as spite fences. Allgor hand painted these signs, mostly unclear and poorly spelled condemnations with some socialist campaign messages.

Here are some excerpts from the dark wooden placards, which offer a glimpse inside the mind of their overzealous wordsmith. We have transcribed these tirades with their original spelling intact:

"The do say don't say who embezzled the farmers relief money it don't say who took the church money who do you say? Ask next door."

"Should a man be obliged to respect the court that refuses to respect itself? Some day they will punish judges for contempt of the people. M Devils pray als Judges who pervert justice, is it because they fear to meet a just judge! And be sure your sin will find you out.

NOTICE J M ALLGOR IS LIKEN UNTO THE MAN THAT CAME DOW FROM JERUSALEM TO JERICHO AND FELL AMONGST THIVES AND THEY TOOK ALL THAT HE HAD. THE ONLY DIFFERENGE THERE ALLGOR GAME OVER FROM SEA BRIGHT TO THE FAMOS RUMSON R AND FELL IN THE HANDS OF A BAND OF THIVES AND ROBBERS WHO TO THAT HE HAD EXCEPT HIS PRINGIPAL THIS THEY GAN NOT STEAL OR BU ?WHAT IS WORSE THEN MURDER? THEY DO SAY THE KIDNAPING AND RAIL.ROADING OF J.M.ALLGOR TO THE N.J. STATE INSANE ASYLUM IS WORSE THEN MURDER. THEY DO SAY THE RAIL ROADING OF BRANDT TO STATE PRISON FOR THIRTY YEARS. FOR WHAT?THE LORD KNOWS AND SOME ONE ELSE BUT THEY WONT TELL. STOP READ.AND THINK.WHY?SHOULD NOT ALL CHRISTIAN GHURCHES TEACH THE UNIVERSAL BROTHER.HOOD OF MAN INSTED OF USING THEM F RECRUITING OFFIGES FOR BOY SGOUTS TO GIVE THEM THERE FIRST LESSON IN THE ART OF WAR MURDER. THEY SAY WAR IS HELL WELL THEN WHO IS FURNISHING THE MATERIAL? DO YOU SAY THE GHRIST. IAN GHURGHES?IF SO I SAY KEEP AWAY FROM THEM AND LET THEM GO TO H—WHAT DO YOU SAY?

I also will laugh at your calamity I will mock when your fear cometh."

"It is said the Rumson Road thieves robbers and parasites did succeed in obtaining pardons for there three comrades Mr. Morse Heike and Walch. By petitions to President Taft and that they will not be contented until they have procured homes for them on the famous Rumson Road. Birds of a feather flock mid them selves. Notice no petition on the Rumson Road for poor Brandt who was railroaded to state prison by master for thirty years for a crime that he never committed.
WHO HAS DISGRACED OUR FLAG?"

As you might expect, the line between visionary, crackpot, and criminal blurred in the eyes of many of Allgor's neighbors. The local government saw him as both a crackpot and a criminal. Allgor was imprisoned in 1911, and in 1912 he was sent to the New Jersey State Mental Institution. After his stint there, he was given another six-month sentence in prison for accosting a man named Charles Halsey (who he had previously called out in sign form) on the streets of Rumson.

The daily grind of being a freedom fighter is no easy weight to bear, and eventually James Allgor was, as he put it, silenced. He left Rumson Road and moved onto a houseboat, which he also emblazoned with his unique signage. Beneath a flag he flew on his boat was a sign he had previously displayed on Rumson Road. It told passersby that the flag "still waves over the land of the parasites and the home of their slaves. They drove me to it."

PUT DRACULA
IN CHARGE OF THE BLOOD BANK

OR VOTING PROFESSIONAL POLITICIANS INTO GOVT.
IS THE SAME THING!
IF WE DON'T GET THE PROFESSIONAL POLITICIAN
OUT OF GOVT.
IF WE DON'T GET THE LAWYER OUT OF GOVT.
IF WE DON'T GET THE MILLIONAIRE OUT OF GOVT.
THEN IT'S ALL OVER   AMERICA IS FINISHED
WE HAVE BEEN BLED AND SUCKED, ALMOST DRY.

THE DUMBEST MAN IN AMERICA   COULDN'T
DO WORSE

VOTE INDEPENDENT   NOW IS THAT TIME
WE MUST GET NEW FACES IN GOVT.
WHEN YOU VOTE FOR THE LESSER OF TWO EVILS
REMEMBER YOU'RE STILL VOTING FOR AN EVIL!
REMEMBER YOU ARE STILL VOTING FOR AN EVIL

THE PROFESSIONAL POLITICIAN
HAS BROKEN EVERY ONE OF THE TEN COMMAND-
MENTS. THEY ARE FORCING YOU TO BREAK THEM.
THEY ARE THE EVIL   THE SATANS IN GOVT.
IF YOU VOTE THE POLITICAL HACK INTO GOVT.
OR FOR THOSE HACKS ALREADY IN GOVT. YOU ARE
COMMITTING A SIN.

I PRAY TO GOD
HE PUT A CURSE ON YOU
THE MOMENT YOU PULL THAT LEVER FOR DEVILS
IN OFFICE THAT BAD LUCK BEGINS FOR YOU AND
YOURS
I PRAY TO GOD THAT EVERY SOLDIER WHO
DIED OR SUFFERED A HORRIBLE DEATH FOR FREE-
DOM THAT HE PUT A CURSE ON YOU AND YOURS
BECAUSE YOU DIDN'T DO YOUR JOB WELL
A SIMPLE JOB LIKE VOTING RIGHT.

This Is The Year for the
Independents to Bring
Democracy Back

The Fabulous Fifty Acres of John Val Jean Mahalchik

I first visited Mahalchik's Fifty Acres in 1976, when my friend Bill and I trekked through Burlington County in search of roads less traveled. At that time, the place was filled with old army buses, locomotives, parts of airplanes, and thousands of military surplus artifacts. It was a truly amazing junkyard.

Signs in front of the place declared Mahalchik's distaste for political authority, including a huge billboard portraying Richard Nixon painted on the body of a bloody red rat, labeled NIXON TRAITOR.

Not seeing anyone around, we took a self-guided tour of this very bizarre place. Rows of rusted cars from the '20s through the '40s were lined up next to upside-down stacks of zeppelin carriages, amphibious military vehicles, and a mountain of canteens and metal ammo boxes. All of this stuff surrounded a huge metal tepee in the middle of the compound.

The owner was John Val Jean Mahalchik (1918–1987), a self-proclaimed freedom fighter, freethinker, and sometime political candidate. Originally he operated a crop-dusting company from the property, but after a freak storm destroyed his planes, he went into the military surplus business. These supplies transformed the land into the Fabulous Fifty Acres that became well known throughout Burlington County.

Mahalchik also began painting billboards that he placed along Route 206, denouncing the government. His first sign went up in 1959, when the county wanted to expand Route 206. Then he began protesting the county's refusal to award him a

junkyard license to sell his inventory, and moved on to encouraging the overthrow of the government.

In 1969, he was arrested for not obtaining proper building permits. The county seized his land, and his house fell victim to a suspicious fire. Once out of jail, Mahalchik found a loophole in the building ordinances and constructed a tepee on the property in which to live.

Mahalchik attracted many supporters. Anonymous donors helped settle some of his tax debts out of their own pockets. In 1972, he campaigned for President on the America First ticket, backed by two thousand followers who called themselves Mahalchik's People, ranging from soldiers from a nearby military base to local farmers fed up with the tax burdens of operating farms. But after losing the bid, he stopped making signs and lived the life of a hermit on his fifty acres of junk. Mahalchik died in 1987, and the contents of his property were sold off.

Twenty-five years later, on a trip that took us down Route 206, I realized that we had stumbled upon the land that the Fabulous Fifty Acres had once occupied. It was all gone, stripped and barren. I stopped the car, and we walked through the muddy fields to find some remnants of what was once a truly weird roadside attraction. All that remained were a few footlockers and some old tires.

Wandering the grounds, one could only imagine the explorations that might have been if Mahalchik had become President. The place will always remain in my memory the way it once was, and I feel fortunate to have seen it.–*M.S.*

The Little American Revolution of Irwin Richardt

Tucked away in a section of Bernards Township ironically called Liberty Corner is Irwin Richardt's farm. Richardt, a self-described Jeffersonian constitutionalist, calls his land Sons of Liberty Farm, and in January of 1999 he felt compelled to protect it from the government's laws of eminent domain.

Local officials and city planners were in the process of condemning a seven-foot-wide, four-hundred-foot-long portion of his "sacred, sovereign land" to widen the neighboring Somerville Road to accommodate the traffic spewing forth from a twenty-six-hundred-home condominium complex known as the Hills. More than a decade ago, Richardt lost a similar battle when a portion of his land was confiscated in order to widen Allen Road.

Richardt's twenty-two-acre spread is covered with maple trees that he taps for syrup, his chosen method of making a living. Part of his outrage stems from the fact that when the government first took his land, they destroyed a number of his trees. "For seventy years, my trees have sustained me with life, liberty, and the pursuit of happiness—and food," Richardt says of the trees.

His mind and lifestyle seem to be a throwback to the late 1700s. The colonial clapboard house in which he was born and still resides has no telephone. He rides a bicycle because he refuses to pay for car insurance. Prior to taking to his two-wheeler, Richardt drove a red-white-and-blue bus emblazoned with the words of his hero, Thomas Jefferson. When he was pulled over, rather than producing an insurance card, he showed the cops a Bible and argued that he already had the best coverage available to a motorist. His refusal to buy car insurance led to a jail stint of two months during 1987.

Probably the most attention-grabbing aspect of Richardt's property is the plethora of crudely made signs that he has posted around the perimeter that expound his own personal philosophies. The most notorious of these is a large American flag next to a sign that reads THAT US FLAG REPRESENTS JUST ONE THING, THE US CONSTITUTION. OBEY IT OR BE CITED FOR TREASON. Richardt once protested the construction of a new police building by displaying a sign urging RAZE THE POLICE STATE.

As one might expect, this embodiment of the Founding Fathers' ideal citizen—the independent and upstanding farmer—grew upset when the municipality again decided to nab some of his land. Richardt threatened to protect his property with arms, saying, "If anyone else tries to confiscate my sacred land, I shall have no other choice than to do what my forefathers did at Concord Bridge." (Concord was the site of the first battle of the American Revolution, where a group of militia fired upon British troops.) "Private property is the lifeblood of America."

Despite general support from the local community in Richardt's favor, the courts have chosen to ignore his grievances and proceed with the construction project. It seems that recent history may be repeating itself in Bernards Township. Richardt still stands alone, fighting off bureaucracy and retaining an ideal straight out of American history.

Irwin Richardt Might Just Have the Right Idea!

Irwin is not wacky. In fact, his ideas and his philosophy are absolutely down-to-earth. He not only believes in what most of us believe in, he actually stands up and says it, something you can't say about very many people. And it is this matter-of-fact manner that gets Irwin in trouble with the local town council. Quite a few people side with Irwin's cause. In one election, he received over five hundred write-in votes! Irwin does not believe the state has a right to dictate to a person that they must buy auto insurance. "They have no more right dictating that than they have telling you that you have to buy milk," he is known to say.—*Captain Lanidrac*

The Device Is in the Brain in Totowa

Have you guys ever heard of the house on Union Boulevard in Totowa with the weirdo signs in the window? There used to be these crudely hand-lettered, poster-size signs filling every window in the house with such inscriptions as: THE DEVICE IS IN THE BRAIN and HEAT FROM THE BODY POWERS THE DEVICE. The guy who lived there (I assume he's gone now because the house looks normal now) must have been really something.—*David Burd*

My husband and I spotted it, this apparently normal-looking white house with signs posted in the windows saying THE DEVICE IS IN THE BRAIN, HEAT FROM THE BODY POWERS THE DEVICE, and other alien-inspired ravings. Whenever we thought about that house, we'd get the creeps.—*J. Burchfield*

The Mind Control Manifesto on Wheels

Last autumn I was leaving my county library here in South Jersey when I spotted an old Chevy Nova, which at first seemed to be covered in stickers. I walked toward it and was rewarded with a truly weird delight—it wasn't stickers, but large sheets of cardboard with black stick-on letters. Carefully laid out on each window, seat, and dashboard was a woman's story of being held captive for forty-three years by a "mind control ring," which used psychic powers and chemical warfare to control her.

She claimed that the "pied pipers" are protected by authorities and their motive is money and power. Messages on the car repeatedly urge readers to not get involved if contacted and to protect your children! The woman must be genuinely terrified because, in addition to the storyboard, which must have been awfully time-consuming to create, there was a large metal chain with a padlock wrapped around the driver's side door handles! I read the entire story, which took about ten minutes, and during that time, no one else stopped to look. Not even when I retrieved my camera from my glove compartment and started taking pictures did anyone seem to notice. I was even starting to become disappointed that no one from "the ring" was approaching, as surely the car itself must be a decoy for the hypnotic victimizers! I still frequent the Burlington County Library, but have never seen her again.—*Monica St. Clair*

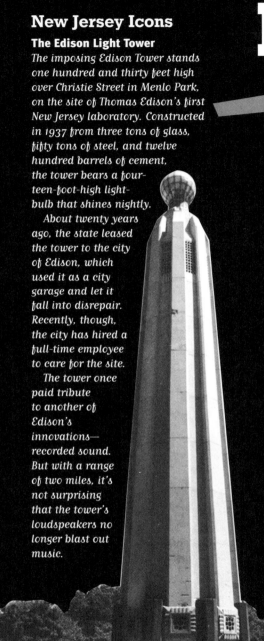

New Jersey Icons

The Edison Light Tower

The imposing Edison Tower stands one hundred and thirty feet high over Christie Street in Menlo Park, on the site of Thomas Edison's first New Jersey laboratory. Constructed in 1937 from three tons of glass, fifty tons of steel, and twelve hundred barrels of cement, the tower bears a fourteen-foot-high lightbulb that shines nightly.

About twenty years ago, the state leased the tower to the city of Edison, which used it as a city garage and let it fall into disrepair. Recently, though, the city has hired a full-time employee to care for the site.

The tower once paid tribute to another of Edison's innovations—recorded sound. But with a range of two miles, it's not surprising that the tower's loudspeakers no longer blast out music.

Roadside Oddities

The saying "It's not the destination, but the journey that[...] been our credo when traveling around the Garden State[...] along the road can sometimes turn your head in disbelief or j[...] fleeting glimpse of tackiness! New Jerseyans are fortunate to [...] such beautiful examples of roadside art, the kitschy and the b[...] shoulder to shoulder along the routes so well traveled in our [...]

As we all know, New Jersey is more than just traffic jams, and mysterious smells along the Raritan River. The Garden St[...] amalgam of many parts, with an identity all its own—architec[...] eccentrically innovative, and downright gutsy in its ability to [...] its two armpits, Philadelphia and New York. How it expresses[...] is often reflected in the things that line our roadways.

Many books have been written about New Jersey's roadsi[...] and highway hangouts, but we've found that another roadside[...] bubbling just beneath the surface—something that nobody ha[...] and documented. We believe these odd and eccentric attractio[...] New Jersey's byways are a part of our fast-moving culture and[...] documentation. We record these thir[...] reflect our lives now, so that future g[...] may see things as they once were.

Many of these sites have gone u[...] for years. Some have become so far[...] we hardly even notice them when w[...] We think that it's time now to slow [...] pull off to the side of the road, and [...] look at some of these roadside odd[...] were seeing them for the first time.

ELEPHANT HOTEL, MARGATE CITY,
AN OLD LANDMARK, ATLANTIC CITY, N. J.
THE ONLY ELEPHANT IN THE WORLD
YOU CAN GO THROUGH AND COME OUT ALIVE

Lucy the Elephant, Margate

Real estate speculator James V. Lafferty built Lucy the Elephant in 1881 to lure property buyers to the tiny shore town of Margate, south of Atlantic City. The sheet-metal-and-timber pachyderm attracted the curious almost immediately. People came from far and wide to check out her observation deck and thirty-six-foot-long trunk.

Unfortunately for Lucy, her appeal as a tourist attraction faded quickly. Within six years, she had been converted into a tavern, and a few years later became a summer cottage for rent. Then came long years when she simply stood and slowly deteriorated.

That all changed in 1966, when the state finally declared Lucy a landmark. Federal authorities soon followed suit and she became a nationally protected site as well. In 1970, she was moved and renovated. Today, Lucy the Elephant houses a museum.

His Master's Voice

Camden once housed the RCA Victor factory, which displayed four stained-glass portraits of its fox terrier mascot, Nipper. After years of vandalism, the fourteen-foot panels have been moved and reassembled. Three have gone to the Smithsonian, Penn State, and Widener University. The fourth is at the Camden County Historical Society Museum, at Park Boulevard and Euclid Avenue in Camden. RCA still employs Nipper, his head cocked to one side, listening to "His Master's Voice" through an old Victrola. But few people today realize the macabre concept of the original painting and slogan. While Nipper listens to his master's recorded voice, he's sitting on his coffin.

The Wantage Totem Pole

Until recently, a grimacing, weathered totem pole stood on Route 23 in Wantage, Sussex County. The pole was constructed in 1920 to advertise a trading post at the site. Shaped from a tree wrapped in chicken wire, the pole featured figures sculpted using Craftex and painted in bright colors.

On Friday the 13th of December, 2002, a police chase that started in New York State ended with the driver of a stolen car ramming into the landmark totem, killing two passengers in the vehicle.

Though the pole was nearly completely destroyed, we've heard rumors that its pieces were collected by the good folks of Space Farms in Beemerville, who hope to reconstruct the totem and display it in their museum.

A Tiny Town and One Big Hoax

In 1938, Orson Welles broadcast a radio adaptation of "The War of the Worlds" that caused a national panic. Six million people heard bogus radio news reports of aliens attacking the nation and went into a mass hysteria. None were as scared as residents of Grovers Mill, New Jersey, a tiny rural town that Welles had chosen at random as the landing place for his Martian invasion. Early in the broadcast, Welles announced that forty townspeople and police officers were lying dead on the outskirts of Grovers Mill.

Local citizens either barricaded themselves in their homes or formed shotgun-wielding posses to fend off the alien invaders. One jumpy mob fired on a local man's water tower, thinking it was a giant robot Martian.

For years, residents of Grovers Mill felt embarrassed by their hysterical reaction to the incident. More recently, though, they have come to embrace it. On the fiftieth anniversary of the broadcast, the town erected a monument in Van Nest Park commemorating the hoax.

As Different as Square and Round?
A Tale of Two Mannas

White Manna means bread from heaven, but it's also the name of a concept diner introduced at the 1939 New York World's Fair. In New Jersey today, two tiny diners claim to be the direct descendants of that original. White Manna at 358 River Street, Hackensack, is a small, square eatery with glass-brick windows, stainless steel frames, and red-painted trim. Twenty low stools surround its front-and-center grill. The other White Mana, spelled with just one n, is at 470 Tonnele Avenue (Routes 1 and 9) in Jersey City. It's round instead of square, with gleaming white enamel outside and thirteen stools around a circular counter. An impressive pattern of hand-laid tiles lends a three-dimensional optical effect to the floor.

The two establishments have more in common than just their name. According to Jeffrey Tennyson's 1993 book "Hamburger Heaven" (Hyperion), they once had the same owner—Louis Bridges. Before Ray Kroc had even thought of McDonald's, Bridges planned to introduce fast food to the masses. He purchased the round, prefabricated diner shown at the World's Fair and introduced a new service concept—the man at the grill could cook your burger, pour your drink, deliver the meal, and ring it up on the register without moving more than three steps. By the mid-1940s, Bridges had opened White Mannas in Jersey City, Hackensack, Springfield, and Elizabeth.

So which came first? It's not really important. Both are originals, and share a unique place in New Jersey's rich diner tradition.

Art for Our Sake

Light Dispelling Darkness

One of the most bizarre roadside attractions in New Jersey is not the work of some eccentric. It is a federally funded work made in 1937 by Waylande Gregory, the head of the New Jersey branch of Roosevelt's WPA Sculpture Project.

"Light Dispelling Darkness" sits in Roosevelt Park, Edison, where it was originally a fountain. The central pillar depicts images of education, industry, and technology in a bold deco relief style and supports a hand-painted globe of the earth. But the work takes a surreal turn with the arches that buttress the central pillar. Each of the six arches features a different horrific sculpture representing greed, materialism, and the Four Horsemen of the Apocalypse—War, Famine, Pestilence, and Death. The fragile terra-cotta used to build the figures has weathered and suffered vandalism over the years, but one can still make out a scythe-wielding, skeletal figure of death riding a lightning bolt, two hideous yet beautifully detailed octopuses writhing in battle with each other, a lustful character covered in festering sores, a Trojan soldier on horseback carrying a shield emblazoned with a skull, and a serpentlike creature with six grotesque human faces.

In its day, with water streaming from its pedestal and cascading over its arches, "Light Dispelling Darkness" must have been quite a sight to behold. Though decades of neglect have left it in a state of disrepair, it is the only remaining outdoor sculpture from the New Jersey branch of the Works Progress Administration. So a project is currently under way to restore "Light Dispelling Darkness" to its original state. Its inspirationally optimistic view of the future, created in the depths of our nation's most desperate depression, makes a powerful statement for the effect that public art can have in our daily lives.

Roadside Robots of Route 54

This proud metal mama rocks her baby in a carriage along Route 54 in Newtonville, near Hammonton, Atlantic County. Beside her, the happy pappy robot bangs on a tom-tom to announce the couple's joy to passing motorists. The little family, along with several members of their extended robot clan, can be seen outside Ralph's Auto Parts yard. They are made entirely of old car parts and are the work of William Clark, who most folks in Newtonville know simply as Robot Man.

Clark, a mechanic by trade, started welding his robot army together back around 1980. What started as a hobby to kill some time soon grew into a lifelong obsession. Some of the spare part creations are as tall as twenty feet; others have headlight eyes that flash.

The Scary Moses

At Clifton's Town Hall on Clifton Avenue, between Van Houten and Colfax avenues, stands a statue that's supposed to be Moses. The cops at the nearby police station have their own nickname for the bizarre statue: Darth Vader Delivering a Pizza. He's also been likened to an evil giant nun. The face and hands, which look like giant claws, are made of stone, held up by wooden beams that are covered with a cloak that is basically just a tarp.

When Weird NJ first reported on Scary Moses, he was living on Franklin Avenue in Ridgewood. But like the original Moses, who wandered the desert for forty years, Scary Moses just can't seem to find a home. The statue used to stand at a church on Route 202 in Suffern, New York. Then it was relocated to Ramapo College and then onto a church ground in Ridgewood. Scary Moses is due to be relocated once again, although the destination is currently unknown. We hope that it doesn't take this Moses as long to find his promised land.

Land of 1000 Milk Jugs (and Then Some)

Not far from Mizpah, on Route 40, stands a unique lawn exhibit of thousands of one-gallon plastic jugs filled with dyed liquid and arranged into a Technicolor work in progress. Lawn artist Josephine Stapleton began the project thirty years ago in an attempt to keep kids off her lawn, and it grew from there. The longest running element in the thirty-year-old project is an enormous red-white-and-blue American flag, but Ms. Stapleton also creates seasonal displays for Easter, Halloween, and Christmas. She has even crafted a life-size self-portrait named Jugabell that hangs beneath the eaves of her front door, wearing a brightly colored housecoat, wig, hat, and glasses.

Visitors have taken to donating their used jugs to support Josephine's art. She hopes one day to build a map of the entire United States out of jugs, with each state represented by a jug from its home state.

Head Scratchers

Some things we see along the road just seem to raise questions like "what the heck was that all about?" These are the sites that we refer to as head scratchers. Sometimes closer examinations reveal the reasons for such sites to be actually quite logical or even mundane. But upon first sight, these roadside oddities will no doubt cause you to raise an eyebrow and ask yourself the big questions.

Whose Ham Came from a What Now?
This puzzling mural can be found on Decker Road on the outskirts of Flemington. Though the owner told us over the phone that he would explain the meaning of it to us in a letter, he never did.

The Route 23 Mystery Poles: Putting High Art on a Pedestal
The first art piece to appear on utility poles along Route 23 showed up in 1994, along the southbound lane near Smoke Rise, Kinnelon. It was a grinning plastic pumpkin that sat atop a thirty-foot utility pole. Other characters followed, including a chicken, a bowling pin, a two-foot-tall beer bottle, a mailbox, a rabbit, a flamingo, and a bright pink pig, all perched on consecutive low-voltage telephone poles.

Kinnelon police captain Elmer Bott has received only one anonymous complaint about the poles, but he stated that it is illegal to affix anything to utility poles. When asked to what lengths his officers had gone to find the culprit, Bott said, "Let's put it this way—we did not stake it out."

The House with the Chair on Top
Located along Route 9 in the town of West Creek, near Tuckerton, is a curious attraction known simply as the House with the Chair on Top. The house, which dates back to 1873, is narrow and tapers up to where the chair stands.

Some have speculated that the chair was a welcoming sign meant to invite passing sailors to enjoy bed and breakfast at the house. But it's not now a bed-and-breakfast, and we do not know if it ever was one. One thing's for sure: This immaculately maintained bayside cottage would be a head turner with or without the chair, but it's the chair that really makes it an attraction!

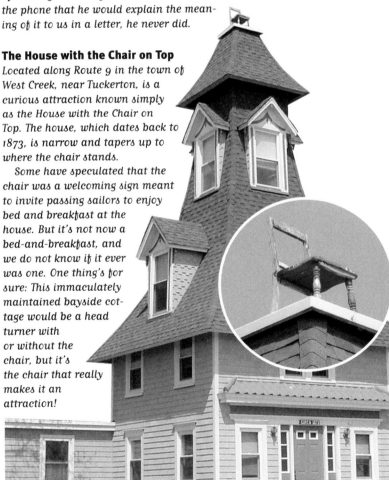

The Boner Bar of Lambertville

Mason's Bar in Lambertille is one place where they really give you the shaft. The quintessential "old man bar" at 51 North Franklin Street comes complete with pine wainscoting, a pool table . . . and a collection of animal penises. Owner Jesse "Jack" Mason prepares each shellacked shaft for mounting, stretching and lacquering the dismembered members of bears, deer, horses, and other animals. He also sells $3 postcards of the collection, each shaft numbered for reference. When you visit, ask what animal number twelve is.

The Egg-O-Mat

Mountain Boulevard in the town of Warren once housed a unique 1950s vending machine. Sadly, the refrigerated Egg-O-Mat, which once offered "Eggs of Distinction," was fried during our first visit in 1998. Then it vanished—poached, we feared, by some hard-boiled souvenir hunter. But not so! The Warren Historical Society had moved it to a safe location to await restoration.

The Cookie Jar House

The old woman who lived in a shoe may have had her imitators, but throughout the United States, only the town of Glendora can claim to have a cookie jar house.

"The house was built in 1947," said John Dobbins, who owned the house when Weird NJ went visiting. "It was built as a speculation house. They were going to make a community of them. Originally, it had a flat roof and a stucco finish. The brickwork was added later, probably because, with a flat roof, it had a lot of leaking problems. I spent a lot of time fixing it up."

The circular three-story steel-framed building has a spiral staircase in the center that leads up to the roof. Touring the semicircular rooms gets disorienting because there are no corners or straight walls at all.

"I do have some problems getting furniture up and down the staircase," said John. "Still, it's very comfortable."

In 1978, Dobbins decorated the house as a jack-o'-lantern for Halloween. He said many people ride by to look at the place. "It's the only attraction in Glendora," he told us.

Eggs are not the only fresh delicacy you can get twenty-four hours a day from New Jersey's roadside vending machines. There are also several Vend-A-Bait dispensers located throughout the state that offer the early morning angler the finest variety of worms and other live baits.

Mary Murray: The Foundered Ferry

A familiar sight to motorists on the New Jersey Turnpike is the beached hulk of an old Staten Island Ferry, the Mary Murray, to the east, near exit 9. After forty years as a Staten Island Ferry, she was purchased by shipyard owner George Searle, whose grandiose plans to use the ship as a restaurant or shopping center have never come to fruition. For some twenty years, the boat has sat on the banks of the Raritan River, rusting away. Searle's daughter told us that her father is now content to just sit on the deck and smoke cigars.

Nautical Jersey

It's surrounded on three sides by water, so it's no wonder that New Jersey has a rich maritime history. Driving around the state, one sees constant reminders of this long nautical tradition. Whether you are close enough to smell the briny deep, or landlocked somewhere high and dry, chances are you're not too far from landmarks that hearken back to our state's proud seafaring heritage.

Absecon's Gas Station Galleon

Many years ago, tall ships sailed the New Jersey coastline alongside such legendary trade routes as Route 22 and Route 35. Few curbside clipper ships remain today, but one galleon-like vessel is moored on Route 30 in Absecon, where she houses an antique shop. She once served as Absecon Beach Camp's rental office and was subsequently converted into a gas station in the 1930s. Let's hope she doesn't suffer the same fate as the ship-shaped building on Route 35 in Old Bridge, which went down in 1993, lost to a suspicious fire. These views of the Absecon Boat House show it as it appears today as an antique shop, as a gas station (not shown), and in its original incarnation as a resort camp.

The Flagship

Eternally sailing eastward into the rising sun, the Flagship takes up a whole block on Route 22 in Union. It was originally commissioned in 1938 as a nightclub, but those luxury cruises are now over, and this once proud vessel is more of a lowly merchant craft—it now harbors the electronics outlet The Wiz. Constructed by a German immigrant named Charles Fitze, it stood for four years until fire destroyed it in 1942. But people weren't ready to have this oddly shaped building disappear from their horizon, and after World War II it was rebuilt and hosted many superstars of the day, including Dean Martin, Jerry Lewis, and Jackie Gleason.

The Flagship eventually closed its doors as a club and at different points in its history housed a dinner theater, a furniture store, and a U-Haul agency. After years in disrepair, the second Flagship building was scheduled for demolition in 1986 when Livingston resident Charles Lubetkin bought it and rebuilt it once again.

These days it is the home of a Wiz appliance store, although not for much longer, as The Wiz plans on vacating the building soon. Hopefully, the Flagship has not seen its last days on the asphalt ocean that is Route 22, and will continue to sail on.

Remembering Menz and the One-Legged Giant

At Menz's Restaurant in Cape May sits a giant statue of Mr. Menz himself. He lost his leg to diabetes, but he would sit outside the restaurant and greet families as they entered. Inside, the restaurant is filled with weird things from ceiling to floor including a jack-a-lope, two-headed calves, and other oddities of taxidermy. Mr. Menz passed away a while ago, and the restaurant is now run by his son, Jay. According to one of our readers, the weird contents of the restaurant are second only to the home cooking you get there—even better than Mom's, they say.

Land of the Giants

Howdy Pahdnas!

Men are thrown off bucking broncos. Calves are lassoed. Steers are wrestled. Are we talking about Texas? Nope—New Jersey. Cowtown is home to the nation's oldest weekly rodeo. Stony Harris began presenting rodeo shows in the Salem County town of Pilesgrove in 1929. The family business continues to this day, as Grant Harris, Stony's grandson, puts a rodeo show on every Saturday night in a four-thousand-seat arena. As you pass Cowtown on Route 40, an enormous statue of a red Jersey cow mooooves you to pull your car over; then the gigantic fiberglass cowboy ropes you into seeing the show.

The Champagne of Propane

This big bottle on Route 9 in Bayville was once an advertising gimmick for the Renault Winery of Egg Harbor City. These megaliter bottles used to be all over the state. Today, only a few survive, including this one, another in Hammonton along the White Horse Pike, and one on Route 30 in Egg Harbor City.

Send in the Clowns!

For fifty years two fun faces leered out from the Palace Amusements building to draw thrill seekers from all along the Asbury Park boardwalk. The nearly identical images, with swooping hairdos, Cheshire-cat grins, and glowing neon, came to be known as Tillie. Tillie's name and ancestry come from the Coney Island amusement park mogul George Cornelius Tilyou. Back in 1897, a face like Tillie's glared out from the glass façade of Coney Island's Steeplechase Park, and appeared on rides, tickets, and advertising until the 1964 closure of the park. Asbury Park's Tillie was painted by a World War II veteran and sign painter, Worth Thomas, who almost certainly intended it to be a sincere form of flattery. There is a strong family resemblance between Tillie and the Steeplechase Park fun face—and George C. Tilyou and his brother, James.

Mr. Bill and His Tipsy Twin

Looking like a pair of homely twins separated at birth, two goofy doofuses stand about fifty miles from one another. One stands twenty-five feet tall on Route 561 south in Winslow and goes by the name Mr. Bill, though he bears a striking resemblance to Mad Magazine's poster boy Alfred E. Neuman, not the clay figure from old "Saturday Night Live" sketches. The big-eared galoot in the floppy hat originally stood in front of a sandwich shop on Route 130, but when the shop went out of business, Ray Giannascoli rescued him and placed him in front of Bill's Drive-in restaurant in Winslow, where he stands today.

Right, New Jersey's largest clown, "Cyclown," stands tall at Display World in Monroe.

Mr. Bill's long lost twin, another dead ringer for Alfred E., stood alongside Route 537 in Jackson near Great Adventure in the Red Cedar Village parking lot until a windstorm toppled him over. He has since been banished to the back of a vacant gravel lot, where he stands lashed to a trailer. Though he might seem a little lost and lonely, he still maintains a brave face and grins that same goofy bumpkin grin.

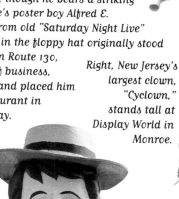

Attack of the Fifteen-Foot Woman
(She's Even Taller in the Heels)

Here's one Jersey girl nobody is going to mess with! Miss Uniroyal stands outside Werbany's Tire World on the Black Horse Pike in Blackwood, as she has for thirty-seven years, her hip thrust provocatively to one side. Man, has she got legs! She looks like she was frozen in time, back in 1966. Owner Ed Werbany recently paid $10,000 for Tire Guy from a competitor's store. Who knows? If the two hit it off, this union just might lead to a whole new generation of Jersey giants!

Jurassic Jersey

New Jersey has a long, storied history with dinosaurs, so it should come as no surprise that there are a number of Jersey-style tributes erected in honor of the reptilian Jerseyans who used to call this place home.

This dinosaur is found at the Gingerbread Castle in Hamburg.

The Route 9 Dinosaur of Bayville

Forever watching over motorists along Route 9 in Bayville, this wire-mesh dinosaur has been a roadside staple since 1932. Bill Farrow purchased the dinosaur from a barn in Howell Township to promote his taxidermist shop in the adjoining building. It is believed that it was once a promotional item from the Sinclair Oil Company, which used dinosaurs as their trademark. The structure has been smashed twice in its history—a truck once sheared off the head, and a bus did heavy damage to the base. It has been rebuilt and reinforced with steel and now has a molded head made out of fiberglass. The original color was white, but over the years it has been known to turn green, purple, and various shades of blue.

Sign Language

Strange Markers and Highways to Hell

Some streets just make you wonder what those who named them were thinking. There is no mountain near the sandy trail that is Mount Misery Road. What personal hell might have inspired Burlington County's Purgatory Road? We don't even want to know what was going down on Double Trouble Road or Life of Agony Road to inspire those charming monikers!

How does that grab you for a road trip?

BANG ZOOM--Straight to the Moon Motel! Route 9 in Howell.

Do you suppose *they send an ambulance or a hearse when a crash is reported from the FATAL ACCIDENT ZONE on Route 15 in Jefferson?*

Roads Less Traveled

Some roads possess an aura that puts people in touch with their most deep-rooted fears. They seem like passageways to the unknown or a window into the subconscious. Many tales of such roads reflect the archetypal imagery of nightmares—ghosts, wild and ferocious animals, and evil, hooded cultists huddled around sacrificial bonfires. Tales of witches and even the devil himself wandering these roads crop up without even a hint of disbelief. Maybe there is really nothing scary to be found on such roads at all. Maybe the road merely serves as a conduit, a pathway to our own innermost demons. If that is indeed the case, then a trip down one of these legendary byways may be a journey of profound self-discovery.

Of course, the people who enjoy traveling such roads may do so purely to scare themselves and their friends out of their wits. Who hasn't at some time, perhaps in their teenage years, piled their friends into an overcrowded car and set off to some allegedly haunted nightspot? Such jaunts usually build to fever pitch before you ever reach your destination, due largely to retelling the legends on the way. Night riders get so jacked up to witness something out of the ordinary that overanticipation alone can cause their eyes to play tricks on them. A stray dog becomes a hellhound, or an innocent jogger transforms into a ghostly running apparition.

Whether these roads are actually epicenters of the hypermystical or merely hot spots for rowdy nocturnal joyriders is a matter for debate. Perhaps they're a little of both. In any case, the abundance of folklore they conjure makes them intriguing. They have proved their potential to strike fear into people's hearts as well as inspire personal reflection and revelry in those who visit them. Whatever the reason, one fact is indisputable: Many roads less traveled throughout New Jersey possess an indefinable yet undeniable power.

Shadowy Past
The Long and Winding Story of Shades of Death Road

Out of all the grim road monikers in New Jersey, none is more foreboding than the infamous Shades of Death Road, which winds alongside Jenny Jump State Forest up to Allamuchy in Warren County. Like many places steeped in local lore, reality and legend have become intertwined over the years, obscuring exactly what can be considered fact. What is known is that for centuries, this road has been a thoroughfare that cuts across one of the more isolated parts of our state. What isn't known is how this street earned its curious name.

One of the earliest folktales explaining the Shades of Death name claims that the area was at one time home to a pack of vicious wildcats. Early settlers referred to what is now Petersburg as both Cat Hollow and Cat Swamp at different times (there is still a road nearby called Cat Swamp Road). Supposedly, Shades of Death earned its name because these vicious wildcats often attacked and killed those who traveled along it.

According to other legends, murder is at the root of the name. One tale says that an unruly band of squatters inhabited the area. Men from this vile gang would often get into fights over women that resulted in death. As the murderous reputation of these bandits grew, the area became known as Shades of Death. As the civilized world encroached, the bandits' control over the meadows diminished to one road that retained the name.

Yet another murder theory says that the road was originally known as The Shades because low-hanging trees formed a canopy over it. Legend says that over time, many murders occurred there, and many stayed unsolved, causing local residents to add the sinister twist to the formerly pleasant name. Anyone who has been around Shades of Death can imagine that murderers would love the darkness and seclusion of the road. In fact, at least three murders did occur there during the 1920s and '30s. A man was murdered with a jack from his car over gold coins; a wife murdered her husband and buried his head on one side of Shades and his torso on the other; and a local resident, Bill Cummins, was shot near his home and buried under a pile of muck. His murder was never solved.

Beware the Fog of Lenape Lane

My friend Rob and I went to Shades of Death at about one thirty this morning. On the way back, we noticed a small road called Lenape Lane. We checked it out and found an abandoned stable. At this time we got really bad chills and decided to leave.

Driving back, the windshield fogged up real bad, and as the fog formed, I saw the shape of a skull appear in it. Rob told me that on his side of the windshield he saw a cross in the fog. We got off Lenape Lane, and the fog disappeared. *–Mike D.*

Still other explanations involve death by natural causes. Shades of Death traverses an area long known as the Great Meadows, which was a vast marshy swampland when it was first settled. Around 1850, malaria-carrying insects were discovered near a cliff face along Shades. The earliest written account of malaria in the area, attributed to a Dr. William I. Roe in 1877, shows malaria's effects upon the community: "The intermittents were very severe and many of the residents expected the usual attacks of chills in the spring while a family moving into the neighborhood from a non-malarial district seldom escaped the ravages of miasma in one form or another."

As the citizens around Shades came to expect deadly outbreaks of this terrible disease every year, the road's name came to reflect their morose attitude. After 1884, when a $100,000 state-sponsored project drained the land, the malaria died down. The name Shades of Death is the last reminder of that darker time.

But there is a lighter side to the Shades story. The unique name on the street signs makes them highly prized by souvenir hunters—so much so that the locals lubricate the signposts to thwart pole-climbing pilferers. On one of our visits, we found an eight-foot-tall pole slathered with dark, gooey grease. At the base of the pole lay two greasy sweat socks, apparently worn as gloves by some would-be thief in a vain attempt to get a better grip.

Shades of Death Road remains a mysterious, foreboding place. Whether its name came from wildcats, wild men, or wild microorganisms, it issues a warning from beyond the grave to those who travel its dark path. Though we may never know for sure how the road actually got its name, it might be a good idea to heed those warnings and say a little prayer when traveling Shades of Death.

The Shades of Death Plague

There was a plague that killed most of the people in town, forcing them to lay dead bodies in the street so some sort of doctor could come pick them up. Some bodies were dumped in Ghost Lake, spreading the plague even more.—*Jennifer B.*

It's Called Ghost Lake for a Reason

My friend and I were sitting in a car at Ghost Lake at about three in the morning. I saw the hay on the ground move, like someone was walking on it. Footprints went all the way around the car for about ten minutes.

There was also an old abandoned cabin right off of Ghost Lake. We were inside it one night. In one of the corners of the house was a hallway with a piano built into the wall. We went upstairs. All of a sudden the piano sounded like someone banged on it. There was a crunching sound like the glass on the floor was being stepped on. This sound came closer down the hallway. Someone shined a light on the area, and there was nothing there. We took off out of there and didn't look back. *—FIVEL*

The Ghostly Lights of Shades

At this one bridge, if you stop in the road, turn off your lights, and honk three times, you will see images of two kids who got killed playing in the road. I tried it, then left. Not three seconds after I started to move, I noticed a light behind me, like the headlight of a motorcycle, but at the height of a big truck. No matter how fast I went, it stayed right with me. As I got to the end of the road and looked in my mirror, it was right on my tail. It disappeared as quickly as it appeared. I looked behind me to see nothing but darkness. I still can't tell you what was behind me, but I will never drive down that road at night again. *—CR1CR*

It Came from the Shades of Death Cornfields

An aunt of mine lives on Shades. One summer, I heard the most unusual sounds I have ever heard coming from the cornfields. They were getting closer and louder. I looked out the window and there it was—a figure in the window. The thing that scared me the most was that I was on the second floor and it was right up by the window. *—FreakVETH*

The Deer Indian Guardian of Shades of Death

The legend was that you had to drive very slow down the road, lest the Indian would get you. The Indian was the guardian of the area. You would see a deer in front of you while traveling Shades, but it was no ordinary deer. It was the Indian in a deerskin. If he charged your car and you did not stop before he reached it, as soon as he passed through your vehicle, you would get into a horrible car accident. *—Alyssa B.*

Sucker Punched by Spooks on Shades of Death

I remember an old barn on Shades of Death Road that my brother told me about. He went there to investigate a rumor that it was haunted. It was really dark there, and his friends walked in, and a few minutes later they came out screaming. One friend was punched by an unseen force. They each thought that he was fooling around, until each one was hit. Some say that some guy hung himself in there. Others say it was murder and that his soul haunts the barn. *—Bob R.*

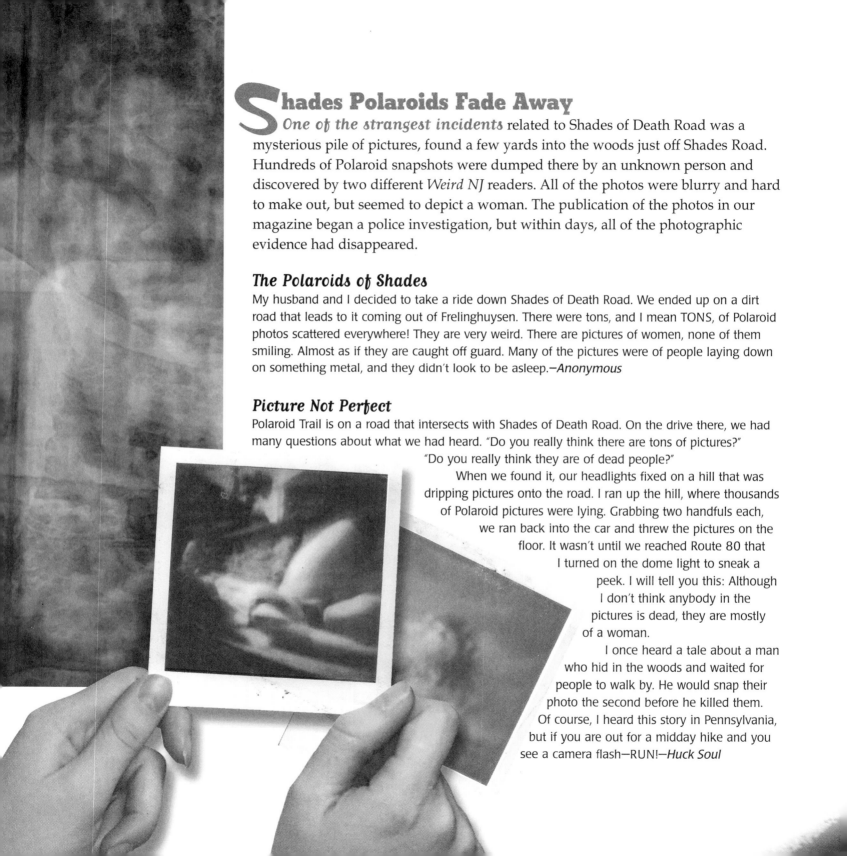

Shades Polaroids Fade Away

One of the strangest incidents related to Shades of Death Road was a mysterious pile of pictures, found a few yards into the woods just off Shades Road. Hundreds of Polaroid snapshots were dumped there by an unknown person and discovered by two different *Weird NJ* readers. All of the photos were blurry and hard to make out, but seemed to depict a woman. The publication of the photos in our magazine began a police investigation, but within days, all of the photographic evidence had disappeared.

The Polaroids of Shades

My husband and I decided to take a ride down Shades of Death Road. We ended up on a dirt road that leads to it coming out of Frelinghuysen. There were tons, and I mean TONS, of Polaroid photos scattered everywhere! They are very weird. There are pictures of women, none of them smiling. Almost as if they are caught off guard. Many of the pictures were of people laying down on something metal, and they didn't look to be asleep.–*Anonymous*

Picture Not Perfect

Polaroid Trail is on a road that intersects with Shades of Death Road. On the drive there, we had many questions about what we had heard. "Do you really think there are tons of pictures?" "Do you really think they are of dead people?"

When we found it, our headlights fixed on a hill that was dripping pictures onto the road. I ran up the hill, where thousands of Polaroid pictures were lying. Grabbing two handfuls each, we ran back into the car and threw the pictures on the floor. It wasn't until we reached Route 80 that I turned on the dome light to sneak a peek. I will tell you this: Although I don't think anybody in the pictures is dead, they are mostly of a woman.

I once heard a tale about a man who hid in the woods and waited for people to walk by. He would snap their photo the second before he killed them. Of course, I heard this story in Pennsylvania, but if you are out for a midday hike and you see a camera flash—RUN!–*Huck Soul*

Indian Curse Road Deptford (Gloucester County)

In March of 1983, the Department of Transportation started construction on a new 7.2 mile stretch of Route 55, just off Route 47 in Deptford, between Mantua and Franklin Township. Two months later, mysterious deaths began to befall the workers involved with the project.

An asphalt roller truck ran over a thirty-four-year-old worker. Another worker fell to his death when he was working on an overpass, swept up by high winds. Soon after, an inspector fell dead on the job from a brain aneurysm. One worker's feet turned black. Then a van carrying five Department of Transportation employees caught fire and blew up.

In a *Star-Ledger* newspaper article, Carl Pierce, the chief and medicine man of the Delaware Indians, explained why. The land was an ancient Indian burial ground, and therefore sacred. "All they had to do was detour around the field," said Pierce, also known as Sachem Wayandaga, "and nothing would have happened."

A DOT employee, who asked not to be identified, told Weird NJ that the site engineer, Karl Kruger, would often speak about the curse. The employee said that Mr. Kruger had recently died of cancer. Yet another victim of the curse?

Indian Curse Road Hits Home

I am local to the area of Indian Curse Road, and the curse has hit pretty close to home for me. My younger brother and two of his best friends were killed on this road. While trying to refill their car from a gas can, they were struck and killed by a drunk driver. There is a memorial posted near exit 50. I drive many nights on that road, and it never fails to amaze me how many cars are parked on the roadside in the middle of the night. I think on any given weekend night there are three or so cars parked there.–*M. A.*

A Healthy Respect for Indian Curse Road

I've lived here in South Jersey almost my entire life. I remember when they were building Route 55, and I remember when (and why) they had to stop building. It's all true—workers were killed, machinery malfunctioned, one man was killed when his own steamroller ran over him! I have never experienced anything really scary there myself, though I use Route 55 often. I attribute this to the fact that I have the deepest respect for the Native American Indians.–*Cris C.*

Gravity Roads

Some of the most common road myths in New Jersey concern "gravity roads," where cars in neutral travel uphill as if forced by unseen hands. We've investigated several of these locations, and the sensation can be very disorienting. The stories told of the various mystery spots have their own twists, but share remarkable similarities—all involve at least one violent death.

To test these roads, you pull your car up to the spot in question, throw it into neutral, and remove your foot from the brake. Ever so slowly your car will begin to travel uphill. Some testers sprinkle flour or baby powder on their car's bumpers to check for signs of ghostly handprints.

The Franklin Lakes Gravity Road legend claims that a young woman was killed at the intersection at the bottom of the off-ramp. When you exit Route 208 at the Ewing Avenue exit in the Franklin Lakes/Wyckoff area of Bergen County, stop at the stop sign. A mysterious force pushes your car backward up the hill. This is supposedly the ghost of the woman warning you of the danger she succumbed to. But she doesn't warn you of another danger.

"The State of New Jersey prohibits any vehicle from backing up on an off-ramp," the police officer said to us as we tested the legend. "We will ticket any vehicle trying out Gravity Road."

Perhaps the incline of the road is merely an optical illusion. The contours of the embankments make it appear the stop sign is at the bottom of the hill, but it could be that the road actually ends on an upward pitch. On the other hand, perhaps a ghost at the intersection pushes your car backward uphill to protect you from harm—but not from a $76 fine and a few points on your license.

Putting Gravity to the Test in Franklin Lakes

One of my buddies was driving. We came to the stop sign at the foot of the hill. He put the car in neutral, and as the legend predicts, the car began to roll backward. After a few seconds, we drove up to the stop sign and did it again. The same thing happened. Finally we decided to go on, and a few seconds later, a cop flashed us to stop.

In the history of moving violations, I don't think any motorist has offered "it was the phenomenon, officer" as an excuse before.–*Mike*

Gravity Not a Law in Holmdel (Monmouth County)

Back when I was a teenager, around 1965, there was a hill just down the side street from the huge Lily Tulip Plant on Highway 35. You would appear to roll right up the hill when stopped at the end by the stop sign. Unfortunately, there was also another hill before the stop sign where you could launch your vehicle off the road. I did it once, and it was very scary. A few years later, several teenagers were killed there attempting to do the same thing. The road was leveled sometime after that.–*Roland M.*

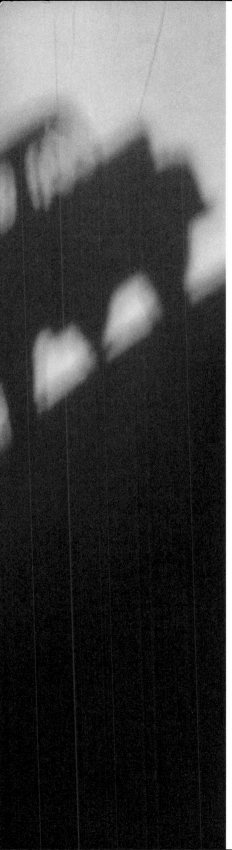

The Hopewell Gravity Road

The Hopewell Gravity Road in Mercer County is located down Route 29 along the Delaware–Raritan Canal between Trenton and Lambertville. Once off Route 29 you'll find Pleasant Valley Road. Travel a mile or so on the thoroughfare and you will notice a small sign on your left indicating where to stop your car. Depending on which way you're headed, your vehicle will either be pulled forward or backward uphill.

One legend of this Gravity Road claims that the adjacent field was once the property of a farmer who came home one evening to find his house on fire, with his family trapped inside. He pleaded with a group of people sitting in a carriage for help, then rushed to save his family. Unfortunately, he and his family perished in the blaze.

The farmer's ghost is the force that moves your car, still asking your help to save his family. The ghost doesn't like vehicles stopping in front of his property, where once people had stopped to gape at his burning home.

Watch for ghost lights farther down the road as the apparition signals passersby with his lantern to help save his family.

More Legends of Hopewell's Gravity Hill

In the early 1900s, a family lived in a farmhouse right off the road. The husband and wife that lived in the house had some problems, and he used to beat her. One day, she fought back and knocked him unconscious. Using the cover of night, she dragged his unconscious body up the hill and across the field that is located directly opposite the house. At the top of the hill across the field she tied his limp body to the lone large tree. From that day on, her ghost has roamed the field and hill and will pull your car up the hill as she did her husband's body so many years ago.–*Jackie L.*

Powerless Against the Phenomenon

I grew up in rural Pennington hearing stories of a Gravity Hill located nearby in Hopewell. The story I remember centered on a husband and wife in an isolated farmhouse. One night, in a fit of rage, the man murdered his wife in their home and attempted to flee via automobile. It is said the murdered woman's spirit tried to pull the car back toward the home, and does the same with everyone who shifts into neutral at the bottom of Gravity Hill.

Another version claims the husband was involved in an extramarital affair. When the wife found out, she hanged herself from a tree close to the home. Now when motorists try the hill, they roll back too far and reach the tree. Then the car loses all power, including electric. Stalling could be explainable, but not the complete loss of current from the battery!–*Edmont*

Heartbeat Roads

While some roads possess an optical
illusion to enhance their mystique, others rely
on sound effects. If you are very, very quiet and listen
closely, you and your date might just hear the distant thump,
thump, thump of one of New Jersey's renowned Heartbeat Roads.

Clifton's Heartbeat Road (Passaic County)

Pavan Road in Clifton was once commonly known as Heartbeat Road.
The faint thump of a constant heartbeat was audible on quiet nights.
Some say it was the ghost of a teenager killed by an automobile while
looking for his girlfriend at this local Saturday night hangout. If you brought
your date to Heartbeat Road, this is the story you would tell.
What you didn't mention was a water pump house alongside the road that
would produce a thump every five seconds. The pump house is still there,
but with the encroachment of housing complexes and industry, its heart beats no more.

A Heart Beats in Montville, Too (Morris County)

In Montville there is a road called Peace Valley Road, also known as Heartbeat Lane. Legend has it that some years ago, in the 1960s, two teens were parked at the boulder, engaged in "lover's lane" activities. Without warning, a crazed woodsman jumped from behind the boulder wielding a large hatchet. The boyfriend jumped from the car and fled the scene in terror, leaving his date to the mercy of the madman. The youth ran all the way home, some five miles. The girl was never found.

Years after the attack, teen couples parked on Peace Valley would claim to hear the heartbeat of the long-dead girl. Teens would park by the huge boulder, turn off their cars, and roll down the windows to listen. In the distance, the sound of thump, thump, thump could be heard. Some teens even claimed to see shadowy figures creeping around the rear of the huge boulder, causing many teen-filled cars to speed down the road in a cloud of dust until they reach the safety of the other end.–*Bernard K.*

The Albino's Revenge on Heartbeat Road

Past Montville there's a road named Heartbeat Road. There is a story about an albino living on the road. All the kids in his school would drive past his house and yell obscenities to him. So to get back at them, he would wait for them to drive down the street, and when they did, he would rip them out of their car and beat them to death on a rock next to the road.–*Chad A.*

Kid with the Red Eyes

Heartbeat Road is a little dirt road off of Pine Brook Road in Lincoln Park. Story has it that a young kid was killed there by the people who live in the woods, who have red eyes. If you go down the road at night, you can still hear the boy's heartbeat, and there is a big rock with bloodstains on it.

It's a good place to take your friends and scare them, especially if you shut off your car's lights. There are no streetlights, and the road is so narrow you cannot turn around. You have to drive down the whole road.–*Jenn R.*

Pump Shed Makes the Heart Grow Louder

The actual name of Heartbeat Lane is Peace Valley Road, but it's so odd—there are no signs at all. It's a normal road, then at the end it turns into a dirt road. It's very dark, and eventually you come to a stone water pump shed.–*Sorcha 666*

The Heartbreaker of Heartbeat Road

The story behind Heartbeat Road is that a young couple was driving when suddenly the car ran out of gas. The guy told his girlfriend to wait in the car with the doors locked until he came back with help. After waiting there for a long while, she fell asleep. When she awoke, her boyfriend's head had been placed on the windshield. Out of fright, she unlocked the door and ran to get help. As she stood there listening and looking around, all she heard were heartbeats. As she got closer to the trees, she noticed that there were human hearts placed on branches of trees. Supposedly there was a killer on the loose, and he would kill his victims, rip out their hearts, and place them on trees.
–*Christie A.*

Split Rock Road

On some roads in New Jersey, the albinos in the woods will not only attack you, but eat you up as well!

Split Rock Road's Albino Cannibals

My sister told me stories about Afro-American albinos living in the woods of the Split Rock area. They are rumored to be cannibals who prey upon any who cruise the back roads of Split Rock. I have since heard similar stories from others.*—CPizar*

Split Rock Road Bandits

Supposedly a band of albino bandits live in the hills around Split Rock Road, which runs from Greenpond Road to the north of Denville (New Hibernia Road). It was a great way to escape traffic when I used to commute to Parsippany from Sussex County. The road is not to be tried without four-wheel drive, because it's not paved and fairly desolate.*—Vic V.*

The Devil's Handprints on Split Rock

Devil's Rock on Split Rock Road is located right after the bridge over the Split Rock Reservoir. There is this big boulder, and it has two handprints in it. They are known to be the devil's because the handprints get deeper and deeper every year as the rock moves closer and closer to the woods off the side of the road.*—PinkPrinces086*

The Split Rock Road Bridge

I recently heard rumors of Split Rock Road in Rockaway. It is a one-lane bridge off a dirt road. Supposedly there have been murders committed in the past by people blocking off the bridge with their cars and trapping the car on the bridge, with nowhere to go.*—Ralph S.*

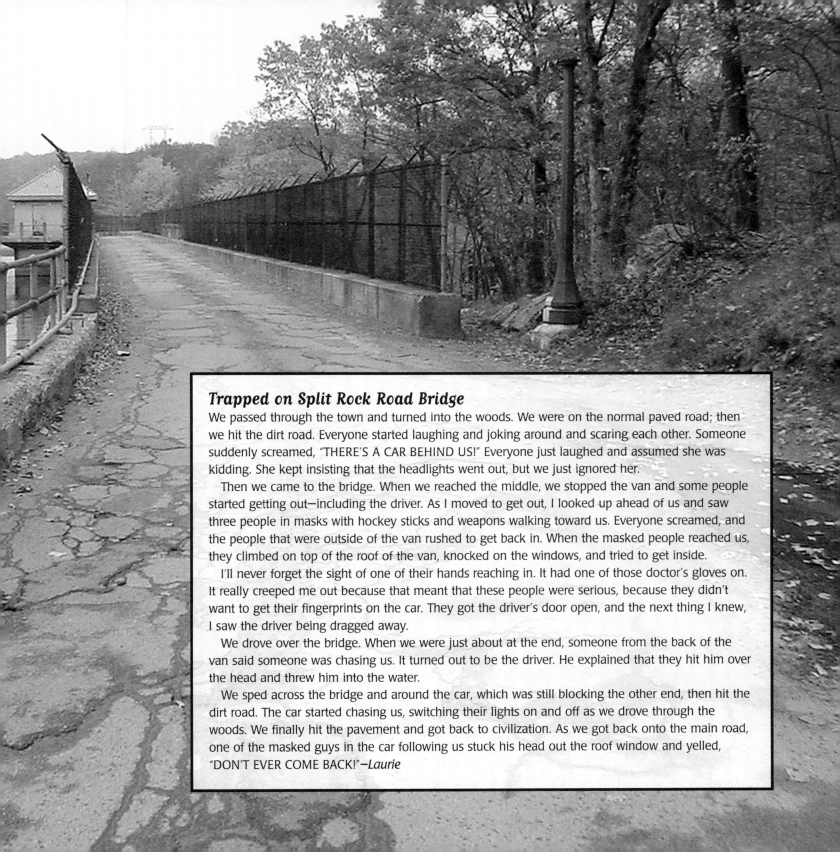

Trapped on Split Rock Road Bridge

We passed through the town and turned into the woods. We were on the normal paved road; then we hit the dirt road. Everyone started laughing and joking around and scaring each other. Someone suddenly screamed, "THERE'S A CAR BEHIND US!" Everyone just laughed and assumed she was kidding. She kept insisting that the headlights went out, but we just ignored her.

Then we came to the bridge. When we reached the middle, we stopped the van and some people started getting out—including the driver. As I moved to get out, I looked up ahead of us and saw three people in masks with hockey sticks and weapons walking toward us. Everyone screamed, and the people that were outside of the van rushed to get back in. When the masked people reached us, they climbed on top of the roof of the van, knocked on the windows, and tried to get inside.

I'll never forget the sight of one of their hands reaching in. It had one of those doctor's gloves on. It really creeped me out because that meant that these people were serious, because they didn't want to get their fingerprints on the car. They got the driver's door open, and the next thing I knew, I saw the driver being dragged away.

We drove over the bridge. When we were just about at the end, someone from the back of the van said someone was chasing us. It turned out to be the driver. He explained that they hit him over the head and threw him into the water.

We sped across the bridge and around the car, which was still blocking the other end, then hit the dirt road. The car started chasing us, switching their lights on and off as we drove through the woods. We finally hit the pavement and got back to civilization. As we got back onto the main road, one of the masked guys in the car following us stuck his head out the roof window and yelled, "DON'T EVER COME BACK!"—*Laurie*

Runyon Road

Bridges found on isolated wooded lanes seem to always fill travelers' hearts with a sense of dread. When such a bridge happens to have the words "KILL YOURSELF" scrawled across its narrow expanse, it might just be enough to set a traveler's imagination running wild.

Exploring Runyon Road and the Kill Yourself Bridge

Runyon Road, located in Old Bridge, is a dirt road. There is a bridge on it that has the words "KILL YOURSELF" spray-painted on it, and legend says that a girl did actually kill herself next to the bridge. A lot of strange people go back there. I personally have been chased in the woods by people with knives and weapons. In the woods off of it are strange things you may come across, such as an Indian burial ground I once found.

I have also seen a bloody wild pit bull that was standing over a deer it had killed. –*Jordan*

The Kill Yourself Bridge

Supposedly a boy killed himself on that bridge, and just before doing the deed, he spray-painted that there for all passers to see. –*Miss. Take*

The Mystery Train of Runyon Road

After the houses of Runyon Road is an old train bridge, which looks like it definitely could NOT support a train. It obviously hasn't been used in a very long time, because trees are growing up through it. After we went under, we heard a LOUD train whistle. It sounded like it was above us. We looked up, but there was nothing there. –*Amanda, South Amboy*

13 Bumps Road

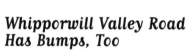

This legendary road is located in the North Plainfield/Watchung area of Union County. Also known as Johnston Drive, 13 Bumps Road is rumored to be the burial ground of thirteen witches, who were either hung or burned or both, sometime before the townsfolk started keeping records of such incidents.

"One thing's for certain," one of the locals assured us, "they have paved over that road to level it out, but the bumps keep coming back. Also, I counted thirteen bumps going down the road, and coming back I counted fourteen bumps. I've done this several times with the same result."

In the right hands, even an uneven road surface can become the stuff of legend.

13 Bumps Road

One week after the paving of the road, thirteen large bumps in the middle of the road appeared. In 1993, the road was finally dug up along with the bumps, leveled off, and repaved. Two days later, the bumps pushed their way up again—all thirteen of them.–*Jason R.*

13 Bumps for 13 Sisters

13 Bumps is said to be thirteen sisters who, in the mid-1700s, killed many of the children in the now abandoned town of Feltville, which is part of the nearby Watchung Reservation. The sisters were put on trial and burned. Their bodies were buried on a dirt road, which is now Johnston Drive, so that whenever the local townspeople would drive over the bodies, they would be reminded of those they had lost.

Legend has it that if you drive over the bumps and count them, then say, "thirteen witches" and turn around, you can see the witches following behind your car. So far I have tried this many times to no avail, but the thirteen bumps are definitely there.–*Kyle*

The Reason for the 13 Bumps

As a person employed in the area of 13 Bumps Road, I have heard many different stories about the bumps. I heard of a witches' burial ground, cult activities, and other strange stuff. But the truth, which I was told by an old-timer, is much more mundane.

The road in question has some steep inclines. The old-timer told me the bumps were built in the days of the horse and carriage. These bumps prevented the carriages from rolling down the declines when the coachmen stopped to make a delivery.–*BG*

Whipporwill Valley Road Has Bumps, Too

Back in the 1800s, there were seven farmers who accused fifteen women of being witches. They had a town trial and decided to burn these supposed witches at the stake. Before the witches were burned, they put hexes on all of the farmers who had accused them, and ten months later they all died of a strange disease.

The farmers were buried ten feet away from the witches, who were buried outside of the cemetery. Supposedly when you drive down Whipporwill Valley Road today (which is still a dirt road), you will feel fifteen bumps under your wheels, and on the way back you will feel seven bumps. We all know what or who those bumps are supposed to be.–*Moonbaby*

Cry Baby Bridge and the Baby Tree

Sometimes on a dark night ride, travelers can get a little turned around and disoriented. Street names get mixed up, and their legends and the sites associated with them get confused. Such seems to be the case with the lore of Igoe and Colliers roads, which border the grounds of the former Marlboro Psychiatric Hospital in Marlboro, Monmouth County. Both roads have stories of trees with babylike growths on them, and a bridge where the wailing of babies can be heard—sometimes reputed to be the babies of nuns, drowned by the priest who fathered them.

To further cloud the issue, the Igoe/Colliers legends seem to overlap with the tales of Whipporwill Valley and Cooper roads, which are located several miles away in Middletown.

Igoe Road's Baby Tree

Down Igoe Road we came to the Baby Tree. The tree has this abnormal growth on the side, in which you can see two babies within a womb formed from it. The story my friend told was of a nun that had refused to throw her baby in the river. The priest ordered that she be killed, accusing her of witchery. So they all hunted her down, and she hid in the opening of a small tree. She remained there until she eventually died, and the tree grew around her. My friend also said that if you bring a piece of the bark from the tree home and sleep with it under your pillow, you will dream about what happened.—*Pawn*

The tree is said to be warm to the touch.—*Greg F.*

The Baby Tree Was on Colliers Lane, Not Igoe Road

When you turn into the wood on Colliers Lane in Marlboro, you will pass a statue of the Virgin Mary. Drive past the statue, and it appears to turn its head to follow you. A minute or so past the statue is the former location of the Baby Tree. It is said that [a] nun hanged herself here after discovering she was pregnant. Growing outside of the tree was a form not unlike that of a newborn baby.—*Michael K.*

Tree Takes on Baby's Shape

There was a story about two sisters that went to school there in the woods of Marlboro. One of the sisters was pregnant, and the other helped her to abort the baby. They placed the body in a tree hole, and as the tree grew around the fetus, it seemed to take the form of a baby. If you do go to see it, it does seem to look like a baby.—*Michele, Keansburg*

Nuns in the Baby Tree Woods

Two carloads of my buddies decided to take a trip to see the Baby Tree. As we drove past St. Dorothy's School, we came to a fork in the road. At the fork was a stone statue of the Virgin Mary. About a thousand feet ahead, our lights shined on this enormous tree. On the tree was the face of a baby. We got spooked and decided to speed it up a bit. Even spookier, we came to a halt right past the tree and watched about a dozen nuns walk across the road into the woods. This was freaky because it was about three in the morning!—*Jason C.*

Trees with Human Shapes on Whipporwill Valley Road, Too

One legend I remember from my high school days is that of Whipporwill Valley Road in Middletown. It's a dirt road that descends into a valley. If you continue on, there is a tree on the right that appears to have a human shape trying to escape from it.–*Darin R.*

Whipporwill Valley Road and the Baby's Cries

I've lived down the street from Whipporwill Valley Road for seventeen years and have heard numerous stories about the road. The weirdest thing I've heard about the road is that if you travel along it at night and stop or shut your car off, you'll hear what sounds like a baby crying somewhere in the distance, and your car will not start up again.

–*Sunday*

Cooper Road and the Cry Baby Bridge

My friends and I look for weird places every chance we get. On Friday the 13th, we decided to take a ride on the infamous Cooper Road in Middletown. Legend has it that a baby drowned in the water under the bridge that is now known as Cry Baby Bridge, and at one a.m. you can hear the baby cry. It also says that if you stop on the bridge and turn your car off, it won't start up again. So at twelve forty-five a.m. we decided we'd stop on the bridge and see if the legend held true.

Two of my friends got out of the pickup truck while I stayed inside, my back toward the right side of the bridge and my window tightly rolled up. Unexpectedly, I felt a cool breeze on my neck. The driver's side window was open, with my friend standing outside of it. I told him to look behind me; when he did so, his mouth dropped and we all heard what sounded like a four-hundred-pound man running through a foot of water. To this day, my friend still swears he saw a man's shadow behind me.–*Kelli and Lisa, Matawan*

The Moaning of Talamini Road

There's a road in Somerset County that has something to say. Well, not really so much something to say, but rather something to moan about. Weird NJ explorers reported an odd phenomenon on Talamini Road in Bridgewater. As you pass the curve on Talamini Road, a moaning sound can be heard—but only from the driver's side of the car, only while traveling in one direction, and only at a certain speed.

We decided to challenge this aural apparition and followed the directions. You must be heading west on the road, you must be traveling thirty-five miles an hour, and just beyond the SLOW, CHILDREN AT PLAY sign the moan will be heard, on the driver's side only.

After attempting the prescribed procedure several times, we determined that a moaning sound can indeed be heard. We describe it more as the faint horn sound of a far-off tractor-trailer truck, but nonetheless, the sound is clearly audible. When traveling at any speed other than thirty-five miles per hour, the phenomenon does not occur.

From the locals whom we've spoken to, the story is that one night a driver, either in a car or truck, tried to take the curve at fifty miles an hour. Some say this reckless act killed a young pedestrian who was crossing the street. Letters we've received state that the moaning is the voice of the driver telling you to slow down. Others say it is the sound of the truck's horn warning of the curve ahead.

After searching through records concerning fatal accidents along the two-mile stretch, we came up with no incidents ever being reported. We looked for a pump house or another structure that might cause the sound, but found no evidence of machinery at work. Checking the pavement for ripples or bumps proved fruitless. The sound is truly a mystery.

Of course, anyone wanting to try this phenomenon should bear in mind that the actual speed limit on the road is twenty-five miles per hour and not thirty-five miles per hour, so testing the legend would require breaking the law. Also, speeding on any road with SLOW, CHILDREN signs may result in tickets for other moving violations. Sometimes we here at *Weird NJ* are forced to break the law in the name of investigative research so that you won't have to.

Talamini Road Says "Slow Down"

The sound is quite monotone and a bit gurgled, but it resembles a man's voice yelling, "Slow down!" Of course, as with most weird things, the driving must be done at night, specifically, past midnight. Furthermore, you have to be doing at least fifty miles per hour and have all windows rolled down, music and air conditioning off. It only seems to occur when traveling in one direction, specifically away from Highway 202-206, heading for the intersection of Country Club Road.
—*Letter via e-mail*

Pig Lady Road
Hillsborough, Somerset County

In Somerset County's Hillsborough area, local legend tells of a grotesquely deformed woman in the woods that border the estate of the late tobacco heiress Doris Duke. The unfortunate woman, known locally as the Pig Lady, is said to attack those who disturb her shadowy lane late at night.

Her origins are a mystery. To some she was a maid of the Duke family, abandoned to a fire at the mansion and disfigured in a fall from the second story. Another tale describes her as a reclusive pig-faced farmer who killed some teenagers who taunted her and buried them in her garden. In another story, she was born so grotesque that her father chopped off a pig's head and put it on her. Now she tries to steal your head if you go down her road.

The Pig Lady's Pig Head

You are supposed to go down this road off of Roycefield Road in Hillsborough that is roped off and honk your horn at night, and her glowing head appears.–*John R.*

Pig Lady roams the area and can be summoned by driving down the road, turning the car off, flashing the lights three times, screaming, "Pig Lady!" and looking in your rearview mirror.
–*Erik W.*

Cries of the Pig Lady

If you drive down Pig Lady Road at midnight, she will jump out in front of your car making loud weeping noises. She weeps in shame of her disfigured face and only comes out at night.

Along Pig Lady Road there are also stone walls. If you walk up to one of these walls and throw a penny backward into a well, you could see her reflection in the water standing behind your back.–*Andrea R.*

The Mysterious Pig Lady Attacks!

Legend has it that in order for her to come out, you must annoy her by flashing your lights, screaming, "Pig Lady," and beeping the horn. Then you must leave someone from the group on the street and drive off without looking back. Once you get to the end of the road, you turn around and go back and see what your friend has witnessed. The whole drive from leaving your friend and coming back takes ten minutes.

We all admitted to being scared, except for my friend Jenn. She was calling us stupid for being scared and taunted the Pig Lady when she got out of the car. We did the routine and sped off. We arrived back and laughing at how scared we all were, except there was no Jenn. We thought she was playing a joke, so we got out of the car. My friend Shannon heard crying from a nearby bush. My friend John carried Jenn out, and we got into the car in silence. After leaving the deserted road, we stopped to get gas. Jenn was still crying, and I turned to comfort her. That's when I noticed the scratches on her face, arms, and legs.

We dropped her off, and she never spoke to us again. She moved one year later.–*The Pig Hunter*

The Pig Woman and the Hall-Mills Murder

Coincidentally, a historical figure called the Pig Woman featured prominently in a local murder story. In 1922, the dead bodies of a local preacher and a married choir singer were found beneath a crab apple tree on a lover's lane in Franklin Township. Reverend Edward Wheeler Hall, forty-one, and Mrs. Eleanor Rinehardt Mills, thirty-four, had both been shot in the head, then carefully laid out side by side, with the minister's dead hand gently set beneath the choir singer's shoulder and neck. Love notes from Mrs. Mills to the married preacher were strewn around the site.

The murder trial that followed made national headlines, and the only apparent witness to the crime was a pig farmer, Jane Gibson, who lived at the end of De Russey's Lane, near where the bodies were found. She told investigators that she had been out that night, patrolling the area for thieves on her mule Jenny. Her testimony was the cornerstone of the prosecution's attempts to convict the preacher's widow and her relatives of the murder.

The press dubbed her the Pig Woman, and her notoriety increased as the trial went on. She was dying of cancer at the time and gave her testimony from a hospital bed that was brought to the courthouse each day by ambulance. But her real fame came from the outcry against her testimony. The Pig Woman's neighbors swore on the stand that she was the biggest liar they had ever met. Her own seventy-six-year-old mother would attend the trial every day, sit in the first row, directly in front of her daughter, and mutter the words "She's a liar."

Certainly, four years after the murder, the Pig Woman's recollections of the crime were much more detailed than they had been at the time of the original investigation— and more like the scenarios put forth by the tabloid newspapers and the prosecution.

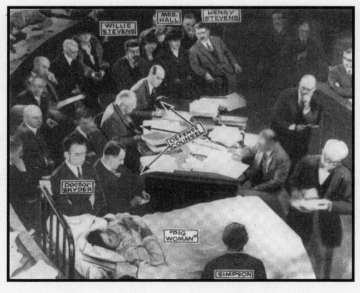

Mrs. Hall, her brothers, and their cousin were all ultimately found not guilty of murder, due largely to the shaky testimony on which the prosecution had built its case. The Pig Woman died shortly thereafter, and the Hall-Mills murder case remains unsolved.

Could the historical figure of the Pig Woman be the inspiration for the mysterious apparition known as the Pig Lady, or is the swine reference and proximity of the two tales merely a coincidence? You be the judge.

Clinton Road—A Dark Ride
West Milford (Passaic County)

One road has spawned more rumors and tall tales by far than any other thoroughfare in the state—Clinton Road in West Milford. Clinton Road seems to strike terror into the hearts of those who travel it. This rugged ten-mile stretch of deserted road right off Route 23 in West Milford is so rich in lore that it has attracted late-night visitors for generations. Where else can you find Satan worshipers behind every tree, sacrificed goats and chickens littering the woods like leftover barbecue, and black trucks chasing innocent teenagers over dark, pothole-ridden roads?

Rumors of bad vibes have been floating in the area since it was first settled. In 1905, J. Percy Crayon wrote about the woods just beyond the Clinton Furnace: "It was never advisable to pass through the 'five mile woods' after dark, for . . . tradition tells us they were infested with bands of robbers, and counterfeiters, to say nothing of the witches that held their nightly dances and carousals at Green Island, and the ghosts that then made their appearance in such frightful forms, that it was more terrifying to the peaceful inhabitants than wild animals or even the Indians, that often passed."

The stories that sightseeing sojourners have brought back with them of their adventures are sometimes harrowing, often terrifying, and almost always intriguing. Many of these tales of midnight joyrides may seem unbelievable, while others leave one wondering just where truth ends and an overactive imagination begins.

Cross Castle: The Unholy Edifice

Castles seem to have always inspired the imagination. The Cross Castle is no exception. Built by Richard Cross in 1905, it looked like something out of a fairy tale. Its walls were three stories high. A fire destroyed the wooden part of the structure, leaving the walls intact as a place where hikers, teenagers, and the occasional Satan worshipers could congregate.

In its abandoned state, the ruins of Cross Castle would become the stuff of legend. For some it may have just been a place to party; for others it was a place of pure evil. In 1988, the Newark Watershed Commission deemed the remaining structure unsound and knocked down the walls. You can see remnants of the concrete today. But the castle on Clinton Road will live on in local lore and weird New Jersey mythology.

Never Get Out of Your Car on Clinton Road!

Cross Castle, which used to be off Clinton Road, had dungeons where many bodies were found. Satan worshiping was active around Cross Castle, and the K.K.K. was also rumored to be active in the area. Never get out of your car, especially at night. It is definitely weird.–*U101*

The K.K.K. and Cross Castle

Two friends, brothers who I will call John and Bill, regularly took excursions through areas of West Milford. They were driving down Clinton Road. Both noticed a bonfire near Cross Castle. As they drew closer, they saw a group of people dressed in robes around a bonfire. They could make out the leader, who was dressed in typical K.K.K. regalia. One of the members of this meeting spotted them and called out to stay where they were. Of course, John and Bill took off to their car and left. Their hooded friends got into their vehicles and began chasing them! John and Bill said they were wielding shotguns.–*Sly C.*

The Writings on the Wall at Cross Castle

I had a friend who lived near Clinton Road. He used to take me on May Day and Halloween's Eve to spy on wiccans practicing in the areas near his house. It was a nice afternoon in 1977. We decided to get our packs, a tent, and a rifle to spend the night up in the woods. I took a journal along with me. When we came upon the castle, we were amazed, as always, at how it stood out in the woods. We entered it and were shocked to learn that someone had put up two huge boards with words spelled out in red paint. The nature of the writing intrigued me, so I copied down what the walls proclaimed, and my friend snapped a picture.

The journal stayed in a box until six months ago, when, after my wife's death, I was going through everything and read it. I went to a local bookstore to match my journal with the *Lex Satanicus.* What was once scribbled down in my youth was now revealed as one of the writings of Anton LeVay of The Church of Satan!

I concluded that the tales about Clinton Road were seriously understated! The satanists who practiced there were not a joke, but a local grotto of people using dark forces to bring forth their evil reign. Now when I go to Clinton Road, I look at everything in a different light.–*Scot*

Spirit Souvenirs from the Inner Circle

I have actually taken three trips to the castle. The first time, we found the castle by accident. We wanted to see if the rumors were true. I will tell anyone: NEVER step over the boundary of the castle. One of my friends did so. She became stiff and ran out of there. She said she saw something in her head—a little boy being slaughtered. We decided to get the hell out of there.

We realized that my other friend had dropped his wallet on the trail. We headed back there around eleven p.m. I was nervous about going back, so the other people did without me. My friend once again started gagging. We drove to our local diner, and I noticed a bruise across my friend's neck.—*Teddi*

Clinton Road Makes Me Sick—Literally

About a month ago, my sister, her husband, my boyfriend, and myself decided to take a ride down Clinton Road. We started from Route 23, and it was around twelve thirty a.m. I can't exactly explain the feeling I started getting. I don't know if my imagination was going wild, but my sister, my boyfriend, and me started telling my brother-in-law to turn around. I felt so scared and sick to my stomach that I couldn't even breathe. It was an oppressive feeling like just pure evil, and I definitely believe that something would have happened if we had just kept going.—*Anonymous*

Partying at Cross Castle

We would tell people the Jackson Whites would cut a tree to block the road. Then, when you would turn around, you'd find that they had cut another one down. That's when they would get you.—*Victor*

Chants at Clinton Castle

We parked the cars, got out, lit a fire, and drank some beer. After a half hour, we began to hear chanting and chains rattling. One of the girls started to go into a seizure. Three of us tried to move her, to no avail. It was like she was nailed to the rock. Then the chanting stopped. The girl came around. We all looked at each other like "What the hell is going on here?"—*G. J. R.*

Satanic Scripture Puzzles Wrecking Crew

A demolition crew came in and destroyed the castle, and all that remained was the basement. On the walls were old satanic scripture. This baffled the demolition crew because there did not appear to be any entrance to this area of the castle.—*Nick B.*

Unearthly Animals

The environs surrounding Clinton Road have always been home for a variety of wildlife, some species wilder than others. Black bears and poisonous snakes have always been present in these West Milford woods, and more recently, coyotes have become a feature of the landscape. The threat that these critters pose pales in comparison to the fearful animal apparitions that some of our readers have told us they've encountered on Clinton Road.

Beware the Grayish Whitish Wolf with Red-and-Yellowish Eyes

I never thought that my first trip to Clinton Road would be horrifying. As we were turning, in the bushes appeared to be a grayish whitish wolf with red-and-yellowish eyes. Later on, NO JOKE, my friend told me about his first trip, where he also saw a grayish whitish wolf with red-and-yellowish eyes running in the bushes.—*Amy, Pequannock*

The Floating Dog

One legend states that Cross Castle rebuilds itself every October 30th, and the K.K.K. sacrifices a goat. I get scared every time I go down the road that leads to that area, because the one time I went down there, a strange figure chased our truck out of Clinton. When I got a good look at it, I screamed and told my friend to drive faster. It was a dog of some sort, but it was floating, not running.—*Kelly B.*

Is There Anything NOT in the Woods of Clinton Road?

One night my sister and her friend were driving down Clinton Road when my sister's friend says, "What IS that?" My sister looks, and there was a MONKEY. They were both freaked out. Monkeys aren't common to West Milford.—*Ryan O.*

The Hellhound of Clinton Road

After once through this ten-mile road, nothing had happened. So we went back and checked out a dirt side road. Nothing was around except for dense woods. It felt very eerie, and the TRESPASSERS WILL BE SHOT ON SIGHT sign did not ease my mind. That's when I noticed something walking toward our car. All eight of us saw the same thing—an animal of some sort. We went sixty down this off road with this "animal" on our back. Finally we got back on Clinton Road and got pulled over by a cop, and the animal disappeared! People say it's a hellhound or the Jersey Devil. All I know is that it was not human.—*Jessica*

The Ghosts of Clinton Road

Probably the most common ghost story that we hear about Clinton Road is that of a dead young boy who hangs out under a bridge and returns coins to you after you throw them in the water. As far as we know, this tale is unique to Clinton Road, but it is difficult to say when or how this story began.

Although he is the most-talked-about apparition to haunt Clinton Road, he is by no means the sole spirit to spook this street.

Small Change

If you ever decide to travel down Clinton Road at midnight, stop at the bridge by Dead Man's Curve. As the story goes, if you sit on that bridge and throw pennies into the river, the ghost of a young boy will throw them back to you.—*Anonymous*

Years before any of us heard about the road, a boy was challenged by his friends to stand on the bridge as they drove to Route 23 and back. Unfortunately, by the time the friends returned from driving to the highway, they found their friend dead.—*Anonymous*

Another rumor of Clinton Road is that if you throw a penny into the lake, the next morning the penny will be on the road. Supposedly there was a kid that drowned there trying to get a ball or something, and the kid is supposed to appear at night and pick up the penny and put it on the ground.—*Gregory MC*

My friends and I decided to find out for ourselves what is true and what is not. We went to the bridge and threw a quarter off. Not but a minute later, you hear the bloop, as if you dropped the quarter in again. The water filled with ripples, and a child's reflection appeared. I flew back to the car. That scared all of us.—*Dina, West Milford*

Ghost Boy Pushes You into the Lake

The story I heard was that a little boy was hit by a car and killed on the bridge when he went to pick up a quarter he saw on the ground. The legend is that if you get out of your car and stand on the bridge, you will see a quarter drop, and if you bend down to pick it up, the little boy will push you into the lake to save you from being hit by the car.—*Anonymous*

The Clinton Ghost Kid Doesn't Want Your Quarters

I threw a quarter off the edge, and we drove away. On the way home at eleven thirty, we passed over the bridge and stopped because Mike wanted to point out the kid's name on the side of the bridge. Just when he said the kid's name, a quarter or something metal was thrown hard against the window of the car.—*Anonymous*

Ghostly Camaros

This girl was racing down Clinton Road toward Route 23 in her blue 1988 Chevy Camaro. She slammed right into the cement divider on the sharpest turn on Clinton Road and was killed instantly. If you tell someone else the story of the accident while driving down Clinton Road, you will see a blue 1988 Chevy Camaro drive by. When my friend Vince told me this story, we saw headlights in the distance, and when the car passed, we made it out to be the Camaro.—*Mike*

Ghost Rangers Patrol the Forest

Hanging out at the old castle was great. Much further up the road on the right there are trails that go up the mountain to a lake called Terrace Pond. The pond was crystal clear and great for swimming. We were camping one night around one a.m., and two park rangers noticed our fire and walked over to us. They were concerned about the fire, drinking, etc. We asked if our vehicles would be okay where they were, and asked if they would be ticketed. They said they were fine and no ticketing would be carried out.

In the morning, we ventured down the mountainside and approached our cars, and they had two summonses per car. West Milford police and Newark Watershed authorities approached us, and we asked them about the park rangers and they looked bewildered. One of the Newark Watershed authorities replied, "What did these park rangers look like and what were they wearing?" We described their appearance, and the authority told us that there were no park rangers patrolling the property anymore, and the two men we saw that night were killed on patrol in 1939.—*Anonymous*

The Odd Characters of Clinton Road

Did you ever have that strange feeling that someone was watching you—that a pair of eyes were fixed upon you from somewhere, but you just couldn't figure out whose, or from where? Well, that feeling seems to be pervasive among the people who travel on Clinton Road. Most folks can just shrug off these feelings as paranoia. On Clinton Road, however, the uncomfortable feeling that someone is watching you is all too often followed by the realization that somebody actually is!

The Boy in the Woods

My friend lived in West Milford right off Route 23 and across from Clinton Road. We used to play in the woods behind her house, and we would pretend that someone was chasing us. The strange thing is that sometimes we would turn around and actually see someone chasing us. It was this dirty-looking barefoot kid. He would chase us all the way to the edge of the woods, but he would be gone by the time we got to my friend's swing set in the backyard. We never knew who he was. We always called the boy Jackson White, although I don't know where we got that name.—*KEM*

The Man in the Woods

About a mile up Clinton Road, we pulled over so we could get out and walk around. With flashlights in hand, we made the journey into the woods. I was leading this bunch of ghost-hunting explorers when I saw a man about twenty feet in front of me. He was about six feet tall, with black pants and a red jacket, and he was staring right at me. I looked back, and my friends were not paying attention to the weirdo ahead of us. The one thought that went through my mind was, "What the hell is this guy doing in the middle of the woods at two o'clock in the morning, staring at me?" I can never remember being that scared before in my life.—*CJ*

The Man Is Watching You

My wife and I used to go swimming on Clinton Road. The last time I went, we received a scare. It was getting a little dusky out, it was a hot summer night, and we were swimming in the pool by the waterfalls. I dove off the waterfall rock in order to swim to the opposite shore. When my head came out of the water, there was this dude standing right there on the edge, staring at me. He wasn't there before I jumped off the rock, and it would be impossible for him to have run up to that spot while I was surfacing. He had this German shepherd and this piece of black felt over his head.

   My wife let out a noise, for she saw him, too. He never said a word, just stood there. I said, "What's up, bro?" in a real shaky voice. He just kept staring with this expressionless face. He didn't reply, so I turned around to tell my wife to jump in so we could leave on the opposite shore. We swam to the side and got out and peered over our shoulders, shaking from pure fear. He was gone!—*Scot H.*

Mystery, Murder, and the Mob on Clinton Road

One factor that makes all of the stories told about Clinton Road even more tangible is the tales of bodies being deposited and discovered along its wayside. Traveling through wilderness along the expanse, even the most law-abiding people might find themselves thinking that this would be a perfect place to dispose of a body.

Peering into the forest on either side of the road, one can't help but wonder what has been found there by accident over the years, what gruesome discoveries are yet to be made, and what might lie out there somewhere in a shallow grave that will never be found.

The Mafia Connection

Clinton Road provides easy access to New York State. Because of this, the New York Mafia would take their victims' bodies into New Jersey and dump them in the woods off Clinton Road. Therefore, if the bodies were ever discovered, the state of New York was not involved in the investigation and the Mafia was safe from prosecution.

People hired by the Mafia will still drive Clinton Road on a regular basis because they are aware of the attention that it has gained, and fear people like you who have made public the fact that Clinton Road is haunted. They are the ones who chase kids out.—*Rebecca T.*

Body Bag on Clinton Road

I've had many weird experiences up on Clinton Road. I was coming home one night with a friend, and we approached the curve located in the middle of Clinton Road. There, laying in the road, was someone in a body bag. The blood could be seen on the bag. I put the car in reverse and went back the way I came. We called the police. They found nothing—no blood, no body, no trace of anyone.—*Bob E.*

The Iceman Cometh

In May of 1983, a bicyclist on a deserted stretch of Clinton Road noticed buzzards circling a tree. When he investigated, he discovered a plastic garbage bag in the woods with a human head sticking out of one end. This murder not only helped add to Clinton Road's dark and mysterious legend, but also helped crack the case of the Iceman murders and earned the murderer, Mob hit man Richard Kuklinski, his chilly moniker.

The corpse had a single bullet wound in the head, which quickly determined the cause of death. What was not so easily determined, though, was the time of death. When the county medical examiner began his autopsy, he noticed that although the outside of the body had begun to decompose, the internal organs were still quite fresh. Upon closer inspection the doctor found ice crystals on the victim's heart. This led investigators to conclude that the body had been frozen for some time to disguise the time of death.

Investigators knew of the victim's association with Kuklinski, and this motivated them to watch the Iceman more closely, which helped lead to his eventual capture.

Kuklinski was convicted of two murders and was sentenced to two concurrent sixty-year sentences. He would eventually admit to icing about a hundred unfortunate associates, though the actual death toll is probably much higher. He is currently incarcerated in Trenton State Prison and will be more than one hundred years old before becoming eligible for parole.

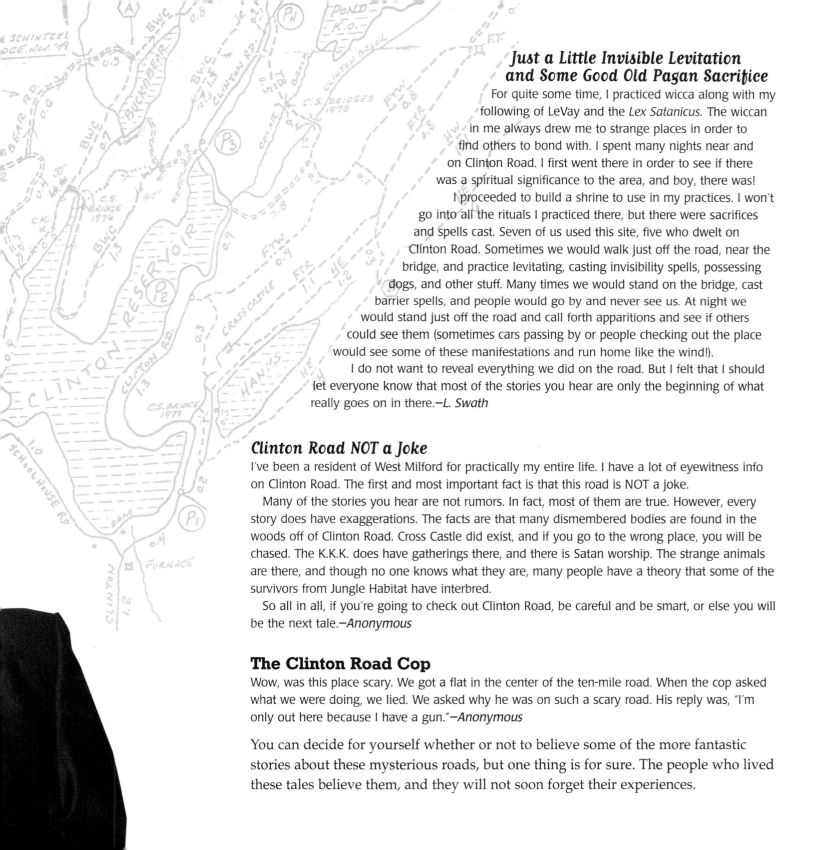

Just a Little Invisible Levitation and Some Good Old Pagan Sacrifice

For quite some time, I practiced wicca along with my following of LeVay and the *Lex Satanicus.* The wiccan in me always drew me to strange places in order to find others to bond with. I spent many nights near and on Clinton Road. I first went there in order to see if there was a spiritual significance to the area, and boy, there was!

I proceeded to build a shrine to use in my practices. I won't go into all the rituals I practiced there, but there were sacrifices and spells cast. Seven of us used this site, five who dwelt on Clinton Road. Sometimes we would walk just off the road, near the bridge, and practice levitating, casting invisibility spells, possessing dogs, and other stuff. Many times we would stand on the bridge, cast barrier spells, and people would go by and never see us. At night we would stand just off the road and call forth apparitions and see if others could see them (sometimes cars passing by or people checking out the place would see some of these manifestations and run home like the wind!).

I do not want to reveal everything we did on the road. But I felt that I should let everyone know that most of the stories you hear are only the beginning of what really goes on in there.–*L. Swath*

Clinton Road NOT a Joke

I've been a resident of West Milford for practically my entire life. I have a lot of eyewitness info on Clinton Road. The first and most important fact is that this road is NOT a joke.

Many of the stories you hear are not rumors. In fact, most of them are true. However, every story does have exaggerations. The facts are that many dismembered bodies are found in the woods off of Clinton Road. Cross Castle did exist, and if you go to the wrong place, you will be chased. The K.K.K. does have gatherings there, and there is Satan worship. The strange animals are there, and though no one knows what they are, many people have a theory that some of the survivors from Jungle Habitat have interbred.

So all in all, if you're going to check out Clinton Road, be careful and be smart, or else you will be the next tale.–*Anonymous*

The Clinton Road Cop

Wow, was this place scary. We got a flat in the center of the ten-mile road. When the cop asked what we were doing, we lied. We asked why he was on such a scary road. His reply was, "I'm only out here because I have a gun."–*Anonymous*

You can decide for yourself whether or not to believe some of the more fantastic stories about these mysterious roads, but one thing is for sure. The people who lived these tales believe them, and they will not soon forget their experiences.

Garden State Ghosts

There are many theories as to why ghosts exist, if in fact they do exist. One popular thought is that ghosts are victims of a sudden death, trapped in a vortex between dimensions. They see us, like the specters in the movie *Poltergeist* looking out from a TV screen, but are unable to move out of their one-dimensional plane of existence.

Sometimes on their journey between dimensions they appear in our world for brief moments, and while among us, tradition says, they may be able to affect material objects. This is where the poltergeist type of entity comes into play. Ghosts are said to communicate best with humans when we are in a light trancelike state, like when we are falling off to sleep or just waking up, which is probably why most sightings occur at that time.

With New Jersey's rich history, legend, and lore, it seems only natural that a few ghosts have chosen to hang around our fair state. At *Weird NJ*, though, we've always faced a dilemma when it comes to stories of a ghostly nature. Unlike so many of the other subjects we feature, ghosts are notoriously camera-shy. This makes getting concrete documentation rather difficult, to say the least. But our ghost files are brimming with firsthand accounts our readers have related to us of their otherworldly visitations. Having never actually seen a spook, specter, or spirit ourselves, we have only eyewitness reports to clue us in on just what such an encounter is like.

Here are some ghostly tales from the darker corners of the *Weird NJ* files. If you are the type of person who believes in ghosts, or has perhaps even seen one yourself, this chapter may reinforce some of your beliefs. If you are a skeptic who thinks that all of those things that go bump in the night are easily explained away, you may see these tales simply as the products of overactive imaginations. Either way, we're sure you'll be sleeping with the lights on tonight. So curl up, get settled in, and read on.

enthslcybp.m,kv-"01x528934zj67q:()&?;
enthslcybp.m,kv-"01x528934zj67q:()&?;

House Ghosts and Uninvited Guests

As a rule, we tend to take incredible stories with a grain of salt. A healthy dose of skepticism helps us to weed out the kooks who are scared by their own shadows. Still, some hauntings are not so easy to explain away. Some stories come to us from folks who have no apparent motive to fabricate a ghost story. Glenn and Jackie Wershing are two such people. This is their own story, in their own words.

The Haunting of Hunt House

Glenn Wershing is an archaeologist who runs a local historical society in Sussex County's Green Township. For a long time, uninvited guests have been materializing at the Wershings' house. We first met the Wershings in 1995 at their home. We didn't know at the time it would turn out to be probably the most haunted house in New Jersey.

Glenn: This is the Thomas P. Hunt house, built in 1835 next to Bear Creek. The house was once an inn, and it's in what was once the industrial center of the town. We moved here in 1961 with three children. As soon as we arrived, we knew there was something strange about the place. On the third floor, we would hear footsteps, then a big thump. I must have run up a hundred times to see who was there, but never found anything. Many times we heard footsteps coming down from the third floor — and footsteps coming right down the wall! Once, we were upstairs and we thought we heard the kids coming home from school. We heard noises and the door open and close. But when we went downstairs, the school bus was just pulling up the driveway, dropping the kids off! Another time, I had misplaced my bankbook. We searched all over for it. A week later, I came home and found it in the bedroom. I said to Jackie, "Where did you find it?" and she said she hadn't!

Jackie: Those were prank things, even kind of funny — nothing harmful.

WNJ: So there was never anything that really scared you?

Glenn: Oh yes! One night my youngest daughter wakes up screaming, and at the foot of the bed was a ball of light, just hanging in the air. I walked over to it, and it went right across the hall. I didn't know what it was — ball lightning, St. Elmo's Fire, or a ghost. There's a fault line that goes under the house, which we thought was causing these balls of light to materialize. We went to Drew University to hear a lecture by the Warrens, who are ghost chasers. We told them what we were experiencing. They asked if we had any girls reaching puberty; they said that may contribute to these encounters. When someone dies, this energy force is left, which can manifest itself in the conscious or the subconscious. It's a reflection of the past, a wavelength that's stuck on the wall. Young children seem to bring these things out.

Jackie: Then, thanks to *Weird NJ*, we were contacted by the show *Sightings*. They brought a psychic counselor, who told us there was an evil entity or presence, and a vortex in the living room that these spirits were emerging from. Then, again because of *Weird NJ*, we had director Tim Burton and the American Movie Classics channel film their Halloween special here in 2000. During the filming, one of the crew went

_*÷¢ĝ!$]@¿#[é½⅝¶§KFZVEYQNPGHDBJROMIWAU
_*÷¢ĝ!$]@¿#[é½⅝¶§KFZVEYQNPGHDBJROMIWAU

A Wershing family *Christmas photo, c. 1963. Glenn (seated), poses with his daughters Diane (standing), Jeanne (center), and son Glenn (seated). No one knows who the transparent child holding the doll at the left is.*

back into the house to get something. We were standing outside when he comes bolting out of the house screaming, saying something grabbed hold of his leg. He refused to go back in to retrieve his equipment.

Glenn: I've said I don't believe in ghosts, but something is happening here.

Jackie: I had an electric typewriter, and one day it started typing by itself. I put paper in to see what it was typing, but it looked like gibberish. I pulled the plug, and it kept on typing!

WNJ: What was the most recent happening?

Jackie: Just last week I was cleaning on the third floor when the door to my son's room—supposedly the "hot" room—slammed shut, but it was already closed! When the rooms get cold, you know they're around. One time I woke up about five in the morning, and the room was cold. There, standing in front of Glenn's dresser, was a lady with extremely long hair who had a flowing nightgown on. I tried not to move, because I didn't want to scare her away. I barely opened my eyelids, trying to see a face in the mirror, but nothing was reflected in it.

WNJ: Was she transparent?

Jackie: No, she was three-dimensional. She just stood there looking into the mirror. And once when Glenn was traveling and I was in bed, the house got bitter cold. I woke up and felt a heavy pressure holding me down. I screamed and tried to get out of bed but couldn't. The next day my ankles had red marks on them from where I was held down.

Glenn: Once, our son said a whirlwind of cold air pinned him to his bed. With his last bit of strength, he threw himself out of bed, grabbed a pair of jeans, tore out of the house, and spent the night at his friend's house.

Jackie: Another time when Glenn was away, I awoke feeling that something was lying alongside of me, behind my back. I could feel the heartbeat. I reached back to touch it, and it had coarse hair, like an animal. Then it started talking through my mouth, making a guttural voice in the back of my throat. That scared the hell out of me! I ran out of the room and stayed up all night. That same week, I slept in my daughter's bedroom, since I didn't want to sleep in my bed. I was awakened again with this ice-cold air. I opened my eyes and felt this whack, and I was flipped over in the bed. I heard the words "Found yoooooooou!" This hit was so hard that two days later this yellow bruise appeared. I called up our other daughter, who lives close by, and I asked to come over. She said, "Is there somebody trying to break in?" I said, "No, it's just the house."

The History and Mysteries of Blairsden: The Dark Mansion on the Hill

Mountaintop mansions with forbidding gates, reclusive religious sects, and dark forests are the stuff of local legend. They inspire the tales that folklore thrives on. And Blairsden has them all.

Blairsden was once the Somerset Hills home of investment banker Clinton Ledyard Blair, and remains one of the finest examples of Beaux Arts architecture in the country. Blair began construction of the four-hundred-and-twenty-three-acre estate in 1898. He leveled the top of a mountain and carved terraces into the hillside down to the North Branch of the Raritan River. Designed by the architects of the New York Public Library, the Italianate mansion boasted twenty-six fireplaces, an indoor swimming pool, and a squash court.

In its heyday, between 1903 and 1919, Blairsden hosted numerous dignitaries, but Blair's fortune eventually dwindled. When he died in 1949, his heirs sold the estate off.

The mansion and fifty acres of land fetched $60,000 and went to the Sisters of St. John the Baptist. Over time, the estate's ominous appearance and the reclusive nature of its occupants gave rise to rumors of evil-doings and ghosts. More recently, its ornate, crumbling front gate has tempted curious trespassers. Their midnight explorations have spawned fantastic stories of crazed nuns and ghosts in the woods.

Weird NJ reader Will Hagerty of Warren wrote to us of his experiences.

"I learned about Blairsden from my friend A. J. in 1997. He told me that the head nun was a practitioner of Paganism and wished to convert her fellow sisters to the Pagan ways. When they refused, they were tortured and slain. In a final act of sacrifice, the head nun took her own life.

"Supposedly, there are two ghosts on the path that ranges from the closed bridge, up to the back steps. The first is a mentally unstable man who was tortured and killed in the house. He appears at the halfway point, near two trees on either side of the path which connect about 10 feet off the ground, giving it the appearance of a gate or doorway. He serves as a devilish deterrent to prevent you from reaching the second ghost. The second apparition is that of the head nun herself. If you get past the 'warning' ghost, you will probably find her near the bottom of the terraces. Rumor has it she tries to lead you into the house to torture and kill you. I've also heard stories of a screaming nun running down the hill, over the bridge, and through a car."

The screaming nun apparition

may have its origins in an actual person, according to Bill Lawton of the Blairsden Association, a nonprofit group that once sought to raise funds to purchase Blairsden.

"There used to be a nun there named Sister Adolphus, I think," Mr. Lawton said. "She was a huge woman, with a thick German accent. If she saw someone biking up the hill, she would bellow commands through a loudspeaker for the trespasser to leave. If she was outside, she would chase you down the hill, barking at you all the way in that German accent of hers!"

The sisters sold the property to investors in November 2002 for $5 million. So far, the group, the Foundation for Classical Architecture, has not announced its plans. Who knows whether the new owners were informed about the ghosts said to inhabit their dark mansion on the hill?

Blairsden's Ram with the Red Eyes

About ten or eleven years ago, some friends and I were told about Blairsden, so late one Friday night, four of us piled into the car to find this place. There are no streetlamps in the area, but you can see the mansion way up on the hill with the lights on. It was a very narrow road that could fit only two cars side by side, and the river was right down the hill from one side, a little too close for comfort.

An old bridge took you over to the property, but it was blocked by a guardrail and falling apart. But you could walk over the bridge with no problem. On the other side was a big iron gate with stone walls on either side. We took out a flashlight and slowly made our way over the bridge. There was no sound except for the water beneath our feet. When we got to the other side, we saw the gates were all grown over with vines and weeds. On either side of the iron gates were these small figurines attached to the walls that I believe were once little fountains. They looked like rams' heads, with a small basin below for the water. The scary thing was that in the pitch dark, we put the flashlight on to get a better look and got a pretty good scare. Someone had painted the eyes of the rams' heads red! That was pretty much all we needed to see, and we got out of there.—*Susan D.*

Blairsden's Nuns Dam the Orphans

According to an old legend, about twenty-five nuns and twenty-five orphans lived at Blairsden. One day the nuns took all the children down to a waterfall halfway down the hill and lined them up across it. They pushed the children off the edge, one by one, and then they all jumped themselves. This was many, many years ago, and as far as I know, the mansion hasn't been inhabited since then. I haven't been up to the house in about a year, but the driveway going up there is all overrun with weeds, and there is a guardrail blocking the entrance to it. I've never seen any ghosts there . . . but I never stay long.—*Sean*

Bloody Blairsden Massacre

The nuns had a vow of silence, and their only contact to the outside was the mother superior. She would walk all the way down the trail to the gate and would meet the grocery boy to pick up their food. One week, the mother superior did not show up. The grocery boy figured she didn't remember or something. The next week she also was a no-show. The grocery boy went to the sheriff, and he investigated. He broke the lock on the gate and drove up the trail. He found all of the nuns' bodies ripped apart and blood everywhere. They locked the place up. Because of the value of the land, it wasn't long before a celebrity moved in. This person stayed one night and refused to ever return again. He had movers come back for his things. Since then, the lock has remained on the gate.—*Carmen Malangone*

Ghosts of the Union Hotel, Flemington

Flemington's Union Hotel stands witness to the media circus surrounding the Lindbergh baby kidnapping and murder case. During the "trial of the century," the hotel's fifty-two rooms and even its closets formed the base of operations for the world's journalists. Today, only the bar and restaurant on the first floor are open to the public. But even though the grand old hotel no longer accepts visitors for overnight stays, some guests, they say, have never checked out.

Weird NJ was invited to tour the vacant rooms and empty hallways of the second, third, and fourth floors. According to the manager, the ghostly tenants have been getting restless.

"One night, after closing," she told us, "the bouncer locked the front doors, then returned to the bar, where a few of the staff were sitting around. The locked doors flew open, and a cold wind swept past us. When he went back to re-close the doors, he saw an empty pair of children's black patent-leather shoes walking up the main stairway. He freaked out and ran, then called us from a pay phone and told us to get out!

"Another time, one of my waitresses was carrying the register drawer upstairs to the office. When she reached the top of the stairs, she heard an unearthly voice humming a lullaby. She dropped the drawer full of money, ran out of the building, and never came back."

The manager has also had experience with spooks in her second-floor office.

"Once, at about three o'clock in the morning, I was doing the books in my office. All of a sudden, I felt something in the room with me. I could feel the pressure of it right up against me, pushing on my chest. It was hard for me to breathe. I didn't feel threatened. I simply asked it to move away and leave me alone. Then it was gone."

Walking the deserted hallways, one can easily imagine what it must have been like there during the media-circus trial of Bruno Hauptmann. Not much has changed in these empty rooms since the 1930s. And if there is a more accommodating residence for a specter, we haven't yet seen it.

Union Hotel Still Haunts a Former Employee

I worked at the Union Hotel in Flemington, and I found it harbored several ghostly residents. Several stories I heard included rooms on the upper floors. Some of the servers said it was like something out of Stephen King's novel *The Shining.* Curious, I decided to go upstairs.

It was still early, and there was plenty of daylight. I could not imagine being spooked. I started down the hall, looking in each room. They were small and nondescript, each with one window. It was very quiet in the hall, and because of this quiet, I heard the door to the main hall behind me slowly creak shut. I turned around in time to see it latch. My heart thundered in my ears, and I realized how alone I was. I turned around and hurried back, pulling on the door, almost expecting it to be locked. It opened easily, and I hurried downstairs. "Okay," I admitted when I returned to the first floor, "it is spooky!"

Late one evening, a waiter asked, "Whose kid is playing in the dining room?" It was nearly midnight, and the dining room had been closed for at least two hours. The waiter asked everyone at the bar if they had a little girl. He came back after a few minutes and said, "I know I saw a little girl in there!" He assured us he had seen a girl of about eight to ten running in the dining room. He said she had long, dark hair and was wearing a fancy dress. One of the regulars laughed and told him, "You just seen a ghost!"

I found out that a previous owner had once brought in a psychic who determined that at various times during the hotel's long history there had been several violent murders. And according to the psychic, there is a little girl who haunts the front hall and stairs.–*Marige*

The Spy House

The Spy House Museum in Port Monmouth has been called the most haunted house in New Jersey. Several popular books on American haunted houses describe the museum, which operates from one of the oldest houses in the state. The seventeenth-century building boasts more than twenty ghosts, publicized in booklets, news reports, and archived accounts of visitors. My first visit to the Spy House a few years ago caused me to upgrade my credibility evaluation from "plausible" to "likely." Approaching the front door, I was unenthused. That came to a close the moment I passed through the front door. In that moment, I crossed an invisible but palpable line. The air became thick, oppressive, and definitely no longer cheerful. The sensation was abrupt and positively real. My two companions experienced the same sensation. The eerie sensation stayed with me until I walked back outside onto the lawn, where everything seemed normal again.–*Randolph W. Liebeck*

Spy House Ghost Boy

One morning, my friend Dave's parents went to visit the old Spy House Museum in Port Monmouth. They were there at the appointed opening time, but the curator wasn't there. After about a half hour of waiting, they said the hell with it and left. As they were getting back into their car, my friend's father looked up and pointed out a kid about ten or twelve years old, looking at them from the upstairs window. The kid had one of those puffy shirts that they used to wear in the old days. Just then, the curator drove up and apologized for being late. They told her that they had seen a boy upstairs, and together they searched the place but found no one.–*Ray*

Ghosts Along the Road

Perhaps it's appropriate in our fast-moving state that many of our most notable ghosts are seen hanging out at the side of the road. Countless motorists have witnessed roadside apparitions over the course of several generations. Unlike the many hitchhiking ghosts so popular in urban legends, New Jersey's street-corner spooks don't seem to have any interest in bumming a ride. They seem to just be content to wander their own stretch of highway, eternally reliving their final moments alive on this earth.

The Ghost of Annie on Annie's Road

Imagine you are driving down a narrow, winding two-lane blacktop. It is around midnight, and the pavement is wet and shiny from a recent mid-autumn shower. Multicolored leaves dance in front of your headlights before settling onto the slick asphalt. To your left, a densely wooded hillside crowds its way to the edge of the shoulderless street. On your right, a low steel guardrail stands between your car and the inky black waters of the Passaic River.

Your headlights illuminate the canopy of tree branches over the roadway, giving the impression that you are traveling through a long, undulating tunnel.

Suddenly you find yourself at a hard right curve in the road and realize you're going too fast. As you begin to regain control, you see something that sends a shiver up your spine—a splash of red on the road and guardrail, trailing off down the edge of the street. Was that . . . blood? Then you see an eerie mist forming on the glassy moonlit river, just ahead of you to the right, and on the left, the gleaming marble stones of a vast, sprawling cemetery. The mist begins to take shape in your headlights, and you clearly make out a distinct figure crossing the road up ahead. You hit the brakes and do your best to negotiate the slippery pavement. Then you watch in disbelief as the translucent but unmistakable form of a young woman in a flowing white dress floats across the roadway inches above the ground, then disappears into the moonlit graveyard.

You have just experienced a close encounter with the legendary Ghost of Annie on Totowa's Riverview Drive—more commonly known to locals as Annie's Road. At night, it is a dark and treacherous drive that leaves little room for error, and it is no stranger to severe auto accidents. But over the generations, this remote and wooded road in the heart of a densely populated area has lured countless seekers of the supernatural to late-night adventures. It's important to remember, though, that to some people, Riverview Drive is more than a midnight joyride—it's home. We at *Weird NJ* strongly discourage anyone from disturbing the residents. It is also worth remembering that places are not given charming little nicknames like Dead Man's Curve, which can be found on Annie's Road, without some good reason.

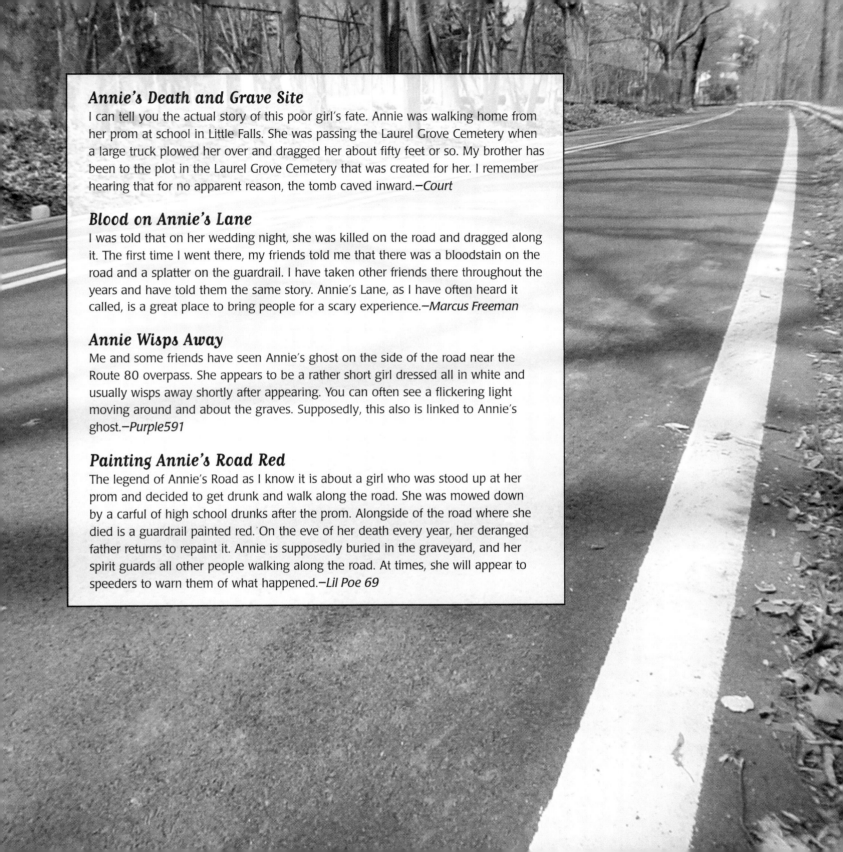

Annie's Death and Grave Site

I can tell you the actual story of this poor girl's fate. Annie was walking home from her prom at school in Little Falls. She was passing the Laurel Grove Cemetery when a large truck plowed her over and dragged her about fifty feet or so. My brother has been to the plot in the Laurel Grove Cemetery that was created for her. I remember hearing that for no apparent reason, the tomb caved inward.—*Court*

Blood on Annie's Lane

I was told that on her wedding night, she was killed on the road and dragged along it. The first time I went there, my friends told me that there was a bloodstain on the road and a splatter on the guardrail. I have taken other friends there throughout the years and have told them the same story. Annie's Lane, as I have often heard it called, is a great place to bring people for a scary experience.—*Marcus Freeman*

Annie Wisps Away

Me and some friends have seen Annie's ghost on the side of the road near the Route 80 overpass. She appears to be a rather short girl dressed all in white and usually wisps away shortly after appearing. You can often see a flickering light moving around and about the graves. Supposedly, this also is linked to Annie's ghost.—*Purple591*

Painting Annie's Road Red

The legend of Annie's Road as I know it is about a girl who was stood up at her prom and decided to get drunk and walk along the road. She was mowed down by a carful of high school drunks after the prom. Alongside of the road where she died is a guardrail painted red. On the eve of her death every year, her deranged father returns to repaint it. Annie is supposedly buried in the graveyard, and her spirit guards all other people walking along the road. At times, she will appear to speeders to warn them of what happened.—*Lil Poe 69*

Images of the White Lady have appeared next to this tree at the southern end of Branch Brook Park in Newark.

The Lady in White of Branch Brook Park, Newark

Like the Ghost of Annie in Totowa, the White Lady of Branch Brook Park in Newark has been giving motorists the heebie-jeebies for many years. The two tales of death by auto and roadside haunting have several similarities, and they have been confused before, but the details tell two distinct stories.

The Lady in White vs. the Ghost of Annie

The "Legend of Annie in Totowa" story has been stolen! The original story happened in Branch Brook Park in Newark to the Lady in White. The story says that her and her groom were riding in their limo to take wedding pictures. Supposedly the limo hit an ice patch and crashed into a tree, where the bride was killed instantly. This young bride can still be seen, mostly in the evenings, and her image appears on the tree where she was killed.—*Laynie*

A Nice Day for a White Wedding

The legend goes that she and her new husband were killed on their wedding night after crashing into the tree. The county put a new road through the park a few years back, and the tree is no longer adjacent to the road. I am not about to wander through there at night to find it!—*Cougar*

White Lady Still Waiting

Many people have told me of the White Lady who haunts Branch Brook Park on the Belleville/Newark border. A teenage boy asked a girl to be his date for the high school prom. The night of their date, they decided to take a drive through Branch Brook Park on their way to the prom. It was raining heavily, and visibility was bad. The car suddenly began to skid out of control and crashed into a tree. The boy was fine, escaping with only some minor scratches. The girl, however, was dead. Today, the tree that they crashed into is painted white in the form of a person. Witnesses have recalled seeing a lady in white next to the tree who beckons them toward her on rainy nights. Perhaps she is still waiting for her prom date to join her.—*Cheryl Laudadio*

Ring Around the White Lady Tree

I used to live in Nutley around Branch Brook Park. Out of sheer boredom, we decided to take a ride through the park. I was sitting in the back seat of the car, so I really didn't notice anything. I felt the car stop, and everyone went silent and stared out the front window. I could not believe what I saw, and I still don't. There was a shadow of a gray-and-off-white woman walking around the tree in a circle. My friend accidentally beeped the horn, and she stopped walking and stared at us. The next thing I knew, she was walking toward us. We sped out of there so fast I don't even remember how I got back to my house.—*Fish*

White Lady Hit and Run

As a kid, I heard all the stories about the White Lady, but I believed that the legend was phony. All this changed on Thursday, April 12, 2001. It was about three thirty a.m. on one of the foggiest nights I'd seen in a very long time. The street through the park was particularly foggy. As I made my turn around the bend, I noticed a white cloud hovering over the road, slightly below the branches. As I drove through this cloud, I got this feeling I couldn't explain, and my friend said, "John, you just ran over a ghost."—*John Spina*

White Lady's Work May Be Done

We went to Branch Brook Park in search of the White Lady, but the road had been rerouted so that it passed away from the tree line. Finally we came across a huge tree with an X etched into it with white paint. This was our tree. Someone had cut off most of the branches, and what was left was a huge trunk with the bizarre white mark upon it. The road originally led right toward it and veered off to the right within five feet of the tree. No wonder there were so many accidents. Ghost or not, it was a tricky turn. My girlfriend, Tracey, said that maybe the White Lady's mission was to warn the passing motorists of the treacherous tree. Perhaps she was trying to prevent any other people from crashing like she did. She said that since the road was rerouted, the White Lady's job was now done, and perhaps her soul may finally be at rest. Ever since then, I'm no longer afraid of driving through the park at night.—*David Zayas*

The Atco Ghost

From the southern New Jersey town of Atco comes the following tale of a young boy run down after chasing his basketball into the street. The tale centers on a dead end on Burnt Mill Road on the fringes of the Pine Barrens.

Atco Ghost Lies Down in Technicolor

If anyone lives in South Jersey, they might want to stop by Atco. There is a story about a boy that was hit and killed by a car, right off Route 30 (The White Horse Pike), and his spirit is seen laying on the road. I saw the outline of a boy full of colors, similar to the ones you see when you look into the sun. There are certain directions you have to follow to see it.—*hiffalump*

Kill the Engine, Kill the Lights, and Walk Away

The Atco Ghost can be seen in a number of different ways. The most common is to drive to this haunted road in the middle of the night, park on the side, kill the engine, kill the lights, and get out of the car. You then walk away from the spot where the ghost appears, and after twenty feet, turn around. You will then see the spectral form of a little boy walking toward you.

—*Manning L. Krull*

Ghost Boy Searches for Those Who Killed Him

I used to row for my college's crew team in South Jersey. A teammate said that if you park at the end of the road with engine and lights off, the ghost would appear and look the car over to see if it was the same one that killed him.

—*Scott Kafarski*

Atco Ghost Follows the Bouncing Ball

You should go at midnight, park in a specific spot, and flash your lights in the road across from the house where the boy lived. The dead boy is supposed to be seen chasing the ball into the street with headlights coming at him. In my own personal experience, a boy did walk toward our car but never actually made it. It was as though he was walking in place. Nevertheless, I was scared out of my wits.—*Kyle*

I've Seen the Atco Ghost!

I spent many nights with friends at the end of this street waiting for the ghost. We never seemed to find him. I had a different experience when I actually followed the instructions on how to see the ghost. The night was rather misty, and it was raining a little bit. My friend and I drove to the end of the road where the factory is located and turned around. We drove up to the second streetlight and stopped the car. I turned off the ignition, and we sat in silence for a while.

Nothing was happening, so we decided to leave. The moment I touched the keys, a sudden wind swirled the mist on the road, and a shadowy shape appeared at the side of the road. It wasn't a shape really, but a break in the low-lying fog that resembled the outline of a small child. We decided to get out of there. As I was racing down the street, I could see the fog swirling faster and faster.—*Zachary W.*

The Parkway Phantom of Exit 82

Any road as legendary as the Garden State Parkway must have a ghost associated with it. Sure enough, since the completion of the parkway in 1955, people have reported seeing the Parkway Phantom waving his arms and trying to cross the road. He appears only at night and only along an eight-mile stretch around exit 82, near the New Jersey State Police's Toms River barracks. The apparition is very tall, with a long topcoat belted at the waist, waving his arms in a distinctive way from the elbow. It has been described as looking like a strange football cheer. State police are reluctant to comment, but a former state trooper admitted that that section of the highway has more than its share of accidents.

Trying to Get Saved in Toms River

As paramedics in Ocean County, we see a lot of fatal accidents. Usually we only see a patient after they die, but one patient wants to be seen a lot more. About five years ago, on a rainy night along the Garden State Parkway, a guy whose car broke down began to walk along the shoulder when a driver hit him, throwing him into the woods and killing him. Due to the darkness and rain, the paramedics could not find him, and when they finally did, it was too late. Several weeks later, the same medic crew saw someone on the side of the road waving them down. By the time they were able to pull over and back up to the spot, the man was gone, but they noticed it was in the same spot where the man was hit only weeks before. They just blew off the event until another crew reported a similar event in the same area. To date, about three teams have seen this. —SeanEms17

The Hookerman Lights of the Flanders Tracks

The legend of the Hookerman is a familiar tale among aficionados of the supernatural. Mysterious lights appear along a stretch of railroad, and legends tell of a night watchman or other railroad worker who lost his arm in an encounter with a train. Some say the accident drove him mad, and he was hospitalized at a local institution for the insane, with a hook to replace his lost hand. After his death, the Hookerman's spirit appeared on the tracks carrying a lantern, searching for his lost arm.

For more than a century, the Hookerman has been sighted in Flanders on North Four Bridges Road, but more recently on the Naugherton Road railroad tracks in Washington Township, Warren County, and off Roycefield Road in Hillsborough, Somerset County. Other reports are coming in from Boonton and Budd Lake. Anthony Muller, a science teacher in Mount Arlington, has witnessed these lights on several occasions.

"The effect is a bright rose to amber-colored light, balllike or disklike in shape, with a diameter of about four feet," said Mr. Muller. "It seems to be ten to twelve feet above the tracks and moves in one direction, about twenty-five to forty miles per hour.

"I researched this phenomenon. Geologists and electrical engineers told me quartz-bearing rocks, under pressure and stress, produce electrical discharges in what is known as the piezoelectric effect. The railroad tracks may focus this electrical energy into ball lightning or something close to it."

In 1976, the New Jersey–based organization Vestigia conducted a study of the Long Valley mystery lights. The group included experts in meteorology, physics, optics, photography, and chemistry. They set up a Geiger counter and methane detectors, and laid four thousand feet of copper wire between the rails, attached to amplifiers and oscilloscopes. At ten p.m. on November 20, 1976, their instruments registered drastic changes as a small but distinct light appeared a foot above the ground and hovered for two minutes before disappearing. The cameras photographed a pinpoint of light, with infrared photographs that showed more density and light range of the object. The team then turned to geophysical science for an explanation. The geodesic maps of New Jersey revealed a major fault, the Ramapo Border Fault, that runs through Peapack and ends at Indian Point, New York. Since 1962, there have been thirty-three minor earthquakes along this fault. Since quartz-bearing rock produces an electrical charge under seismic stresses and the railroad bed in Long Valley is granite, a very good conductor of electricity, a scientific explanation had been reached. Fortunately for New Jersey night riders, this explanation doesn't dampen the mystique of the legend. As long as there is a place to see the ghost lights, New Jerseyans still set out to find the Hookerman, as they have done for over a century.

Hunting for the Hookerman

Back in the 1960s and 1970s, the Hookerman site was a big teen attraction. A friend of mine would often go down to see the lights, and on hot summer nights, there would be a crowd of fifteen to thirty teens! The Hookerman, he said, generally appeared right before a train was to pass by. Usually it appeared as a yellowish hazy ball that bobbed about the tracks. One particular night, he became a true believer. As a train slowly approached, the Hookerman light appeared about thirty feet down the tracks. The train got closer, and the light moved down the tracks as well. Just before the train reached the group, the engineer dimmed his headlight, then turned it on again at its highest brightness. For a second, in the rays of the bright light, the group saw a translucent figure of a railroad worker in overalls with one arm, and that arm was waving a lantern side to side. As the train passed, a crewman shouted, "Did you see that?"

One last intriguing fact: In the 1920s and 1930s, the Central Railroad of New Jersey had a notation in their employee timetable not to stop for any lantern signals in this area—that's how common the Hookerman lights were!–*Paul Tupaczewski*

Hookerman May Be Just a Lot of Gas

There used to be a Central Railroad of New Jersey line from High Bridge to Greenwood Lake Junction (where it met the Lackawanna). This line closed about 1974, and the tracks were ripped out west of Flanders. Sometime in the early part of this century, a track worker was supposed to have been killed by a train. Since then, he has been haunting the old line with a lantern between Flanders and High Bridge, with many sightings around Bartley and Long Valley. People see a glow in the air along a hiking trail. Some say that the explanation is gas leaking from a pipeline, but people have seen the Hookerman years before the pipeline was installed. I read that Rutgers University had done tests and that a possible reason for the lights was triboluminescence. This is a photoelectrical phenomenon in which strain (striking the material, for example) produces a flash of light. In the Hookerman case, Rutgers speculates that small tremors or earthquakes strain the rocks under the roadbed, causing the glow. Anyway, it's a cool recurring story.–*David Goessling, Technical Information Analyst*

Encountering the Hookerman

Three of my friends and I went down to Four Bridges Road in Chester to look for the Hookerman. We parked and headed down the abandoned railroad bed. A few minutes later, we thought a car was coming down the tracks, until the four bright lights merged into one, then headed toward us. It got real faint as it got closer. It was the Hookerman! As it came closer, we ran for that foggy light. We got within twenty feet or so, then it disappeared. As we looked down the bed past the car, it reappeared. We ran past the car, down the bed on that side of the road. It had disappeared again. We looked back at the car, and the light was doing loops around it. It started as foggy light, changed to green, then bright red, then shot up about ten feet and disappeared. Three of us swear on our grannies' graves on what we saw. The fourth is in denial. He says the bright lights were from a helicopter, and the light looping around his car was a radar detector! Go figure.–*Don in Andover*

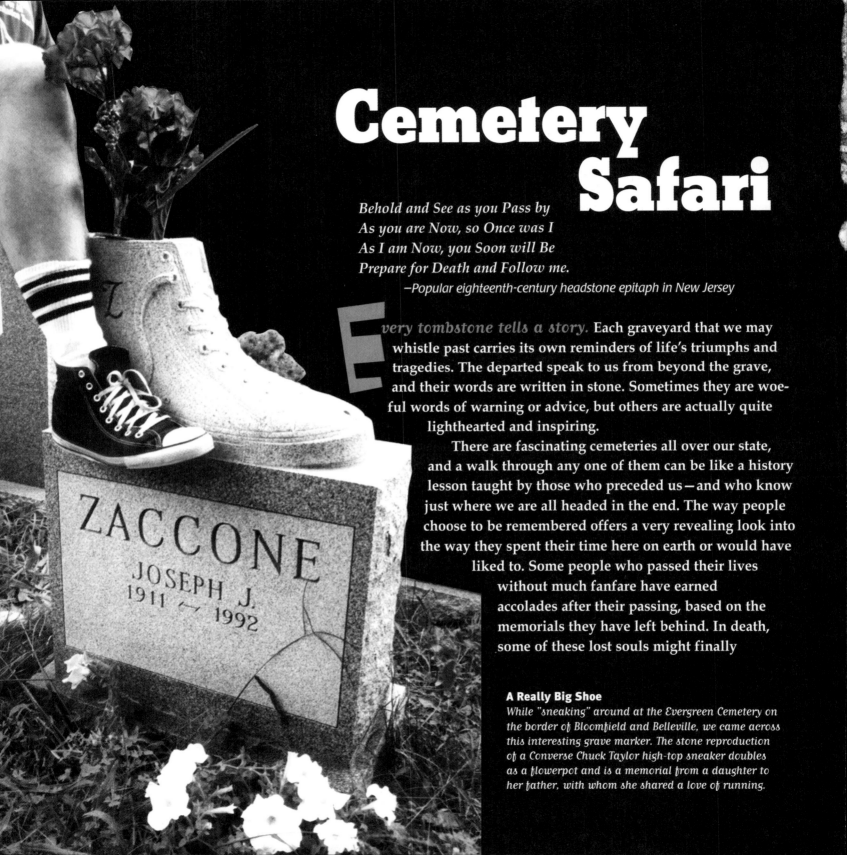

Cemetery Safari

Behold and See as you Pass by
As you are Now, so Once was I
As I am Now, you Soon will Be
Prepare for Death and Follow me.
—Popular eighteenth-century headstone epitaph in New Jersey

Every tombstone tells a story. Each graveyard that we may whistle past carries its own reminders of life's triumphs and tragedies. The departed speak to us from beyond the grave, and their words are written in stone. Sometimes they are woeful words of warning or advice, but others are actually quite lighthearted and inspiring.

There are fascinating cemeteries all over our state, and a walk through any one of them can be like a history lesson taught by those who preceded us—and who know just where we are all headed in the end. The way people choose to be remembered offers a very revealing look into the way they spent their time here on earth or would have liked to. Some people who passed their lives without much fanfare have earned accolades after their passing, based on the memorials they have left behind. In death, some of these lost souls might finally

A Really Big Shoe
While "sneaking" around at the Evergreen Cemetery on the border of Bloomfield and Belleville, we came across this interesting grave marker. The stone reproduction of a Converse Chuck Taylor high-top sneaker doubles as a flowerpot and is a memorial from a daughter to her father, with whom she shared a love of running.

Ear to the Limestone
This tombstone, located in West Long Branch, makes you wonder just what this woman is listening for.

garner the recognition that they probably felt they deserved all along.

There are hundreds of notable people buried here in New Jersey who made a name for themselves while alive. There are historic figures like Grover Cleveland and Aaron Burr, world-renowned writers and poets such as Stephen Crane and Walt Whitman, and great entertainers like Sarah Vaughn and Joey Ramone.

But these people have had their time in the sun. In this chapter, we're going to place the spotlight on those New Jerseyans who waited until after death for their turn to really shine.

Going Out in Grand Style

For thousands of years, great rulers and religious figures have erected great monuments to themselves. These days, many people do the same thing in humbler ways. These folks are just not content to commemorate their time here on earth with a plain gray slab of granite or marble. They have led unique and interesting lives, and they want everyone to know it. Or are these memorials an ego trip or a reluctance to accept the finality of death? Are they a tribute from their families? Perhaps it's just that the deceased wanted to exit this world in the same way that they lived in it— in grand style.

The Lightbulb Grave—Laurel Grove Cemetery, Totowa

On a random drive-through of the Laurel Grove Cemetery in Totowa a few years ago, we happened upon one of the must unusual gravestones we had ever seen. It's a four-foot-tall black marble stone carved into the shape of a lightbulb. Engraved on it was a hand grasping a fistful of lightning bolts, encircled in gold letters with the words World's Greatest Electrician. Below the hand was an electrician's license number. The base of the stone bore the name and smiling face of Sal Giardino and a golden two-socket wall outlet. Laid in tribute on the ground in front of the stone was a very large electrical fuse.

After we published a picture of this monument in our magazine, we heard from Laurie Giardino, daughter of the World's Greatest Electrician. She told us that when her father passed away, she contacted Sgobba Monument Works of Totowa to help her with the memorial. She drew up some sketches, and the plan was under way.

We interviewed Laurie Giardino and Anthony Sgobba at Laurel Grove and gained some insight into the man and woman behind the stone—as well as the man beneath it.

WNJ: You didn't chisel that by hand, did you?

AS: Yes. Years ago, we probably wouldn't have been able to cut something like the lightbulb—with the shine and all. It was sanded by hand, then polished and sandblasted on the lathe wheel. It took about nine months.

LG: We kept saying, 'There's no rush. Dad's not going anywhere.' Bad jokes were flying all over the place.

WNJ: Do cemeteries have standards you have to follow, or do you have a free rein?

AS: Years ago, cemeteries would allow any kind of stones, with different widths and heights. Then they got away from that and made it regulatory sizes.

WNJ: When we first saw the lightbulb, the caretaker told us your family wanted to install a lightning rod next to the bulb!

LG: No. We're not putting any additions on it. Although it wouldn't be a bad idea!

WNJ: I think you've set a new standard for the century.

LG: I think I'm going to start a consulting firm. Look around—it's all gray rectangle, and they're all so faceless. This cemetery here I really grew up with. When you were young,

you'd play hide and seek. When you're a teenager, you'd park with your boyfriend; when you were in your twenties, you make it a meeting place; and when you're in your thirties, you're burying your parents. A real rites of passage. That's why I can handle it, not in a comical way, but in a lighter way. I've been around it my whole life.

AS: There are more dead people in Totowa than living residents. That's a statistic. It was listed in *Ripley's Believe It or Not.* The area is surrounded by four cemeteries.

LG: My father was such a character, a real comedian. This is a perfect memorial to him. He was such a jokester that even when he got sick, he said, 'If I'm dead by Christmas you can hang my balls on the tree!' Whatever costume he had on for Halloween, he would put it back on for Thanksgiving and carve the turkey in it. I have many pictures of him carving turkeys in weird costumes.

He was the best. He gave nine million kids from this town jobs as electricians. Before the stone was in, we left a big fuse box at the site. We also left some BX cable and some other offerings.

WNJ: Now you've got me thinking about what I want my tombstone to look like.

LG: We'd have to interview you and look at pictures. Let me know when you're ready.

Tragically, Laurie's sister Kim died in a motorcycle accident just a few months after Sal's death. Laurie again paid tribute. Kim's monument is also black stone with real gold lettering, and depicts a globe at the top with a peace sign superimposed over it. Kim's unique stone sits right beside her father's.

The Shrine of Singin' Sam Stevens

Located in the Evergreen Cemetery in Hillside is another impressive black-and-gold memorial. This commemorates a legend of the music world who nobody seems to have ever heard of—Singin' Sam Stevens. The multipillared monument is adorned with music-related motifs, including a larger-than-life Gibson electric guitar, music notes, and a giant record listing all of Sam's greatest hits—which again, no one has ever heard. Beneath the record are the words Singer, Song Writer, Peace Maker. The tribute looks very much like one you might expect to see at Graceland to immortalize the King of Rock 'n' Roll, but here it sits in Hillside, an homage to a lesser-known musical icon.

Gypsies, Tramps, and Singin' Sam

I uncovered some information about Singin' Sam Stevens from a friend in the funeral business. Singin' Sam was a gypsy. The gypsies were the forgotten people, never granted a homeland, traveling from place to place. Most of the graveyards and funeral homes in Union County and the surrounding areas will not deal with them. The adornment of his gravestone with guitars and music notes more than likely has nothing to do with any musical fame. The extravagant headstone was probably the result of his friends and family wanting to make it as impressive as they could. As they travel with big cash, they would have no problem taking up a $30,000 or $40,000 collection to pay for it.—*Kevin*

My friend told me at one time the little marble table beside the grave actually had some kind of music box that would play some of Sam's "hits." Unfortunately, that has long since disappeared.—*Nick Clemente*

The Man in the Iron Casket

Everybody has heard the expression "They'll never take me alive." One New Jersey resident went to great lengths to ensure that nobody would take him after he was dead.

Smithville in Burlington County was once known as Shreveville, but when a fire consumed a factory central to its economy, it took on a new identity. An enterprising New England inventor named Hezekiah B. Smith acquired the town, renamed it, and began to mold it in his own vision.

Smith invented new types of machinery, including versions of both the automobile and helicopter. But he earned acceptance among the townsfolk when he won

the contract to make Star bicycles, which revitalized the local economy. He used the bicycles to build one of his most bizarre inventions—a bicycle railroad that carried people to and from work.

When his wife Agnes died, Smith had a statue of her erected on his front lawn. He handled his own death in an even odder fashion. He had himself buried in an iron casket, with instructions that the casket be encased in cement and bracketed between two more slabs of iron. When his family tried to remove his remains to return them to New England, they found that his body was absolutely immovable.

Hezekiah Smith had made a permanent home for himself here in New Jersey.

Who's Exhumin' Whom in Smithville?

I work for the Burlington County Division of Parks. Our office is located at the Smithville Mansion in Eastampton, New Jersey. Most of your facts about Hezekiah Smith are correct except for one important one. Agnes wasn't his legal wife! He did marry Agnes, but he never divorced his first wife, Eveline. She wouldn't give him a divorce. He was buried next to Agnes in an iron casket like you stated. But the reason behind the iron casket was he knew his son would try to take his body back to Woodstock, Vermont, to their family plot, next to Eveline. But he wanted to be next to Agnes.

His son by Eveline did place a headstone in their family plot with Hezekiah's name on it to make people think he moved the body, but he couldn't, because of the iron casket and the concrete encasement. He also supposedly sent a dummy casket back to Woodstock to make people think he had successfully exhumed the body.

Also, as for the statue of Agnes you mentioned: After he died, his son Elton had the statue destroyed and the pieces thrown into the Rancocas Creek. The workers were told to pulverize the statue to make sure no relics were left.—*Tami Bozarth*

A Stylish Ride to the Other Side— The Stone Mercedes-Benz of Ray Tse

In the peaceful setting of the Linden Park Cemetery in Union County stands a monument to one young man's love of an automobile. The final resting place of Raymond Tse is impressive enough with its marble pillars, urns, and relief sculptures of Oriental lions. But what really puts this tomb in the luxury class is the full-size granite replica of a Mercedes-Benz 240 Diesel. The sculpture is an exact scale model of the German four-door sedan, chiseled from a single block of stone. There it sits, parked out back, fully loaded and bearing all the manufacturer's insignia, eternally at the ready to whisk the dear departed away to the hereafter. It even has personalized license plates bearing the name Ray Tse.

Weird NJ spoke with Richard T., a tenant of Ray's older brother David, and one of the mourners at the funeral.

"David owned several luxury cars," Richard told us, "and promised to buy Ray one for his seventeenth birthday. David was about twenty years older than Ray. Ray lived in Hong Kong, but he visited David in America often. When Ray died, his parents could not accept the loss and shipped the body over here for burial. They didn't even attend the funeral.

"At the service, we were all given play money and fake gold bars to throw into a can of fire so that Ray would have wealth in the afterlife. They also gave out real money. I was given $30, which I threw in a drawer and did not touch for five years.

"Ray's mausoleum and Mercedes take up forty cemetery plots and cost $500,000 back in the '70s. David is said to still visit the grave every day. "

The monument is a wonder of the modern stonecutter's craft. The car's grill, windshield wipers, tire treads, textured taillights, and even the exhaust pipe and muffler are rendered in painstaking detail. The only things missing are the sideview mirrors, which would have protruded too much and been broken off.

Anthony Sgobba, who carved the lightbulb gravestone in Totowa, gave Weird NJ his insights into this amazing sculpture.

"They took a big chunk of granite and chiseled away," he said. "It's all done by hand chisels. It probably took a year and a half to cut that stone."

That would mean that by the time this car rolled off the assembly line, it was already a late model, just like its owner.

Rock of Ages Carved for Thee

I'd like to share some facts about the stone Mercedes. First, the car is made of a single block of stone quarried at the Rock of Ages in Graniteville, Vermont. It was transformed into the stone Mercedes at their craft center. It was paid for by Ray Tse's older brother. There is a Chinese custom that if you promise something to someone and they die before the promise can be fulfilled, then you must try and do your best to keep the promise to the deceased person. *–Ray Makul*

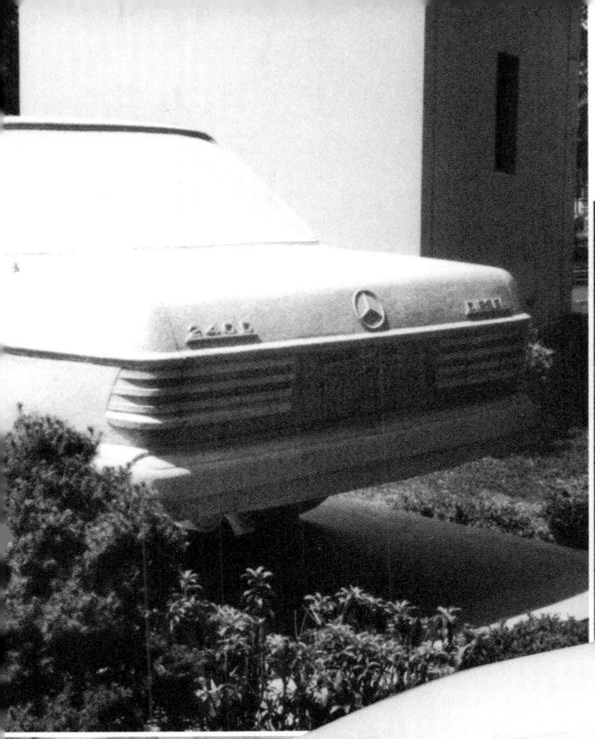

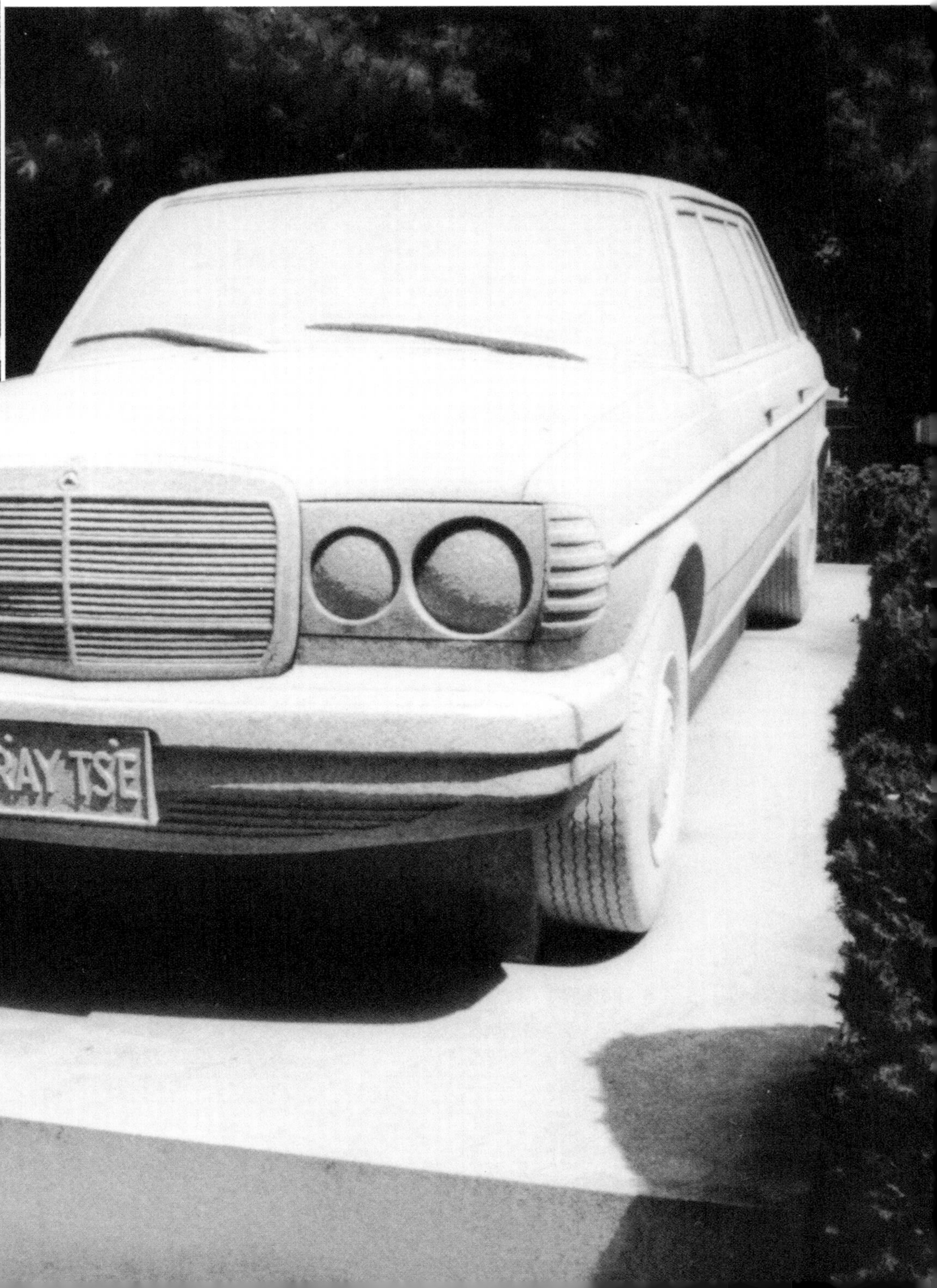
RAY TSE

Glowing Graves

What can be more frightful than a grave that glows? A local legend of the Montville area, located off Church Road, does just that. The secret is to turn into the church parking lot and ride along the fence until you have your car door even with the eighth fence post from the end. Look to the right of the middle tree and toward the very rear of the graveyard. You can see the tombstone glowing orange and yellow. Some believe the trick is produced by the angle of the tombstone and by a streetlight that happens to hit it in just the right spot. Recent condo development in the area has marred the view somewhat, so be sure to go there on the darkest of nights.

The Glowing Grave of Readington

I know of a glowing grave located in a small cemetery off Route 202 South in Readington. The cemetery in the churchyard has a headstone that glows at night. We walked right up to it to see if the stone possessed any phosphorescent qualities, which did not appear to be the case. We then looked at the streetlights in the area to see if they were creating the glow, and they were not. It only glows on a clear night.—*Lorri Passin*

For Whom the Stone Glows

Legend has it that a soldier of the battle of Trenton was buried there after being burned to death.—*JersJ*

Going Toward the Light in Readington

My buddy and I solved part of the mystery about the glowing grave in Readington. We drove to this road that curved around a hill, and he pointed out the window. I looked up, and sure enough, there was this headstone at the crest of the hill shining like the sun in the middle of the dark cemetery. As we climbed up that steep hill, it seemed to get even quieter. I looked up at the headstone. That sucker was absolutely blinding! As we crested the hill, I was able to really admire its glow. We walked slowly up to it, and when we were about eight to ten feet away, the headstone suddenly went dark. It was no longer glowing, but the grave site itself was illuminated in a perfect block of light!

I watched as this guy's hand cast a shadow across the grave when he touched the headstone. That was when I realized what was happening. The headstone was perfectly positioned to reflect the light from the streetlights below. For a certain time, at a certain angle, you are actually seeing the light reflected from the one streetlight. As you lose that reflection, it picks up the second streetlight. As you get to the grave, your angle of sight changes and you can now see the light reflected onto the grave itself.—*Samuel M.*

General Robert Erskine's Grave and the Blue Light

At Ringwood Manor in Ringwood, you'll find the grave of Robert Erskine, a Revolutionary War hero who provided Washington with accurate maps essential to the American victory. Erskine made his home in Ringwood after the war and was buried on the property. There is something peculiar about this grave site. The bricks that make up his crypt just won't stay in place and seem to keep falling out. Legend has it that Robert is digging his way out of the grave.

People have witnessed a mysterious blue ball of light, which appears above the crypt. Sometimes the light will follow you. Some believe it's Robert sitting on top of his own crypt waving a lantern with a blue flame. For a tour of the house, make sure you go before a storm—that's when most of the paranormal activity is said to occur.

General Erskine's Ghostly Mist

I took this picture of the replacement tomb of General Robert Erskine in September 1986. At eleven a.m., I took a series of photos depicting the masons and helpers bricking up the tomb. The morning was bright and sunny as I routinely clicked away.

When I got the film developed, I thought that one of the photos was spoiled. The photo had a partially transparent cloud over the tomb. The white, bright, smokelike cloud seemed to radiate as if the tomb were emitting some sort of energy. Some of the curators related ghost stories and experiences, including one about Erskine walking the grounds, carrying a lantern shining blue light.—*William Trusewicz*

The Green Light Cemetery of Middletown

Nestled in a quiet corner of Middletown, in Monmouth County, is a graveyard nicknamed the Green Light Cemetery. The Bayview Cemetery off Hosford and Stillwell roads got its more descriptive name from an eerie green light that appears high above the trees there. The legend surrounding this light tells of a caretaker who once resided on the hill behind the cemetery. After his death, the caretaker's ghost would light a green lantern as a beacon for lost spirits, which gives the hill its nickname—Beacon Hill.

The Green Light Mystery Solved?

I could see the Green Light from the second-story window of my room, through the trees. The source of the light may have been an old lighthouse that sat up on the hill. I have talked to older members of the community who said that lighthouses used to help boats in the bay to find the shore, but the one off Kings Highway became irrelevant as the trees grew to a height that blocked its beacon.—*Paul Erol*

Let the Spirits Move You

Not far from the legendary Green Light Cemetery is another well-known local graveyard attraction—the Dancing Jesus of Middletown. It is said that if you visit the Mount Olivet Cemetery near Chapel Hill Road at night (which is probably illegal) and shine your car's headlights on the statue of Christ, it will begin to shimmy and shake for you.

Savior Last Dance for Me

You are supposed to look at it at night with the headlights on and then after ten seconds shut them off. If you do it right, the Jesus should do a little dance or wave. I saw it, and it looks like it's waving to you. Whatever it's doing, it's damn strange.–*Bob in Hazlet*

The Final Parking Place of Mary Ellis

For the past one hundred and seventy years, Mary Ellis has resided on what she probably thought would always be a stately piece of property in New Brunswick overlooking the Raritan River. But for the better part of a century, Mary has been monopolizing a prime parking space, outside what is now the Loews Cineplex on Route 1. How poor Mary came to rest beneath the asphalt is a romantic and tragic story.

As the legend goes, Mary Ellis came to New Brunswick in the 1790s to stay with her younger sister, Margaret. Around this time, she met and fell in love with a sea captain. When the captain sailed down the Raritan and out to sea, he vowed that the two would be wed when he returned. He even left her his beloved horse to look after in his absence.

Every day, Mary would ride his horse from her sister's house on what is now Livingston Avenue down to the river to watch for her lover's returning ship. In 1813, she purchased a parcel of farmland that overlooked the river to maintain her daily vigil. Fourteen years later, she died there, still faithfully anticipating her captain's return. She was buried on the property, along with her sister, some other family members, and according to local lore, the captain's horse.

Over the years, the land changed hands several times, and the neighboring area suffered a blight of strip malls and discount outlets. Mary's farm was paved over, and for many years it was the site

of the Route 1 Flea Market. Her grave stood in the parking lot in a sea of tarmac and bargain hunters' vehicles. For most of that time, the small, grassy island was enclosed by a chain-link fence and sporadically maintained by Mary's descendants. Often, though, the weeds grew so tall that they obscured the two-and-a-half-foot-tall marble headstone inside.

Those who did take note of the parking-lot grave have always been curious about and sometimes even inspired by it. It's been alleged that the early 1970s pop hit "Brandy" was really an ode to Mary. The Looking Glass, the band that wrote and recorded the song, were in fact from New Brunswick, and did record other songs based on local sites. Brandy, a fine girl according to the song, was in love with a ship captain who could not leave his true love, the sea, to marry her. Sound familiar?

When the Loews Cineplex replaced the Route 1 Flea Market, the parking lot was regraded, making Mary's grave stand even taller than before. Still parked in a prime spot, Mary's grave has been given a new retaining wall, and a few small trees have even been planted close by. The final resting place of Mary Ellis seems to have been given an extended lease. It's just too bad the new theater isn't a drive-in.

There Was Something About Mary

I read your Mary Ellis article and was intrigued. I grew up in New Brunswick and spent many hours playing in the woods along the Raritan River around the grave site. The grave was on a mound about ten feet up from the clearing floor. Surrounded by the remains of an iron fence, the mound was swathed in thorny wild rosebushes. At the top, the tombstone lay flat, and the epitaph was very clear. The top of the mound offered a panoramic view of the Raritan, which must have been truly magnificent in Mary's day before the Route 1 bridge was built. The area had a dreamlike quality to it. It was never creepy or scary, even to a little kid like myself. *–Andy Bernstein*

Murderer Mysteries

Everybody loves a good murder mystery. Here in New Jersey, you don't even have to buy a book to hear a chilling story of murder and mayhem. Just take a stroll through any number of our state's graveyards, where the spine-tingling tales and whodunits are written in stone.

Crossroads Killers

Any mention of a crossroads in a rural county is fodder for legends of ghosts, devils, and the occasional murder. This probably stems from the custom of burying murderers at the crossroads nearest to where their victims had died. New Jersey has its very own crossroads in Changewater, a small village along the Musconetcong River in Warren County. At the intersection of Asbury and Anderson roads is a place known as Murderer's Bridge, named for a famous quadruple murder that occurred there long ago.

On May 2, 1843, a local resident discovered farmer John Castner lying murdered in a ditch along the road. On his way to the Castner house, the man discovered the bodies of John's wife, Marie, the couple's three-year-old daughter, Matilda, and Marie's brother, John Parke.

Two years after the murder, Joseph Carter and Peter Parke (a relative of the murdered John Parke) were tried for the homicides. Both men professed their innocence, and many believe they were convicted on circumstantial evidence. They were hanged outside the county courthouse in Belvidere and their bodies were carted to the crossroads and buried.

Today, three large rocks and two small metal signs mark the spot where Carter and Parke are buried, which happens to be in the backyard of Kathy Knudsen. Kathy invited us to take a look at the stones and offered us some history on her unusual lawn ornaments.

"Visitors came by in droves to see the burial site after a book was published called *Murder Along the Musconetcong*," said Mrs. Knudsen. "But the circumstances are no different than any crime. It's like Lee Harvey Oswald; you'll never know the real truth of what happened that night."

The graves of the murder victims can be seen in the Mansfield Cemetery in Washington Township, near Route 31. Marie and her child were buried together, and the inscription reads, "Our mingled blood cries out to God for vengeance."

The Grave of the Unknown Woman Murdered in Rahway

One grave in the Rahway Cemetery marks a murder mystery over a century old. This is actually a double mystery—the question being not only who was the murderer but who was the victim? The headstone simply says, "An Unknown Woman Found Dead March 25, 1887."

The story began on a cold March morning in 1887, when four brothers on their way to work at a mill on King's Avenue found the body of a young woman with her throat slashed. There were signs of a struggle, with a trail of bloodstains and clothing scattered about. Nearby was a basket of eggs. There were no signs of robbery, since the woman's jewelry was still on her person. Nearby were other pieces of evidence— a bloodstained jackknife with a turquoise handle, an embroidered handkerchief bearing the name K. Nooz, a man's footprints, and a straw hat.

After her body was embalmed, the victim was dressed in the clothes she was found in— a green cashmere dress with green feather trimming and a cape—and photographed. The photographs were circulated in hopes of identifying her. At first glance, it would seem to be an easy case to solve. The woman, one might reason, must have lived locally—how far would a person travel on foot carrying a basket of eggs? But although a special train ran from Jersey City to Rahway and Ryno's Morgue was mobbed with people filing through to view the body, she was not identified. The pictures were exhibited at the 1887 Chicago World's Fair, and engravings of them appeared in the *Police Gazette* of April 1887, with the offer of a $250 reward for information. None was forthcoming.

More than a century later, Edward O'Donnell, the caretaker of the cemetery, would like to get this crime on *Unsolved Mysteries*. He has been writing to the show's producers, hoping that someone will recognize this woman from an old family photo album.

"An unsolved murder case is never closed," said O'Donnell.

Princess Doe of Blairstown: Dead Among Strangers, Remembered by All

Of all the unsolved crimes in New Jersey, 'dump jobs' are often the coldest cases of all. When unidentified bodies or body parts are tossed like garbage along a roadside, the cases garner a lot of publicity but very few leads.

One such case is that of Princess Doe of Blairstown, one of the nation's most puzzling mysteries and coldest cases. The inscription on her grave—donated by the people of the town where she was found—says simply, "Princess Doe, Missing From Home, Dead Among Strangers, Remembered By All. Born?—Found July 15, 1982."

The body of this white teenager was found by workers at the Cedar Ridge Cemetery on Route 94 in Blairstown, Warren County. She was five feet two inches tall, weighed about a hundred and ten pounds, and had been dead five to ten days. She had been beaten to death with a blunt instrument, her face beyond recognition, and thrown into a ravine near the cemetery. Medical examiners noted defensive wounds on the girl's arms and hands, and discovered alcohol in her system. The body was found fully clothed, in a V-neck sweater, a red-white-and-blue wraparound skirt, and wearing a gold necklace with a rosarylike cross. Her left ear was double-pierced.

The Blairstown police department first called her Princess Doe—not plain Jane Doe like most unidentified females—because of her young age and small size. The department and the FBI used every available means possible to identify her, including mass media appeals. HBO featured the case in a twenty-minute segment on their show *Strange Crimes*. A novel, *Death Among Strangers,* used the case as a backdrop. On June 30, 1983, Princess Doe became the first person entered into the FBI's national computerized unidentified deceased files. The case became a textbook course taught at the FBI Academy in Quantico, Virginia, but no one has ever been charged with the killings and the identity and origins of Princess Doe remain a mystery.

Recently, the Warren County police department pieced together some more facts about the anonymous young girl. Tips from a detective in Ocean City, Maryland, indicated that Princess Doe was

Police computer *composite portrait of what Princess Doe might have looked like in life.*

probably a runaway who may have worked as a hotel housekeeper under several aliases. Leads sent to the New Jersey police have uncovered up to six people alleging to have information about Princess Doe's true identity.

Another eerie fact has also emerged. Police Lieutenant Eric Kranz, who was second in command at the Blairstown Police Department at the time of the murder, believes he met the killer on numerous occasions. Kranz received a report from witnesses who had seen a man frequenting the grave site of Princess Doe.

PRINCESS DOE
MISSING FROM HOME
DEAD AMONG STRANGERS
REMEMBERED BY ALL
BORN?—FOUND JULY 15, 1982

Not one to dismiss any lead, Kranz went out to meet the mysterious cemetery visitor. As it turned out, the man had a history of criminal violence and was traveling on business before the crime. But Kranz could find no physical evidence linking this mystery man to the murder.

Kranz interviewed the man's brother, who said that the suspect was capable of committing such a brutal crime. Despite the viable lead, the case's prosecutor instructed Kranz not to interrogate the suspect until the girl's identity was known.

"I have a very strong suspicion he is the killer," Kranz told the *Pocono Record*. "I am the only one on God's green earth who really thought the guy did it, and I was never given the opportunity to pursue that the way I thought it should be done."

After an exasperating two years on the investigation, Kranz retired from the police force. He now says the suspect has moved from Blairstown in the past decade, and his whereabouts are currently unknown. So is the identity of the dead girl we have come to know simply as Princess Doe.

Gone but Not Forgotten

Like Princess Doe, the next few graves fall into our "Gone but Not Forgotten" category. Although these sites and people may no longer be with us, they will live on forever in the hearts and minds of those who remember them.

In Clifton, They Remember Frankie Lymon

Frankie Lymon was not from New Jersey. He didn't live here, die here, or get buried here. So why, you might well ask, is his tombstone standing in the window of a record store in Clifton?

Frankie Lymon was a young teen rock star of the 1950s. He formed his vocal harmony group, The Teenagers, in 1954, and went on to record such hits as "Why Do Fools Fall in Love?," "I Promise to Remember," and "The ABCs of Love." Lymon embarked on a solo career in 1957 and scored only one hit, "Goody Goody." By that time, he was addicted to heroin, which eventually killed him in 1968.

You can view Frankie Lymon's tombstone at Ronnie I.'s Clifton Music Store on Main Avenue. The store's owner, Ronnie Italiano, proudly displays the stone on a riser of fake grass, surrounded by artificial flowers. In 1976, Ronnie founded a group called the United in Group Harmony Association (U.G.H.A.) to promote the street-corner harmony music of the '50s and early '60s. Today, he says his shop is the largest retail outlet of vocal harmony records in the world.

But why is Lymon's tombstone in Clifton, New Jersey, when his body is buried in St. Raymond's Cemetery in the Bronx?

"In 1985, his actual grave was unmarked," Ronnie told us. "We [the U.G.H.A.] contacted Frankie's widow, Emira, in Georgia about raising money to buy Frankie a headstone. She liked the idea, so we had a benefit with a few vocal groups. We rented a hall and charged people $10 a ticket and raised about $3000 and had this stone made."

But then Emira asked the U.G.H.A. to hold off on placing the stone on the grave because of some legal problems. Apparently, at the time of his death, Lymon was actually married to three women, and they were fighting in court for royalty rights from the estate. "Just before the movie of Frankie's life came out (*Why Do Fools Fall in Love?*), Emira ran down to the grave and put a headstone on it," Ronnie explained. "But we see this one as the official headstone. It makes a good conversation piece here, don't you think? Sometimes people will come into the shop and ask me if I'm a stonecutter and if I can carve a stone for them. No, I tell them, I'm just a fan."

The Chapel of the Dead Nun

While the Chapel of the Dead Nun in Morristown is not a true grave, legend has it that for a time it did contain a hermetically encased body. For anyone growing up in the Morristown area in the '60s, this site, located just a few yards off Western Avenue, was a must-see for any Friday night date. The dead nun, we are told, was enshrined within the tiny shedlike building with an iron gate through which visitors could peek at the supplicant sister.

Today the Dead Nun no longer resides in the roadside shrine. She has been replaced by a somewhat less awe-inspiring plastic manger scene.

Goin' to the Chapel and We're Gonna Get Weird

There was a two-lane country road going past the convent and a roadside chapel built into the side of a hill. The front of the chapel faced the road, and since a hill sloped up and away from the road, the one-story building actually went into the hillside. This resulted in it always being cold and damp inside the chapel. From the road, you really couldn't see any other buildings of the convent except the roadside chapel.

We walked up to the doors, and they seemed to be wrought iron with stained glass. We pushed them open and went in. It was dimly lit by religious candles. As we approached the front of the chapel, I could see what appeared to be a small altar and a glass partition, evidently to keep onlookers away.

As I looked through the glass, I could see a body lying in some kind of a coffin, which was open. Inside the coffin there was a human figure that seemed to be covered in a thin whitish substance, maybe wax—no one really knew.

I was told that this was a nun who founded the convent. I'm sure that she wasn't a saint or even in the process of being beatified, but there was something special about her, and there was certainly a special reason for her being displayed like this.

As I stood there, I guess that the coldness and dampness got the best of me, because I was suddenly aware of how spooky and weird this whole thing was. I decided to wait outside by the car. Several years after this, I heard that the body of the Dead Nun was missing, either stolen or removed. –*Al Evans*

Too Young to Die

There is probably no sadder experience in this world than the death of a child. We who are fortunate not to have known such tragedy can only imagine the anguish it must cause to the mournful parents. Some of that heartache can still be seen today in cemeteries throughout the state, even though many of those grieving fathers and mothers left this life themselves many years ago.

The Cave Grave

Located alongside Route 621 in the town of Newton is a peaceful little graveyard nestled alongside a wooded hillside, right near the heart of the old town. Most of the nineteenth- and twentieth-century stones here are the usual upright limestone or granite variety, but one memorial is very different. The marker is about fifty yards into the woods beyond the cemetery's boundary, mounted upright against the sheer rockface of the hill. It seals off the entrance to a cave.

The stone bears the names of James, Margaret, and J. Howard Lewis, and the year 1909. As the story goes, young Margaret went into the then unprotected cave and got lost. Seeking to save their sister, the two boys soon followed her into the dark cavern. They were never seen again. Despite all efforts to locate the missing children, their bodies were never found. The decision was made to place a marble tablet over the cave's entrance to mark the final resting place of the three lost children and also prevent any others from suffering a similar fate.

After we first published the story of the Cave Grave of Newton, the Sussex County Historical Society contacted us. They wanted further information about the site. All we could tell them was that like many of our stories, this came to us from people local to the area. How much of it is true and how much is legend, we could not say for sure. They shared their own information on the Lewis grave. All they could tell us was that cemetery records indicate that three children are indeed interred at the site. Even an extensive search through genealogical records failed to produce any additional information.

This we know: Three children died, and the plaque that marks their grave seals off the entrance to a cave.

The Dollhouse Grave

When Lizzie Eckel died at age 12 in 1882, her father Emmanuel placed a dollhouse next to her tombstone in the cemetery of the Trinity United Church in Warren. The miniature dwelling had a red gabled roof and chimney and was constructed of wood and glass. Inside, one could see a child's tea set, a small table, a doll in Victorian dress with a porcelain head, and a children's book entitled *Little Pillow*. A small obelisk-shaped stone marks Lizzie's grave, bearing the inscription, "She was loving, she was fair, and for a while she was given; then an angel came and claimed her own and bore her home to heaven."

In 1973, someone stole the dollhouse. A few days later, pieces of the contents were discovered discarded in a field in nearby Martinsville. The church gathered up the fragments and moved the structure indoors. We are told that it remains there to this day in the church's attic.

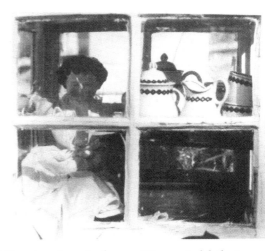

Little Mary Ann's Grave

There is an old cemetery on Old Mine Road, right before the Milford Bridge in Montague, in Sussex County. Way in the back of the cemetery is the grave of a little girl named Mary Ann Perrigo, who died over a hundred years ago. What makes this so interesting is the collection of toys that have been placed on this little girl's grave over the years. There is a doll that looks like it's about twenty years old, and some other little toys that look like they were from Happy Meals of years past. I wonder who this little girl was.—*M. Higgins*

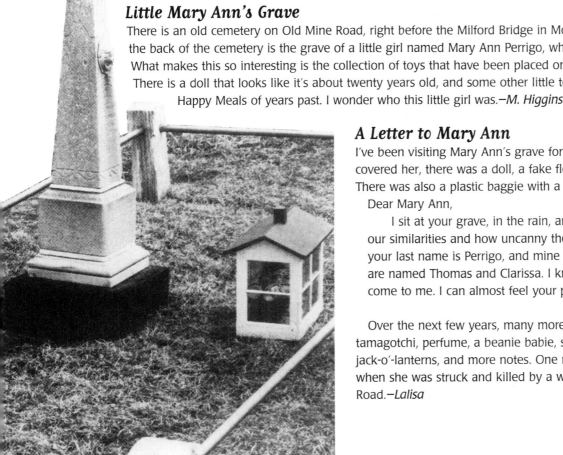
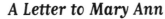

A Letter to Mary Ann

I've been visiting Mary Ann's grave for over seven years. The first time I discovered her, there was a doll, a fake flower, and some change on the grave. There was also a plastic baggie with a note that read something like this:

Dear Mary Ann,

I sit at your grave, in the rain, and think of you. Think of all of our similarities and how uncanny they are. My name is Mary Ann too; your last name is Perrigo, and mine is Perry. In fact, both of our parents are named Thomas and Clarissa. I know if I wait long enough, you will come to me. I can almost feel your presence behind me.

—The Glorious Ghost

Over the next few years, many more things appeared: an Indian doll, a fake tamagotchi, perfume, a beanie babie, shells, rocks, fake flowers, a rosebush, jack-o'-lanterns, and more notes. One note said that Mary Ann reportedly died when she was struck and killed by a wagon train passing along Old Mine Road.—*Lalisa*

Little Pets Rest in Peace

Some of the most interesting and moving graveyards that we've explored are in pet cemeteries. Some people are really attached to their little furry friends and commemorate them with touching tributes. The stones are often much more representational than those you'll find in the human boneyards—there must be at least a dozen fire hydrants in the Blairstown Pet Cemetery alone.

We've located five pet cemeteries in the state so far, but we're sure there are many smaller ones. We asked the proprietor of one cemetery about the animals interred in her yard.

"Well," she said, "we have a gorilla buried here, but we also have cats, dogs, birds, chickens, chimpanzees, and horses."

Who would bury a chicken? That sounds like a missed opportunity for a barbecue to us.

"The horse was the saddest burial. He was sick, and to spare the owner the expense of getting a crane, they just placed a ramp down into the grave and walked the horse right in. Then they shot him and he was covered over." Yikes!

"We don't have lavish burial services here, just simple ones," she added. Especially for horses, we gathered.

Lad, a Dead Dog

Years before Lassie made her debut, there were Albert Payson Terhune's collie books. He wrote over twenty-five children's books about the cuddly canines that roamed his estate, Sunnybank, which overlooks Pompton Lake in Wayne. Some titles include *Lad, a Dog, The Further Adventures of Lad,* and *Lad of Sunnybank.*

Terhune loved Lad, so when Lad passed away at sixteen, Terhune had him buried on the property. The tombstone reads, "Lad, Thoroughbred In Body And Soul, 1902–1918."

Also located on the property are monuments carved in stone to Terhune's other estate-bred collies, including Sandi, Tippy, Lady, Bobby, Wolf, and Fairellen. Viewing hours are nine to five at Sunnybank, off Terhune Drive (Route 202) in Wayne.

Elsie the Cow

Poor Lobelia. This famous symbol of the Borden Dairy Company was on her way to an appearance in Chicago when she was involved in an auto accident. She was listed in critical condition and brought back to her home at the Gordon Walker Farm in Plainsboro, where she passed away. A tombstone was set on the site of the farm to mark her final resting place, though she's not really buried anywhere near the stone.

YOU'LL DO LOBELIA
A PURE BRED JERSEY COW
ONE OF THE GREAT ELSIES
OF OUR TIME
1932   1941

Performing Pets Take a Final Bow

A little town called Linwood outside Atlantic City is the last stop on the show circuit for many a performing pooch. The town is home to the two-acre Clara-Glenn Pet Cemetery. More than three thousand animals lie interred here—dogs, cats, horses, monkeys, guinea pigs, mice, canaries, parrots, and more.

The cemetery opened in 1918 and boasts some famous guests, including the Diving Horse and Rex the Wonder Dog from Atlantic City's Steel Pier. Rumor has it Petey, the ring-eyed canine from the *Our Gang* series, is also there. Celebrity owners who buried their pets there include Irving Berlin, Eddie Cantor, Ed Wynn, Paulette Goddard, and Billie Burke—Glinda, The Good Witch of the North from *The Wizard of Oz*—and financier J. P. Morgan.

The *Ocean City Sentinel Ledger* printed an article in 1959 describing the biggest funeral ever held in Atlantic City. It was for a bartender's dog named Night Life, so well known that when he died, a collection was taken up to bury him. Night Life was known to hail cabs—all the cabdrivers would stop when they saw him standing on the corner and give him a lift. Whenever he saw a tipsy patron on the street, he would guide the inebriated biped on his way. He was of "dubious backstreet ancestry," but when he died, he was laid to rest in a white satin coffin. A five-hour procession filed past his casket to pay final respects. There were twenty limousines in the line of cars behind his hearse, six human pallbearers, and an Atlantic City newspaper publisher who read the eulogy.—*Judy Branin*

Abandoned in New Jersey

By Mark Moran

There are probably no places in New Jersey weirder than abandoned sites. Whether they are vacant houses, forgotten amusement parks, or decommissioned military installations, they possess an aura of history and mystery. Some abandoned places are humble, some are great marvels of architecture and engineering that languish in anonymity, as if waiting for someone to recognize their grandeur. Some are towering monuments to visionary ideals, while others are merely hollow husks of ill-fated follies. Wandering through these places today, one cannot help but wonder what they must have been like in their day. But there is often a melancholy sense of loss that these once grand places are now no more.

A number of my most vivid memories from childhood are those of exploring abandoned places. Stepping into a strange world that others once inhabited is a weird sensation. Who had once lived here? Why did they leave, and where did they go?

These are the questions I would ask myself while walking through these forsaken monuments of rotting wood and broken glass. There usually weren't many clues; maybe some furniture, perhaps some clothes, and, if I was really lucky, old books or photographs. With these discards, I would try to answer the riddles of the former inhabitants, much like an archaeologist trying to reconstruct an unknown species of dinosaur using just a few fragments of bone. The key element of this suburban archaeology was imagination—trying to envision people living in another time. It was curiosity about these forgotten people and places that led me to my fascination with the unrecorded history of New Jersey.

Paradise Lost

There may be no sites in New Jersey more nostalgic than its abandoned amusement parks. Seeing their festively colored ruins strangled by vines of poison sumac, one cannot help but feel a sense of lost innocence and irretrievable youth. Perhaps the heightened vitality that these now defunct places once enjoyed reminds us of our own mortality.

When I was about six years old, I saw a black-and-white movie called *Carnival of Souls* on TV late one night. It had a profound impact on my young, impressionable mind. In the film, a young woman accidentally drives her car off a bridge and into a river. After she swims to shore, she is haunted for weeks by ghoulish apparitions that try to communicate with her. In the end, they finally surround the helpless girl at an abandoned seaside amusement park on the outskirts of town. The final scene of the movie shows workers dragging the woman's car from the depths of the muddy river, her lifeless body still in the driver's seat. As a kid, that low-budget B movie scared the hell out of me and started my lifelong fascination with abandoned amusement parks.

The New Jersey landscape is dotted with derelict cabana clubs with names like Pleasureland, Sun Valley, and Crystal Lake, their turquoise swimming pools now brackish ponds filled with tadpoles and sunfish. Once, these fun spots were popular summer attractions, alive with the screams and laughter of happy children. Now they lie silent, slowly being reclaimed by nature. Perhaps some of these humble abandoned family parks will be spared so future generations can see what life in our state was like in a simpler time, before recreation meant satellite TV, Universal Studios in Orlando, and X-Boxes.

Asbury Park: A Carnival of Sorts

Perhaps the most impressive and depressing of all the abandoned amusement parks in New Jersey is the waterfront area of Asbury Park. The Asbury Park that I knew and loved in my younger days was not the wholesome family resort that it was from the late nineteenth through the mid-twentieth centuries. In the early 1980s, it was a seedy, run-down seaside town, struggling to recapture summer vacation revenues that had steadily been moving farther south to places like Seaside Heights and Wildwood.

Yet vestiges of its former glory remained. Bracketing either end of the half-mile white-sand beach were two ornate structures. At the north end was Convention Hall, a massive 1930s brick building with pastel-colored terra-cotta sculptures of winged sea horses and huge green copper lanterns. To the south was the casino, which had jutted out on its spindly pilings over the breaking surf since 1903, adorned with reliefs of seashells and sailing ships. At the southern end of Ocean Avenue stood the one-hundred-year-old copper-and-glass carousel house, its antique hand-painted wooden ponies prancing around and around behind windows emblazoned with the screaming visages of Medusa-like faces.

Occupying a whole block on the corner of Lake Avenue and Kingsley Street was the minty aqua-green façade of the Palace Amusements building, a turn-of-the-century fun factory advertising rides like the Twister, the Scooters, the Fun House, and the Tunnel of Love. Inside, there was another antique merry-go-round and a one-hundred-year-old Ferris

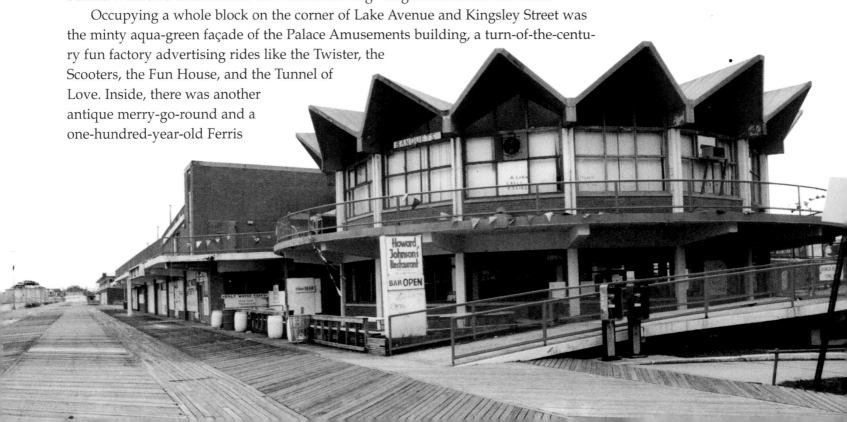

wheel, though what was most memorable was the deranged grin of the two huge faces that gazed down from the palace walls. The character was given the name Tillie, and he had greeted visitors with his wide-eyed, almost demonic glee since he was first painted on the building back in the 1940s.

On a sunny day a couple of years ago, I decided to pay Asbury Park a visit, after almost a decade's absence. I was not prepared for what I found. I drove past the Palace Amusements building, which was tightly shuttered and looked dilapidated. I noted an unusual lack of cars parked on the street. As I made the turn from Asbury Avenue onto Ocean, I could see all the way up to Convention Hall. There was not a single soul or vehicle anywhere in sight. Every single store was closed for business, and many were boarded up. To my dismay, many of my favorite places had vanished altogether, empty lots where they had once stood.

I parked my car near the beach to stroll on the boardwalk. Surely there, I thought, I would see people. I was wrong. Everything on the boardwalk was shut down tight. The shops looked as though they had not been opened in years. I began to get the feeling that I was in an episode of the *Twilight Zone.* It was a beautiful day at the Jersey Shore, the Atlantic Ocean was sparkling, the sun hung suspended in a clear blue sky, and here I was, the last man on earth. The place was a real honest-to-God ghost town.

When I got home, I tried to find out just what had gone wrong in Asbury Park. I found some answers in an article *The Star-Ledger* published on May 22, 1994.

"Whatever could go wrong in Asbury Park, did. The locals rioted. The

upper class bolted. *The economy crashed. The working class ran out of work and became the welfare class. The mental patients and druggies moved in. So did the prostitutes.*

"The city gave away too much in a desperate attempt to secure developers who promised too much and went bankrupt. The only construction accomplished after nearly a decade of effort was either torched or halted mid-way.

"If there is a single symbol of the state of the Asbury Park redevelopment, it's the monstrous, traffic blocking, steel-and-cement hulk on Ocean Avenue. It is the skeleton of the luxury condominium high-rise that developer Joseph Carabetta abandoned in mid-construction four years ago. One city official said: 'People hate it so much they would pay to blow it up.'"

The article goes on to quote a former Asbury Park councilman, Angelo Chinnici, referring to the oceanfront area as "Sarajevo-by-the-sea," and city manager Alan Feit calling it "the dead zone."

In March of 2003, when Mark Sceurman and I heard that the Palace Amusements building was soon to be demolished, we set out to visit Tillie one last time. As I looked up at the casino from down on the beach, I could see straight up through the broken windows of the grand old building, through its cavernous interior, and right up through the gaping holes in its roof to the gray skies above. Sand dunes swept over the top of sections of the boardwalk. Around the Palace Amusements, the entire block and bordering streets were cordoned off with yellow police tape and orange plastic barrels. The paint of the building's once brightly colored exterior was chipped and flaking off. The multicolored neon lights, which once framed the ever-smiling faces of Tillie, hung broken and swaying in the breeze. The March wind was rhythmically banging a huge piece of sheet metal against the skeletal frame of that ill-conceived luxury high-rise. The mournful echo of that clanging toll seemed like a death knell for the Asbury Park I once loved.

Nuclear Jersey's Nike Missile Bases

In Livingston, where I grew up, everybody knew that there was a missile base at the top of the highest hill in town. But most people didn't realize that the cold war was being fought right in our own suburban backyards. Nike missile bases in Middletown, Old Bridge, South Plainfield, Livingston, East Hanover, Wayne, and Mahwah shielded New York City with radar-guided missiles designed to intercept and destroy incoming Soviet air squadrons. Other bases in the southern New Jersey towns of Marlton, Pittman, Lumberton, Swedesboro, and Berlin-Clementon guarded Philadelphia.

Though most have been abandoned or redeveloped, the one in Livingston has been preserved and opened to the public as Riker Hill Park. The old barracks and command center, part of the Essex County Parks Department, have been leased to local artists and craftspeople as studio space.

Weird NJ cold-war correspondent Donald Bender explains the history of the Nike program this way:

"Named for the Greek goddess of victory, the Nike program began during the last months of the Second World War. Unlike conventional antiaircraft artillery, the Nike missile could be continuously guided to intercept an attacking aircraft even during evasive maneuvers. Nike's mission within the continental U.S. was as a last-ditch line of air defense against Soviet bombers, in the event that the Air Force's long-range fighter-interceptor aircraft failed to destroy them. Due to the short range of the original Nike Ajax missile, many bases were close to the center of the areas they protected.

"For two decades, from 1954 through 1974, South

Jersey housed no fewer than five U.S. Army Nike missile installations. In the late 1960s, the number of operational Nike bases within the continental U.S. was steadily reduced. During 1974, the nationwide Nike air-defense system became inactive, and shortly thereafter, the Army Air Defense Command (ARADCOM), which administered this system, was closed down."

Weird NJ was fortunate enough to interview the one-time commander of the Livingston/East Hanover Nike facility, Colonel Joseph Evangelist (U.S. Army, Ret.). Though he was very candid, the Army apparently still has some questions it does not want answered.

WNJ: How much of an arsenal did they have down in East Hanover?

Col. Evangelist: When it was a dual site of Nike Ajax/Hercules, it had six magazine rooms, or kits, as we called them. Each kit had four launchers. They were underground in the pits, with eight- to ten-foot-thick walls, and they had their own self-generated power. The Ajax was a smaller missile, about twenty-seven feet, I think. They carried only high-explosive warheads in the nose and center body. The Hercules missiles had a nuclear capability . . . they weren't designed to just take out one aircraft. You had one missile to take out a fleet.

WNJ: The base was surrounded by regular suburban neighborhoods. Did you ever have any problem with curiosity seekers?

Col. Evangelist: Sometimes we had some problems with kids—kids will be kids. The security was very tight, but more so in the launch area, where the missiles were. Down there, we had three fence lines and security dogs that patrolled the area during the hours of darkness. We would open up the fire control area, but not the missile area, once a month and give people unclassified tours and briefings to try to educate them. People assumed that we had nuclear there, and that we were going to have an explosion on the ground.

WNJ: But these missiles didn't really have nuclear warheads, did they?

Col. Evangelist: I can't say anything on that.

WNJ: What became of the underground bunkers where the missiles were stored?

Col. Evangelist: Measures were taken to ensure that they wouldn't cave in. Then the openings were welded shut. I suppose that they're still down there.

WNJ: I was over at the East Hanover base just recently and saw all the abandoned houses for officers and enlisted people. It's just a ghost town. All the doors and windows are broken or fallen off. It's kind of eerie.

Today, weeds and wildflowers push their way up through cracks in the concrete launchpads. Tangled vines climb the rusty steel radar towers of the remaining abandoned facilities. But once upon a time, in a day when death and destruction might rain down from the heavens at any time, these bases allowed New Jersey's bedroom communities to sleep a little easier at night.

Paulinskill Viaduct

Of all the abandoned places that Weird NJ has explored over the years, none can match the magnificence of the Paulinskill Viaduct. The viaduct, or Hainesburg Trestle, is a long-abandoned railroad bridge over the Paulinskill River near Blairstown.

Built by the Delaware, Lackawanna & Western Railroad, the seven-arch reinforced concrete span is an awesome eleven hundred feet long and towers one hundred and fifteen feet above the Paulinskill River. When first constructed in 1908, the bridge was the largest structure of its kind in the entire world. The train line went out of service in 1979, the railroad tracks were torn up in 1985, and the viaduct was abandoned. It is now owned by the New Jersey Department of Transportation.

Beneath the railbed are stepladders that allow the explorer to travel through the inside of the structure. Each tower between the arches is hollow, with cavernous graffiti-scrawled rooms inside. Manholes located along the railbed provide access to the top of the bridge from within. The railbed provides a breathtaking view of the valley for miles around, looking down at the tops of tall trees, but several guardrails are no longer in place to keep adventurers from the abyss. Though trespassing and even bungee jumping have long been popular at the abandoned site, both activities are illegal . . . and life-threatening.

The Satanic Bridge

Just outside of Blairstown, there is a bridge in the woods. As you go down the road, this massive bridge towers above you out of nowhere. If you park your car on the side of the road and walk up a steep hill, you can climb into the bridge. There are tunnels in it with satanic symbols all over. Some people even say satanic rituals are held in the rooms inside the bridge. *—Kristen*

Poured in Cement, Worker's Ghost Wanders the Trestle

A man is supposed to haunt the trestle. He was buried alive in the cement when it was built. The spot is marked in one of the arches. *—Marcella Walgren*

Bungee Jumping from the Paulinskill Viaduct

One time we were having a party under the second trestle, right next to the river. People were bungee jumping from the top of the trestle. They were coming down right over the river. After thirty minutes of watching them, we heard a splash. A rope had broken. We leaped into the water and pulled the guy out. The first words out of his mouth were, "Do I get a refund?" *—Tim*

Deep Within the Belly of the Beast

I belonged to the Blairstown Local Rescue Squad. For some of my training, we used the viaduct for rope rescue training, and just for fun, rappelled off the side of it. A few times when we were up there crawling through the passageways, it felt odd. There was this feeling that someone else was in there, watching us. One time I got so nervous I didn't feel safe to be there anymore. We packed our equipment up and left. It has been five years since I've been there, but my old friends still feel a presence there sometimes. *—Bryan*

Weirdness in the Woods

Many interesting abandoned sites can be found in the heart of wooded areas. There, unobserved by anyone who might destroy them, they flourish in a full-fledged afterlife of abandoned glory.

Jungle Habitat: Wild, Free, and Abandoned

Anyone old enough to remember Mood Rings, Pet Rocks, or Bicentennial Minutes will probably recall TV ads for Jungle Habitat. Located way up north in West Milford near Greenwood Lake and the New York State border, this African safari theme park featured drive-through fields where lions, zebras, and elephants roamed. I remember going there myself as a kid of about thirteen, clad in a pair of striped bell-bottom trousers, desert boots, and a shirt with a collar large enough to rival the Flying Nun's. The park, which was operated by Warner Bros. in the early to mid-1970s, closed more than twenty years ago.

One day, back around 1997, someone suggested that we go check it out. "Everything is still there," our tipster said, "as if it closed yesterday."

Turning off the Greenwood Lake Turnpike in West Milford, we headed up a hill toward the small Greenwood Lake Airport. An old billboard on the side of the road said NAIROBI AIRPORT, a vestige of the Jungle Habitat days. Right next to the mountaintop airfield stood massive gates bearing the words Jungle Habitat in giant wooden letters. Walking through these gates was like entering the gates of *Jurassic Park,* not just because they looked like the scene in that movie, but because we traveled back in time as we crossed the threshold.

Everything was overgrown and reverting to a wilderness state, but I could still recognize the place from my visit there over twenty years before. In fact, at the main exhibit area, the ticket booths, picnic tables, bathrooms, food kiosks, souvenir shops, and even the little zebra-striped safari cars were still there! We toured the animal pens and the reptile house, and I recognized the exact spot where I had once had my picture taken sitting on the back of a giant lumbering tortoise. Everything at Jungle Habitat was indeed still there—except the animals.

Afterward, I couldn't help wondering what went wrong at Jungle Habitat. It turned out that the park's hasty closing in 1976 was not the only messy affair in its history. Only months after it first opened for business in the summer of 1972, an Israeli tourist named Abraham Levy rolled down the window of his cab to get a better look at the animals. Two lions attacked the car and mauled the twenty-six-year-old tourist, lacerating his face and shoulder, and earning the park a ton of negative publicity—though Levy publicly took responsibility for the incident.

By year's end, West Milford residents raised an outcry about escaped animals. Emus and baboons were known to have escaped the park, and sightings of peacocks were reported. But rumors also spread about more dangerous animals, including a pack of wolves and a lion. On December 16, 1972, *The New York Times* ran an article on the fears of West Milford residents. The rumors are still running rampant today. We've been told tales by West Milford residents of seeing ostriches wandering through their backyards. Another recalled a band of baboons running amuck in the town's pharmacy.

Jungle Habitat is gone now, but not forgotten. Most of the structures that stood during Weird NJ's visit have since been torn down. The sign that once stood at the gate now resides in the backyard of one West Milford resident. Several proposals have been made for the land the park once occupied, including a BMX bike park to be called Extreme Habitat. For me, though, there will always be just two Jungle Habitats: the hot and smelly wild safari park of my youth, and the abandoned ruin I explored later in life, when things started getting really weird.

Obey the Law of the Jungle—or Else!

On the opening day, Jungle Habitat created a twenty-eight-mile traffic jam full of overheated cars. The park became a booming success, yet it closed after a few years because the township of West Milford would not allow them to do what they pleased. Warner Bros. wanted to make Jungle Habitat even bigger.

While the safari was open, a lot of animals escaped on numerous occasions. Once, an emu escaped the park, and since emus can run very fast, they were unable to bring him back. A lot of people spotted this particular emu and still remember that incident to this day.

One year, a taxicab driver attempted to feed a lion with a piece of meat and the lion mauled the man, injuring his arm. This story was in the papers and was used to warn other visitors to follow the rules!—*Erinn Johnson*

Kangaroo Sighting, Jefferson

About 1990, we noticed a big animal crossing the road in White Rock in Jefferson. When we got closer, we realized that it was a kangaroo. We both told our parents, but they didn't believe us.—*Mike McCall*

The Bus Stop Emu

Back in the early '80s, a few friends and I drove into Jungle Habitat in a couple of Volkswagen Bugs. It was pretty cool, like driving into a ghost town. It was like they just pulled up stakes and blasted town. I recall an article in the paper about kids waiting for a school bus by the old A&W root beer stand up the road from the entrance. Supposedly a large ostrich or emu came out of the woods and hung around for a while.—*Brian Ringers*

Jet in the Woods

The most unexpected thing that we've found abandoned in the West Milford woods so far is a military fighter jet plane. *Weird NJ* reader Doug G. brought the crash site to our attention when he wrote to us:

"I have lived in West Milford for over forty years. One morning in December some years ago, I was hunting deer in a patch of woods off Macopin Road. I saw something shining in the distance through the early morning fog. As I moved closer, I saw that it was a jet that had crashed and broken into pieces. All of the gauges were out, but the cockpit was still intact. The wings were broken off, and the tail was some fifty-five yards away. The strange part was that trees were all grown up around it. Everyone I spoke to after that said that they had never heard of the jet in the woods."

Even after the original publication of Doug's letter, the origins of the Jet in the Woods remained a mystery to us for at least another year. Then we received the following letter that seemed to solve the riddle.

"In a recent article in West Milford's Action News, there was a story written by retired police sergeant Bill Genader about the Jet in the Woods. Many hikers and adventure seekers have been asking about what happened, and Genader was the first on the scene after the jet crashed in the woods near Echo Lake.

"It was the summer of 1967 when the West Milford police department first got a call from residents reporting that they witnessed a plane crash off Macopin Road. Genader and

another officer jumped in the squad car to find out what happened. He was dropped off at Vreeland Cemetery after observing treetops were sheared off and smelling burning grass. He followed the trail that led to the downed plane. Although the plane was not on fire, the ground around it was.

"He looked into the cockpit, but no one was in it. Then he saw a dazed pilot sitting on one of the wings. The pilot said he was not injured, but he had a buddy with him in the plane. They found him thirty feet away sitting against a tree. He had injuries, but none were life-threatening.

"The military later took the engine out of the jet by helicopter, dropping it off at Greenwood Lake airport. They left the wreckage in the woods and painted orange **X** signs on the wings to mark it as a military crash site." *–Bill Bassett*

The Metal Cage of Dover

Another strange find in the woods is an old two-room jail cell rusting away at the perimeter of Hurd Park in Dover. It had two side-by-side cages, each with the remains of two fold-down bunk beds and a swinging iron-bar door. One cell's door was locked; the other swung open freely. The trees growing up through it indicated that it had been in the woods for years.

Because St. Clare's Hospital parking lot ended a few yards short of the cell, the cage was rumored to be a retaining pen for unruly patients. While this makes a great story, our research would indicate that the jail cell and the hospital actually had nothing at all to do with one another. Dover historian George Laurie told Weird NJ that the cage was the first lockup for the neighboring town of Wharton. When the Wharton police station was remodeled, the antique jail cell was donated to the Dover Historical Society and moved to an old mansion that used to stand where Hurd Park is located today. Sadly, the mansion is now gone, as is the old iron hoosegow.

The Cages at Dover

Near Dover General Hospital there is a cage that was built to keep the violently insane. It was far enough from the original hospital that the patients couldn't hear their screams. It still stands, no roof, no running water, just a cage. It is a real eerie sight and a dark mark on the history of "mental health."—*Brian Z.*

Cage a Mystery, Even to Hospital Staff

I've worked at St. Clare's Dover for about a year, and didn't know of this cage until issue number 15 of *Weird NJ*. We asked a nurse about it. She tried to cover up by telling us it used to hold oxygen tanks for patients. She said they'd put the patients in the cage so they wouldn't mess with the tanks. I don't know about all that, but I'm gonna keep asking around to see if I can find the real use. I just don't want to know why they held the patients in the middle of the woods.—*Diane G.*

Playing Cops and Robbers

The cage used to sit in the woods at the end of Edgewood Terrace in Dover. It was dragged out and fixed up for Dover's two-hundred-and-fiftieth anniversary celebrations in 1972. It was moved to its current location when the Bonneview Mansion was used as a museum. The mansion was torn down by the local hospital to make a parking lot.—*Tom*

Say Good-bye to the Dover Mental Cage

I am writing to inform you of dire news. The cage is gone! My sister, a few of her friends, and I walked there yesterday only to find it had completely vanished. There in the bottom of the trees, which had grown around it, were the marks of the bars. Those marks are the only remaining evidence of the Dover Mental Cage. It is sad.

We had many memories of that cage: locking our friends in there during sleepovers, climbing all around it when we were small enough to fit in the locked side, etc. An era has ended. It's such a pity that the next generation of Dover/Wharton/Mine Hill kids will never know the rush of being crammed into a mental cage by their best friends on a Friday night.—*Shirley Clark and Dijon Urban*

The Iron Door

Yet another metallic mystery abandoned in the woods is the Iron Door of Federal Hill, on the border of Riverdale and Bloomingdale. Weird NJ had received numerous letters about a mysterious doorway in the side of a rocky mountain that led to a secret room. But nobody seemed to remember how to get there.

We knew that Federal Hill had been the site of an American Army mutiny during the Revolutionary War, and the location of a German-American bund camp called Bergwald prior to World War II. This history was enough to set us off on a quest to find out just what lay behind this iron door.

We found one reference on the Internet, written by Cal Deal, who had lived in the area years ago. Mr. Deal describes the site this way:

"In 1917, a building was erected on the base of Federal Hill for the purpose of making ammunition for World War I. The foundations of this building can still be seen along with a small cave where ammunition was stored. The 'cave' was a small storage area carved into the side of the mountain . . . about the size of a large closet."

So was the elusive metal door a remnant of a fort or a munitions factory? Or was it left over from the days of the bund?

On our first charge up Federal Hill, armed only with a hand-drawn map provided by a reader, we found plenty of artifacts but no steel door. After two hours of hiking, we began seeing stone fire rings, some recently built, others quite old. We noticed old galvanized buckets, white enameled metal bowls and coffeepots, and the rusted skeletons of steel cots. We came upon two crumbling stone foundations with fireplaces and chimneys, with stone steps and walkways laid around them. I was sure that this was the site of the old bund camp. We found several more foundations, but the object of our quest eluded us.

A few weeks later, another *Weird NJ* reader—Bob from West Milford— offered to take us to the site. Before long, we were deep in the dense forest halfway up the mountain. With no path to follow, we stumbled over tangled vines and moss-covered rocks. All of a sudden, Bob pointed toward a dark recess in the rocks. There it was, the Iron Door! It was rusty, but still in working order. I reached down, swung it open, and peered into the inky blackness.

The cave was made from a

natural cleft in the mountainside, sealed at the cracks with stones and mortar. It was about twelve feet deep, the floor was flat and damp, and there was a brick step up to the doorway. The most intriguing thing was that the Iron Door locked from the inside! The two heavy sliding latches could only be put into place from within the cave. The bunker was a hiding place not for some*thing* but for some*one*.

So who built this stony fortress, and why? Although we had located this long-lost artifact, it would seem that the Iron Door may forever hold on to some of its mysteries like the proverbial steel trap.

Insane Adventures: Inside New Jersey's Abandoned Asylums

There is no better way to get that creepy feeling than to explore an abandoned insane asylum all alone. Not knowing what or who might lie in wait around the next corner, down the next dark corridor, gives such a heightened sense of awareness that every cell in the body seems to be living a life of its own. Wandering the vacant hallways of these spooky old buildings, one cannot help but imagine the suffering of the unfortunate souls once imprisoned within those walls. These feelings are made all the more poignant by the artifacts left behind. Patient records, fingerprints, and mug shots spill forth from overflowing file cabinets. Antiquated surgical tools litter the floors of operating rooms. Padded cells, electroshock tables, draconian restraint devices with leather straps, and human cages are all part of the abandoned asylum tour experience.

In times past, New Jersey has had a dubious reputation when it came to its treatment of the mentally ill. As early as the mid-nineteenth century, Dorothea Dix crusaded against mistreatment of the insane in our state. Dix was appalled that the insane were forced into almshouses for the poor, or tossed into cells with murderers and thieves, or even auctioned off to homeowners charged with their care but who often forced them into labor instead.

By the early to mid-twentieth century, hospitals for epileptics, sanatoriums for the tubercular, and almshouses for the destitute had become places to warehouse the mentally ill, locked away from society. Many complexes were like entire towns unto themselves, with their own train stations, livestock and vegetable farms, slaughterhouses, barbershops, and even bowling alleys. Now many of them stand all but forgotten on the outskirts of towns such as Marlboro, Montgomery, and Blackwood. Some have been abandoned for so long that it's hard to believe that they were actually overcrowded during their heyday.

So where have all the patients gone? Some institutions, like Greystone in Morris Plains, Overbrook in Verona, and Ancora in Winslow, still house the mentally ill, though in much smaller numbers than they once did. Medical advances in the care and treatment of the mentally ill made many of the others obsolete. We no longer lock up the mentally ill away from the rest of society. So now several of New Jersey's asylums stand empty, tall and foreboding, reminders of a darker time.

Welcome to Hell: The Essex Mountain Sanatorium

In 1896, Essex County purchased three hundred and twenty-five acres of farmland on the border of Verona and Cedar Grove to establish what was then being referred to as the Essex County Asylum for the Insane. Upon its opening, the facility came to be known as Overbrook, due to its positioning just above the Peckman River. Buildings quickly sprang up as part of this complex in close proximity to Fairview Avenue, which was then a dirt road that served as the main thoroughfare of Overbrook.

In 1907, another facility was established just up the hill from the asylum on the border of Caldwell and North Caldwell. The Newark City Home for Consumptives cared for those suffering from tuberculosis, and became known as the Essex Mountain Sanatorium or simply the Hilltop. Eventually, eleven other buildings would sprout up on the property. But after advances in medicine made tuberculosis a treatable disease, the number of patients there decreased dramatically.

Eventually, all of the buildings at the top of the hill were abandoned. Rumors began to spread over the decades about the isolated asylum at the hilltop. Some said that outdated surgical implements, patient records, and medieval-looking devices of restraint were still intact inside. Tales told of escaped or forgotten lunatics roaming the grounds and hallways of the derelict buildings, making their homes in the vast labyrinth of subterranean tunnels beneath the facility.

One warm, sunny afternoon a few years back, I decided to investigate this abandoned sanatorium for myself. It was about five thirty on a late-summer afternoon. Long shadows had already begun to lay down tracks across my path as I set out on my adventure. I parked my car at the foot of the hill and began to walk up the long, arrow-straight Sanatorium Road, heading toward the hospital at the top of the hill. The pavement was old and cracked, with a single hopelessly faded yellow line running down its center. Densely overgrown weeds and thickets covered the rolling hills and spilled out over the roadway. Overhead, large unkempt tree branches swayed in the warm breeze, throwing skittish shadows down to the sun-dappled asphalt.

After walking for what seemed like nearly a half

mile, I began to see buildings poking up through the forest ahead of me. The first one that I came upon was a three-story yellow brick structure with every window broken. The parking lot behind it was piled high with office furniture. A little farther down the road was another building with broken windows and pigeons fluttering through the darkened attic dormers. The sun was sinking low in the sky behind me as I approached the open front door. My shadow preceded me up the steps and over the threshold. Upon entering the cool, dimly lit shell of a building, I looked up to see the spray-painted greeting, WELCOME TO HELL, over an inside doorway.

The building had two wings stretching in either direction away from the main entrance. These shadowy hallways were lined with small rooms, each containing a bed, a small dresser, and a stand-up locker. Paint and plaster was chipping from everywhere, and all of the windows were shattered. I was surprised, though, that much of the furniture was intact. Most of the metal bedframes were still fitted with a fairly tidy mattress, and the dressers were still complete with their drawers. I made my way slowly down the hall, peeking into each room and listening for any sounds of life. At the end of the hall, I found a pile of records strewn about the floor. I picked up a night-shift watch report from New Year's Eve 1978. "All quiet," it said. All quiet it was, and it was starting to bother me.

Up the stairs to the second floor, I was greeted by a horned demon. The pig-nosed, spray-painted portrait seemed to harbor a genuine contempt for my presence. I begged its pardon and descended to the lower regions of the building. Below ground level, the air was cool and damp. Plaster and paint from the walls lay in powdery piles against the baseboards. As I made my way down the long, dim corridor, slowly pushing open one door after another, I found that some rooms had been torched and were charred black from floor to ceiling. I became conscious of each hushed step of my own feet. It was then that I saw it, there in the dust where I had not yet walked—a single footprint. I suddenly heard my father's voice inside my head, coming to me from when I was young. "Someday," he said, "you're going to disappear in one of those places, and no one is ever going to know what happened to you."

He might have been onto something there. I hadn't told anybody where I was going, and if I did disappear, this was not the first place that I would be looked for. What if the lunatics had indeed taken over the asylum, as the rumors alleged? I decided to cut my visit short and get back out into what remained of daylight.

Heading down the hill, I encountered another explorer. I asked him if he knew anything about tunnels under the complex. "All the buildings are connected by a network of tunnels," he replied. "But I won't go in them. I've even been down to the old morgue, but I won't go in those tunnels. There could be gas in there now, or God knows what!"

"Did you ever hear of escaped lunatics roaming around up here?" I asked.

"There were homeless people and vagrants living up in the sanatorium. I heard rumors that they were former inmates that came back and moved in. Anyway, between them, the vandals, and the satanic graffiti all over, the place was getting quite a reputation."

Demolition of the main hospital of the sanatorium began in August of 1993. The remaining outlying buildings were razed over the next nine years. By the end of April 2002, the sanatorium was no more.

The Snake Pit Called Skillman

In Montgomery Township is an abandoned mental institution originally designed for research and treatment of epilepsy. Until its closure in 1998, it went by many names, including Skillman, the State Village of Epileptics, and, more recently, the North Princeton Developmental Center. Perhaps most telling of all its nicknames, though, is the Snake Pit of New Jersey.

These days, the network of medical and residential buildings stands vacant, derelict and ramshackle. The Epilepsy Foundation of New Jersey and the New Jersey Developmental Disabilities Council are currently seeking to preserve and renovate one building, a one-hundred-and-sixty-year-old house, as a museum devoted to the evolution of institutional life in the United States.

Freaky Poetry and the Morgue at Skillman

I recently took a series of trips to Skillman, determined to find the morgue. It was small, only four drawers. It smelled like the inside of a mausoleum. There were burned candles on one of the trays. A locker room we found looked like people had been in a mad rush to leave. Family photos, cans of food, hospital gowns, and freaky poems were all scattered about. I usually don't scare easily, but we heard noises so scary that we fled the building.
–Karen W.

A Cold Slap in the Face at Skillman

Immediately after entering the building, there was a feeling of dire mistake. It was like a slap in the face—it was pure darkness and extremely cold. My feet instantly lost feeling. Goose bumps formed that were so hard it was like my arm had Braille on it.

We shouldn't be here, I thought. The halls contained hundreds of doors, all wide-open. We turned the corner and found ourselves inside the morgue. The smell of stale air was inescapable. To my right on the counter were full bottles of formaldehyde and embalming fluid. The drawer where the body was kept was wide-open.

Down the hall, we found a room with a bed that had restraints on it. In the closet, we found the patients' files, a bloodstained nurses gown, and an EKG machine that still had lines on the printout from the last patient it was used on. That made the hairs on the back of my neck stand at attention.—*Brittany G.*

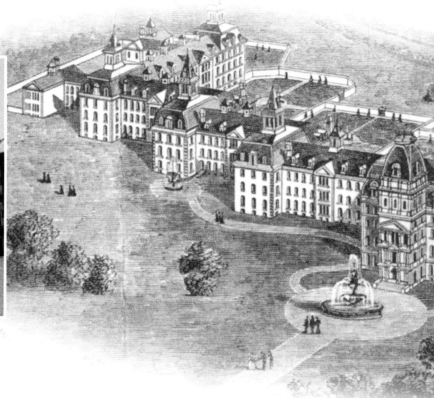

Greystone Becomes Gravestone

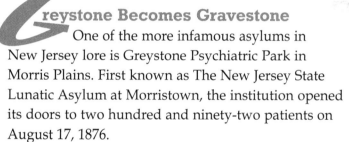

One of the more infamous asylums in New Jersey lore is Greystone Psychiatric Park in Morris Plains. First known as The New Jersey State Lunatic Asylum at Morristown, the institution opened its doors to two hundred and ninety-two patients on August 17, 1876.

In its day, Greystone was a landmark in progressivism. Designed by Thomas Kirkbride, the complex was linked by a series of underground tunnels and rails. Until the Pentagon was constructed, it possessed the largest continuous foundation in the United States.

The hospital provided uncrowded conditions, fresh air, and touted the notion that mental patients were curable. Over time, the humane reputation became tarnished. Overcrowding became the norm. In the 1880s, attic and exercise rooms were converted into dormitories, and by 1953 the hospital packed 7674 patients into a building designed for only a few hundred.

One of the hospital's more famous patients was folksinger/songwriter Woody Guthrie. Woody suffered from Huntington's disease, a hereditary degenerative nervous disorder that proved terminal. During his stint at Greystone from 1956 to 1961, Woody referred to it with sardonic humor as Gravestone. This nickname might prove more prophetic than Woody imagined.

Many of the Greystone buildings went abandoned long ago. The hospital was recently ordered closed altogether because of sexual abuse of patients, patient on patient violence, and multiple patient suicides and escapes. Though historical societies have expressed a desire to preserve the older buildings of Greystone, the fate of the grand old asylum is still up in the air at the time of this writing. Sadly, the time of these massive abandoned behemoth asylums may soon come to an end. But the experience of exploring them in their abandoned state is still indelibly etched in the memories of those who once ventured inside.

Hopefully, some of these awe-inspiring asylums and other great abandoned places will survive demolition and redevelopment so that future generations will have a place to point to, telling tales of what may lie beyond their darkened thresholds. We all need mystery and wonder in our lives, and there may be no better way to fire the imagination than to let your mind go wandering into places where your feet dare not tread.

In the end, whether all these stories of ghosts, demons, and mythical beasts are true or not doesn't really matter. All that really matters is that the stories of them are still alive and being told and retold and enjoyed by people of all ages throughout the state. As New Jerseyans, this is our collective history and shared modern folklore. These tales are all part of our Weird NJ, and yours.

INDEX

Page numbers in **bold** refer to photos, illustrations, and captions.

PICTURE CREDITS

Page 2 bottom left © Todd Gipstein/CORBIS; 2 bottom right © Skot Olsen; 11 © Todd Gipstein/CORBIS; 13 © Bettmann/CORBIS; 14 © Bettmann/CORBIS; 16 © Jim Zuckerman/CORBIS; 21 © J. L. deZorzi/CORBIS; 22 © Thom Lang/CORBIS; 27 © Bettmann/CORBIS; 34 center © Bettmann/CORBIS; 38 © Bob Krist/CORBIS; 44–45 © Phil Ranko/CORBIS; 48 top © Bettman/Corbis; 48 bottom © PEMCO – Webster & Stevens Collection; Museum of History & Industry, Seattle/CORBIS; 49 © Bettmann/CORBIS; 50 courtesy Jefferson Township Historical Society; 54–55 © Nozima Kowall/Corbis; 60 © Hulton Deutsch Collection/Corbis; 62 © David G. Houser/Corbis; 63 © Bettman/Corbis; 64–65 Library of Congress; 66 © Bettman/Corbis; 67–69 The MacMillan Company 1923; 70 © Corbis; 71 ©John Springer Collection/Corbis; 72 and 73 courtesy Gail and Michael Mendelsohn; 77 © H. Armstrong Roberts/CORBIS; 88 © William Whitehurst/CORBIS; 91 © Roger Ball/CORBIS; 94 © George B. Diebold/CORBIS; 96 © Loston Wallace; 101 © Brian Quinn; 103 © Loston Wallace; 112, 114, 115 © Christine Back; 120 © Robert Piersanti; 121 © Bettmann/CORBIS; 124 © Skot Olsen; 126 © Mark Moran; 127 courtesy Alexander Hartenstine; 131 © Kevin English; 132 © Joe Oesterle; 139 top right courtesy Dave Ewan; 151 © Henry Diltz/CORBIS; 154–155 *Life* Magazine, September 1, 1967, Volume 63; 162 top © Mark McMurray; 174 top © Rich Warren; 174 bottom © Kevin Haipt; 175 top right © Mark Moran; 180 © Thomas Brummet/CORBIS; 183 © Todd Gipstein/CORBIS; 184 © Nathan Griffith/CORBIS; 185 © Ricki Rosen/CORBIS SARA; 186–187 © Chuck Keeler Jr./CORBIS; 193 © Bettmann/CORBIS; 194 © Horace Bristol/CORBIS; 198 © Robert Dowling/CORBIS; 203 © Chase Swift/CORBIS; 207 © Bettmann/CORBIS; 210 and 211 courtesy Glen and Jackie Wershing; 216 © Brian Quinn; 220 © Brian Quinn; 222 courtesy Peter Jordan and Vestigia; 232 © Gary Zimmermann; 233 © William Trusewicz; 243 Alan A. Siegel and the Warren Township Historical Society; 245 © Underwood & Underwood/CORBIS; 250 bottom left © Phil Buehler; 263 © Ross Juliano; 267 bottom © Phil Buehler.

EDITORIAL CREDITS

Pages 152–155: Excerpt from *The Boys from New Jersey*
© 1992, The William Morrow Company, Inc., New York, NY.